Enterprise XML
Clearly Explained

Enterprise XML
Clearly Explained

Robert Standefer

Morgan
Kaufmann

An Imprint of Academic Press
A Harcourt Science and Technology Company
San Diego San Francisco New York Boston London Sydney Tokyo

This book is printed on acid-free paper. ∞

Copyright © 2001 by Academic Press

ACADEMIC PRESS
A Harcourt Science and Technology Company
525 B Street, Suite 1900, San Diego, CA 92101-4495, USA
http://www.academicpress.com

Academic Press
Harcourt Place, 32 Jamestown Road, London NW1 7BY, UK
http://www.academicpress.com

Morgan Kaufmann Publishers
340 Pine Street, Sixth Floor, San Francisco, CA 94104-3205
http://www.mkp.com

Library of Congress Catalog Card Number: 00-106077
International Standard Book Number: 0-12-663355-X

Printed in the United States of America
00 01 02 03 04 IP 9 8 7 6 5 4 3 2 1

Contents

Chapter 1: Introduction 1

Who Should Read This Book? 2

What You Need to Use This Book 2

A Bit of XML History 3

    SGML 3

    HTML 4

    XML 5

Acknowledgments 6

Chapter 2: XML Overview 7

What is XML? 8

    XMLs Goals 9

Why XML? 11

    Share Your Data 12

Create Your Own Markup Language 12
How XML Works 13
Structuring XML 13
Document Type Definition 14
XML Schema 15
XSL 16
Valid and Well-Formed Documents 17
Linking with XML 18
XLinks 19
XPointers 21
Absolute Location Terms 22
Relative Location Terms 22
XPointer Support 23
Advanced XML Features 24
Namespaces 24
Summary 24

Chapter 3: XML Tools **27**
Parsing Tools 28
xmlproc 28
Xparse 30
DOMParser 30
XML Authoring Tools 32
Macromedia Dreamweaver 32
Microsoft XML Notepad 33
XMetaL 34
Visual XML 34
XML Pro 35
Adept Editor 35
WordPerfect SGML 36
Adobe FrameMaker+SGML 36
Content Management Tools 37
SGML Database Editorial System 37
Astoria 37

Oracle 8i 38
Object Store 38
Summary 39

Chapter 4: Applications of XML 41

Extensible Forms Description Language 42
XFDL Form Structure 42
XFDL Compute Structure 47
Sample XFDL Forms 49
Vector Markup Language 51
Mathematical Markup Language 57
Semantic and Presentational Tags 58
Channel Definition Format 60
How Active Channel Works 60
Implementing Active Channel 61
CDF Element Definitions 66
Active Channel Example 73
Resource Description Framework 74
Summary 74

Chapter 5: Real-World XML 77

XML in the Web Browser 78
The 3.0 Browsers 78
Internet Explorer 4.0 79
Internet Explorer 5.0 80
Netscape Navigator 6.0 84
Mozilla 87
XML on the Server 87
XML Enabler 88
XML-based Middleware 89
Summary 93

Chapter 6: Developing XML-Enabled Applications 95

The Document Object Model 96
  DOM Requirements 96
  Nodes in a Tree 101
Programming XML 104
  Visual Basic and XML 105
  Perl and XML 109
  Active Server Pages 112
  PHP and XML 117
Summary 119

Chapter 7: XML in the Data Tier 121

The XML-Data Schema 122
  Defining Schemas 122
  Schema Information Access 124
XML as a Data Source 125
Oracle 8i and XML 130
  Oracle 8i XML Support 130
  Oracle 8i Platform for Java 133
Microsoft SQL Server 2000 and XML 134
  FOR XML Calls 136
Summary 138

Chapter 8: Case Study: DVDmdb.com 141

The Objective 142
The Database 144
  The Data Model 144
  Sample Data 147
The XML Documents 148
  Structuring Documents 149
  Building the Front Page 156
  Creating the XSL 158
Publishing the Stories 169
  Uploading 169

Delivering 176
Summary 177

Appendix A:XML 1.0 Specification *179*

Status of this Document 180
Abstract 180
Extensible Markup Language (XML) 181
Version 1.0 181
Table of Contents 181
1. Introduction 182
    1.1 Origin and Goals 183
    1.2 Terminology 184
2. Documents 186
    2.1 Well-Formed XML Documents 187
    2.2 Characters 187
    2.3 Common Syntactic Constructs 188
    2.4 Character Data and Markup 190
    2.5 Comments 191
    2.6 Processing Instructions 192
    2.7 CDATA Sections 192
    2.8 Prolog and Document Type Declaration 193
    2.9 Standalone Document Declaration 197
    2.10 White Space Handling 198
    2.11 End-of-Line Handling 199
    2.12 Language Identification 200
3. Logical Structures 202
    3.1 Start-Tags, End-Tags, and Empty-Element Tags 203
    3.2 Element Type Declarations 205
    3.3 Attribute-List Declarations 209
    3.4 Conditional Sections 214
4. Physical Structures 216
    4.1 Character and Entity References 217
    4.2 Entity Declarations 220
    4.3 Parsed Entities 222

4.4 XML Processor Treatment of
Entities and References 225
4.5 Construction of Internal
Entity Replacement Text 228
4.6 Predefined Entities 229
4.7 Notation Declarations 230
4.8 Document Entity 231
5. Conformance 231
6. Notation 231
Appendices 233
A. References 233
B. Character Classes 235
C. XML and SGML (Non-Normative) 236
D. Expansion of Entity and Character
References (Non-Normative) 237
E. Deterministic Content Models (Non-Normative) 239
F. Autodetection of Character
Encodings (Non-Normative) 239
G. W3C XML Working Group (Non-Normative) 242

Appendix B: Resource Description Framework **243**

Status of This Document 244
Table of Contents 244
1. Introduction 245
2. Basic RDF 247
2.1. Basic RDF Model 247
2.2. Basic RDF Syntax 253
2.3. Qualified Property Values 262
3. Containers 263
3.1. Container Model 263
3.2. Container Syntax 265
3.3. Distributive Referents: Statements
about Members of a Container 268
3.4. Containers Defined By A URI Pattern 270

3.5. Containers Versus Repeated Properties 271
4. Statements about Statements 273
4.1. Modeling Statements 274
4.2. Syntactic Shorthand for
Statements About Statements 279
5. Formal Model for RDF 279
6. Formal Grammar for RDF 284
7. Examples 293
7.1. Sharing Values 293
7.2. Aggregates 294
7.3. Non-Binary Relations 295
7.4. Dublin Core Metadata 298
7.5. Values Containing Markup 301
7.6. PICS Labels 301
7.7. Content Hiding For RDF inside HTML 303
8. Acknowledgements 305
Appendix A. Glossary 306
Appendix B. Transporting RDF 308
Appendix C: Notes about Usage 309
Appendix D: References 310
Appendix E: Changes 311

Index 313

1

Introduction

Extensible Markup Language (XML) has been touted as the greatest advancement in Web technology since Java, or even HTML. There is a great deal of excitement about XML and its capabilities because it offers a level of flexibility that is simply not offered in HTML. The beauty of XML is that it offers both flexibility and simplicity.

XML has already started to gain acceptance on the Internet, and with the release of XML-enabled browsers, such as Internet Explorer 5.x and Netscape 6, there are many reasons to deploy XML on the Internet. But what about corporate IT departments? What about intranets? Does XML have a role in these environments? This book aims to answer those questions and more.

Who Should Read This Book?

This book aims to inform you about XML in the enterprise. The objective of this book is not to teach you XML, but to offer an overview of how XML can work in your organization. I hope that when you finish this book you come away with a better understanding of XML application development, the benefits of using XML, and how to begin implementing XML at your organization.

This book assumes a thorough understanding of the Web and HTML. XML exposure in some aspect is very helpful, whether it comes from a white paper or another book. A lack of understanding of XML will not prevent you from understanding this book, but it will slow you down a bit. If you do not know XML you can use this book to help you decide if it is worth your time and effort learning it.

For those readers who have no knowledge of XML, it is covered topically in Chapter 2. XML tools are covered in Chapter 3, while Chapter 4 offers a discussion of XML applications, such as Vector Markup Langauge. Chapter 5 covers XML in Web browsers and programming languages, and Chapter 6 moves us on to developing XML applications using the Document Object Model. Chapter 7 covers schemas and database support of XML, while Chapter 8 offers a case study of a Web site that uses XML.

This book covers developing XML applications using other technologies, including Active Server Pages, Perl, and JavaScript. Familiarity with one or more of these technologies would prove quite helpful. In the very least, an understanding of HTML and how the Web works is required.

What You Need to Use This Book

The examples in this book will work with any XML parser and validator, including the one shipped with Internet Explorer 4.0. However, to use the examples related to directly viewing an XML document in your browser, you will need Internet Explorer 5.0.

There are specific programs mentioned in this book that only run on certain operating systems. For instance, Microsoft XML Notepad, covered in Chapter 4, runs only under Microsoft Windows NT, Windows 95, and Windows 98. Conversely, Macromedia Dreamweaver, also covered in Chapter 4, runs under Windows NT, Windows 2000, Windows ME, Windows 95, Windows 98, and MacOS.

For those of you who use UNIX or a UNIX-type operating system, the Java-based XML tools and Perl XML libraries will be of particular interest. The Java tools were tested using Sun's JDK 1.1.6, and the Perl libraries were tested using Perl 5.006.

Testing was performed on a Dell Dimension XPS R and a PowerMac G4. Perl and Java programs were tested in Windows 98, Windows 2000, and Red Hat Linux 6.1.

A Bit of XML History

XML is a close relative of two other technologies, SGML and HTML. SGML (standard generalized markup language) is a very complex markup language designed to deal with large sets of data. HTML is a markup language used to format data for rendering in a Web browser.

SGML

SGML has been around for quite awhile, even predating HTML. SGML is very powerful and could be called the grandfather of XML.

SGML defines its markup through a Document Type Declaration. HTML is SGML's best known DTD, and HTML gets some of its best features from SGML. SGML is intelligent and adaptable, and its best uses are in managing large sets of data, such as dictionaries and encyclopedias.

SGML is a popular language for document management systems. I once had a client who required a UNIX-based document management system to maintain an enormous number of maps and corresponding surveying documents. The application was primarily written in C and documents were cataloged through SGML.

Unfortunately, SGML is not without its limitations. Where SGML is weak, HTML is strong. SGML lacks power in linking, simplicity, and portability. Since SGML is so complex, it is unattractive to most authors. Add to that the fact that SGML tools, such as FrameMaker+SGML, are very expensive and SGML seems less and less like the ideal technology. My client in the above example spent close to $3000 on SGML parsing libraries for C.

HTML

In 1990, in order to counter the complexity of SGML while still retaining some of its power, Tim Berners-Lee created HTML. Unlike SGML, HTML does not require a DTD. Since HTML does not require a DTD, it is optimized for transport over a network protocol.

HTML is so easy to learn and use that practically anyone can do it. In 1994, there were very few people who could write HTML and contractors were in extremely high demand. By the beginning of 1996, however, HTML was no longer the primary skill in demand since most everyone knew it.

HTML authoring tools, such as FrontPage, took the simplicity even further and shielded the user from actual HTML tags. This further pressed the popularity of HTML as an authoring tool.

Once HTML had gained wide acceptance, it became less of an authoring tool and more of a design tool. Formatting markup, such as <B> and <CENTER>, became interspersed with semantic tags, such as <TABLE> and <H2>. Netscape and Microsoft added their own extensions to HTML that were not necessarily readable by the other's browser.

Despite all of this, the Web caught on. Companies embraced the Web with full force, creating large and expansive sites to show off both their products and their creativity. The Web moved to the internal network, creating a new technology and a new word: Intranet. HTML was hugely popular, and complemented by technologies such as Java, ActiveX, and JavaScript, poised to take over the world.

But HTML has its limitations, and they became painfully apparent. As corporations moved entire software systems to the intranet, they began to rely on relational databases and server scripting languages such as Active Server Pages to build complex structures of documents using custom tags.

Everything started to get out of hand. Companies were coming full-circle to discover their problems could have been solved by SGML in the first place. However, SGML was still too complex and costly to implement. A new solution had to be created, and it was: XML.

XML

In late 1996, Jon Bosak of Sun Microsystems started the World Wide Web Consortium (W3C) SGML working group to devise a scaled-down version of SGML, one that offered the simplicity of HTML while maintaining the power of SGML. This group evolved into the XML working group, and the scaled-down version of SGML came to be XML.

The intention with XML was to create a markup language that retained the power and extensibility of SGML and still be easy enough to understand so that authors would not snub it.

The first official draft of the XML 1.0 specification came into existence in November 1996. It was at about that time that custom markup languages started to appear, including Chemical Markup Language by Peter Murray-Rust, and MathML, jointly developed by various companies including IBM and Waterloo Maple.

One of the very first applications of XML was released by Microsoft in 1997. It was called Channel Definition Format (CDF), and was designed to push Web pages to users. If you have installed Internet Explorer 4.0, you probably have noticed the Channels bar that opens when you run Internet Explorer 4.0 for the first time. This is CDF at work. CDF is more fully covered in Chapter 9.

The W3C approved the XML 1.0 specification in early 1998, and XML was officially born. XML has exploded onto the scene, with many projects on the table or in works. Vignette has released StoryServer, which utilizes

XML. IBM has announced profound support of XML and plans to integrate it into some of their products. Netscape released the source code for Mozilla and it has support for XML. More recently, Netscape has released their Gecko-based browser, Netscape 6, that is 100% compliant with the XML specification. Internet Explorer 5.0 has direct-viewing of XML capability built in. There is so much going on in the XML world that it can sometimes be hard to keep up. XML shall prove to be very exciting.

Acknowledgments

Writing a book is a difficult endeavor, no matter how simple or complex the topic is. I want to thank the following people for giving me the oomph to bring the book to fruition:

- Thomas Park, Associate Editor, for his patience throughout this endeavor.

- My wife, Amanda, for being there when I needed her.

- Nathan Shulman for helping out with the code in Chapter 8.

- Brian Roberts for his rush to Dallas to help fix my computer two days before deadline.

- Chris Van Buren, my agent, for handling all of the details and being my link to the publishing world.

RES

2

XML Overview

XML may seem like a complicated technology at first glance, but it was designed to be easy to use and maintain. XML is known for its flexibility and adherence to user-defined structure.

In this chapter, we discuss how XML operates and how it works with user-defined structure. We cover the basics of what XML is, why it's used, and how (in short terms) to structure it.

What is XML?

Simply put, XML is a language for describing data on the Web. While HTML uses a predefined set of tags to describe how data looks, XML allows you to create your own custom tags to describe your data.

Unlike HTML, XML does not describe the formatting of a document. Formatting can be added to the document via XSL (discussed below), but the formatting instructions are not part of the XML document itself. The XML document only contains tags that describe the content of the document.

HTML is different from XML in that HTML lets the author issue content and display markup in the same document. HTML is a mixture of formatting tags, such as <B> for **bold** and <EM> for *italics*, and structural tags, such as <DIV> and <P>.

Consider this HTML code, which displays an album from the author's personal collection:

```
<UL>
<LI>Format: CD
<LI>Artist: Radiohead
<LI>Title: The Bends
<LI>Genre: Rock
<LI>Sub Genre: Alternative
<LI>Year: 1994
</UL>
```

The data is described using an unordered list. This code does not say anything about the data contained in the tags. It's almost as if the information is just floating out there. In XML, the same data could be marked up as:

```
<?xml version="1.0" standalone="yes">
<album>
<format>CD</format>
<artist>Radiohead</artist>
<title>The Bends</title>
<genre>Rock</genre>
<sub-genre>Alternative</sub-genre>
<year>1994</year>
</album>
```

The XML code clearly shows what the data is. The tags actually mean something. This is important in two different ways: The tags are meaningful to a human who might be maintaining the code or trying to glean information from looking at the document, and the tags are meaningful to automated programs, commonly called robots, that are performing index operations on the document.

The idea behind XML becomes clear if you think of the markup tags as database fields. If you have a database called ALBUMS with the fields FORMAT, ARTIST, TITLE, GENRE, SUB-GENRE, and YEAR, you have a database that corresponds to the XML tags shown above. The difference is that in a database program, the software shields you from how it knows what fields correspond to what tables and how it all relates. In XML, this definition is left up to you.

XML's Goals

The W3C XML specification sets out the following goals for XML:

1. XML shall be straightforwardly usable over the Internet.
2. XML shall support a wide variety of applications.
3. XML shall be compatible with SGML.
4. It shall be easy to write programs that process XML documents.
5. The number of optional features in XML is to be kept to the absolute minimum, ideally zero.
6. XML documents should be human-legible and reasonably clear.
7. The XML design should be prepared quickly.
8. The XML design shall be formal and concise.
9. XML documents shall be easy to create.
10. Terseness in XML markup is of minimal importance.

Let's cover these individually:

Item one basically says that users should be able to view XML documents as easily and as quickly as they can view HTML documents. This item indicates that XML browsers should be as powerful as HTML browsers, and the current browser market indicates that this is so.

Item two says that XML should extend to a variety of applications, including authoring, content analysis, browsing, and document management, among others. This item is saying that XML shall not be narrowly defined, such as a specific application. Instead, XML is extensible, so it can be used to create many different applications.

It only makes sense that a language designed to be as powerful as SGML should maintain compatibility with SGML. Item three guarantees this. A lot of the people involved in XML come from an SGML-heavy backround, with large investments in SGML. XML was designed to be compatible with existing technologies while offering new capabilities in delivering structured documents.

Item four is of particular interest because it offers reassurance of XML's simplicity. In other words, it should take about a month for an average programmer to develop a program that can process XML.

Item five addresses one of the biggest problems with HTML today: the fact that its support is not standard across the browsers. This item is meant to address the problems experienced by users when they want to share incompatible documents.

Item six basically says that a normal human should be able to read an XML document. This means if you do not have XML browsing capability and you receive an XML document, you should be able to view the XML document as text and figure out what the content means.

Item seven is meant to address the overall slowness of standards efforts. XML met an immediate need and was developed very quickly.

Item eight corresponds in a way to item four. It means that XML must be expressed in Extend Backus-Naur Form and must be amenable to modern compiler tools and techniques.

Just as it should be easy to create XML processors, it should be easy to create XML documents. Item nine ensures this. This item says that people should not have to rely on a piece of software to create their documents for them. XML should be easy enough to write by hand.

Finally, item number ten says that XML markup need not be concise. This differs from SGML in that a lot of SGML markup was designed to minimize typing. Concise tag names can be difficult to understand by looking at them, so XML says they aren't required.

The latest version of the XML specification (as of December 1999) can be found in Appendix A.

Why XML?

Organizations have embraced the Web as a medium for sharing information, selling products, gaining marketing momentum, and, in the case of software companies, deploying product updates. When HTML gained acceptance in corporations worldwide, new opportunities sprouted up and the world changed forever.

HTML was a great invention and to this day is still a technological must have. Unfortunately, HTML can only go so far. Somewhere along the line, especially in corporate environments, design and format takes a back seat to the data. I have personally seen entire sites that were simply black text on white backgrounds, with no images and very little formatting. These sites were built entirely by a Perl program using dynamic data from a database and were more dependent on data than appearance. That was in 1996; current technologies allow us to do exactly what these corporations were trying to accomplish and still harness the other great parts of the Web, including its marketing capabilities. XML is one of these technologies.

So what does that mean? XML allows developers to create sites that are information-centric, rather than design-centric, yet still maintain the design aspects of the HTML way of doing things.

Share Your Data

XML allows you to share your data among a multitude of sources. XML is an official specification of the World Wide Web Consortium (W3C). It is a nonproprietary format, which means it can be be used as a language to share data between applications. For example, Microsoft Word is an extremely popular word processor for Windows and Macintosh machines. Microsoft Word has a proprietary document format. What happens if a Word user wants to share a file with a UNIX user who is using a different word processor, such as emacs or FrameMaker? The Word user either has to export his document to a format that the UNIX user can read, or the UNIX user has to import the document into his application. Either way, the original formatting of the document will almost certainly not be retained.

XML changes all of that. If XML serves as the format for sharing the data, it will be read in the same manner on either machine. That was the intention of HTML, but HTML had too many limitations, so Microsoft and Netscape created their own custom tags which their browsers supported indepent of the other. That kind of problem does not apply to XML because the author can include his Document Type Definition (DTD) and Extensible Style Sheet (XSL) document with the XML data, and it will be rendered the same, no matter where it goes.

Create Your Own Markup Language

XML allows you to create your very own markup language. This has significant advantages in the financial and scientific worlds. For example, HTML does not have the capability to render mathematical notation. Enter MathML, a custom markup language developed in XML that allows an author to utilize mathematical notation, such as pi (π).

A good example of creating a custom markup language is the case of Peter Murray-Rust, who created Chemical Markup Language (CML). Originally an SGML application, CML gradually transformed into an XML application. Murray-Rust identified a need for a markup language that could support the specifics of chemical equation notation, so he developed a markup language to support his need. Murray-Rust also created JUMBO, an XML browser written in Java.

There are so many possibilities for custom markup languages that it borders on the unimaginable. You can create your own custom markup language to suit your needs, or you can find someone who has already created what you need. All of this happens without the necessity of a plug-in or any other custom software.

How XML Works

XML may seem complicated at first, but it really is quite simple. The first thing one must do to understand XML is release the HTML paradigm. Although XML complements HTML and has some similarities, it is by definition a separate and different markup language, and should be treated as such.

The best way to explain how XML works is to refer back to the previous database example. XML functions in a manner similar to how a database describes its data. The principal method for retrieving data from a database is via SQL. In the case of XML, however, you do not retrieve the data. The data is already there, described by tags, and via XSL you can format the data however you want. The basic idea is still the same. HTML describes how your data *looks*, XML describes how your data is *structured*.

At its simplest, an XML application consists of three parts: the XML document itself, the DTD, and the XSL document. Although the XML document can exist on its own, an XML application is more rigid if a DTD is included and more attractive if complemented by an XSL document.

Structuring XML

Good document structure is paramount to successfully utilizing XML. Besides adhering to XML's rules, a good document structure can help you tremendously when you need to make changes to your data.

The United States Marine Corps, for example, is famous for its structure, a set of orders passed down by the chain of command. Without this structure, the USMC would not be the well-oiled fighting machine that it is.

This structure is what gives the Corps its strength. Although there is a lot more to the Corps than its chain of command, every Marine knows he can depend on his commanding officer to give him the orders he needs to carry out his mission.

The correlation to XML is that where the Marine Corps has its chain of command for its structure, XML documents have a schema.

The schema defines the elements that can appear within the document and the attributes that can be associated with an element. It defines the structure of documents, including relationships between elements, what type of data the elements can store, and how many of that element can occur.

In this book, I'll be using the word schema in two ways: schema as it is defined, and schema as in XML Schema.

Document Type Definition

One type of schema for XML documents is the Document Type Definition (DTD). A DTD is a set of rules that defines the structure for an XML document.

The importance of DTDs goes beyond creating structured documents. DTDs can be shared across networks to define how a whole set of XML documents should be structured. DTDs help different people and different programs read each other's files.

The DTD can either reside in the document, or it can be stored in a separate file referred to by each file that is to conform to the DTD. Linking to the separate DTD really comes in handy when there is a large set of XML documents that must all conform to the same DTD. This feature is very similar to the one afforded by Cascading Style Sheets, where the .css document can be linked to from within a HTML document.

This code illustrates how to link to a separate DTD:

```
<?xml standalone="no" version="1.0">
<!DOCTYPE doc SYSTEM "myrules.dtd">
```

Notice the standalone="no". This indicates that the XML document depends on an external file. This external file is identified in the <!DOC-TYPE> tag. Note that the path to the document, contained in quotes, can follow the path syntax of HTML, such as "/myrules.dtd", "../myrules.dtd", and so on.

It is important not to confuse document type definition with document type declaration. The document type declaration *contains* the document type definition. The distinction is that the document type definition contains all of the declarations of the document s elements, attributes, and entities, while the document type declaration is the <!DOCTYPE dtdname [...]> statement, and all of the declarations are placed between the brackets.

Think of DTDs as templates. A DTD serves as a template to pour data in and arrange it without the template being aware of what the data is. While XSL separates the data and structure from the formatting, a DTD separates the structure from the data.

XML Schema

XML Schema, like DTDs, can be used to specify the schema of a particular class of documents. XML Schema, unlike DTDs, uses XML syntax. This is an advantage for the user, who doesn't have to learn a new language to define the grammar of XML documents, just to declare attributes and elements using XML Schema.

XML Schema offers other advantages over using DTDs, including support for data types, a content model, and the XML Document Object Model (covered in Chapter 6).

An example of a schema would be:

```
<?xml version="1.0" ?>
<Schema name="schema_example"
xmlns="urn:schemas-microsoft-com:xml-data">
<ElementType name="Sample1" content="textOnly">
<ElementType name="Sample2" content="textOnly">
</Schema>
```

XML Schema is covered in further detail in Chapter 7.

XSL

While XML provides powerful mechanisms for describing your data, it does not inherently provide any means for formatting your data. XML lacks that feature by design. If you want to add formatting to your XML, you use XSL.

An XSL style sheet is made up of one or more rules, with each rule containing a target and an action. The target is the XML tag to which the rule applies, while the action is what the rule performs for that particular tag. The root element of an XSL style sheet is <xsl>, with each rule following contained in the <rule></rule>.

Here is an example of a simple XSL style sheet corresponding to the album collection XML document:

```
<xsl>
<rule>
<target-element type="artist"/>
<LI/><children/>
</rule>
```

This style sheet says that any text between <artist> and </artist> should be rendered as a line item. The resulting HTML is simply:

```
<LI>Pearl Jam
```

Almost any HTML tag can be used within an XSL style sheet, as well as JavaScript code and built-in XSL functions.

To prepare an XML document for presentation, the XML document and its associate XSL style sheet are fed into an XSL processor to produce an HTML document. This document is output as a file, which can be posted on the Web for all the world to see. Displaying XML, including converting XML to HTML, is covered in Chapter 4.

There is a lot more to DTDs than what has been covered here, but this should serve as a good basic introduction to how they work. DTDs can get complicated, but their underlying design is for simplicity.

Valid and Well-Formed Documents

If documents conform to a DTD or schema, they are said to be *valid*. If they do not conform to a DTD or schema, but still conform to the XML 1.0 specification, then they are said to be *well-formed*. Thus, all valid documents are well-formed, but not all well-formed documents are valid. For the sake of our discussion, we'll imagine using a DTD.

Valid Documents

Since the structure of your documents has been planned, the resulting documents should be complete since they conform to that structure. The process of validation includes checking the structure of the documents against the document type definition that has been defined for them.

Assuming a validating parser is used, document validation is handled at the time the document is parsed. Any document that corresponds to the DTD will not validate if it does not follow the rules set forth in the DTD. For example, if the DTD specifies that each <album> can contain only one <format>, then this XML code will not validate:

```
<?xml version="1.0" standalone="yes">
<!DOCTYPE album [
<!ELEMENT album (format)>
<!ELEMENT format (#PCDATA)>
]>
<album>
<format>CD</format>
<format>LP</format>
<artist>Pearl Jam</artist>
```

The <!DOCTYPE> tag says that the <album> tag must contain one <format> tag (which itself must have Parsed Character DATA). Since our code has two <format> tags, it does not validate.

It is necessary to know the syntax for defining DTDs. In the case of the code sample, we know that the <!DOCTYPE> only allows one format per <album> because the <album> element is defined with only one child of a particular type. If it were to allow one or more elements of <format>, it would be declared <!ELEMENT album (format+)>.

Well-Formed Documents

A well-formed document meets the minimum set of requirements defined in the specification that a document must satisfy to be considered an XML document. These requirements ensure that the correct language terms are used and that the document is logically coherent in the manner described by the XML specification. A fatal error occurs when the XML processor detects that the document failed to meet one or more of the requirements for well-formedness. When this happens, the XML processor stops the application using it.

To illustrate this, look at Internet Explorer 4.0. If an HTML document is not well-formed, Internet Explorer 4.0 renders it anyway. That is why there are so many problems getting HTML code to work from browser to browser. If HTML were required to be well-formed, then the browser would refuse to render the HTML.

Linking with XML

Can you imagine surfing the Web without links? Linking is one of the things that makes the World Wide Web so powerful and so useful. It only makes sense that the power of linking is harnessed within XML.

Extensible Linking Language (XLL) offers the capability of linking between documents but goes beyond the simple URL-based hyperlinks and anchors available to HTML. Want to link to an arbitrary point in a document? XLL allows you to do that. Need multidirectional links? XLL allows you to do that as well. These things make XLL perfect for advanced linking uses such as footnotes and cross-referencing.

Since XML documents can be converted into HTML, the HTML syntax for linking can be used by XML documents. However, HTML linking is very limited. For example, HTML links are limited to one specific URL, which means one specific document. HTML links cannot point to a specific word in a specific sentence in a specific paragraph in a specific document without the use of named anchors, which you must insert yourself. The linking mechanism in HTML does not think for you.

Linking in HTML is decidedly one-way. Documents know where they are going, but they do not know where they came from. Although most browsers maintain a history, this information is not accessible through HTML and is not always correct. Have you ever pressed Back twice rapidly in Internet Explorer 4.0? The history gets confused and replaces the second document with the first. Multidirectional linking simply is not possible with HTML.

With XLL, however, it is. XLL has the capability for linking in any direction. XLL is the sum of two parts: XLink, the XML Linking Language, which defines how one document links to another, and XPointer, the XML Pointer Language, which defines how individual parts of a document are addressed.

XLinks

Linking in HTML is performed through the <A> tag. The <A> tag in HTML allows you to link to another document or, with named anchors, link to a specified position in the current document. The <A> tag is the only method of linking in HTML.

XML does not have this narrow limitation. Almost any tag in XML can be a link; elements that include links are known as *linking elements*. Each linking element is identified by the xlink:form attribute and contains an href attribute. Just as in HTML, the href attribute is the value of the URL of the resource to which it is linked.

Simple and Extended Links

An XLink can be either simple or extended. Simple links are similar to HTML links, while extended links are more complex. The following are examples of simple XLinks:

```
<artist xlink:form="simple" href="artist.xml">Pearl Jam</artist>
<genre xlink:form="simple"
href="http://www.rockmusic.com">Rock</genre>
```

Each link target attribute's name in the example above is href, with a specified value in the form of a URL. These tags, rather than describing their function, describe their content, with the information that the elements are links included in the tags.

Now, here is an example of a document that uses extended links:

```
<company>
<office xlink:form="extended">XYZ Company
<locale href="http://www.xyz.com.au">Australia</locale>
<locale href="http://www.xyz.com">United States</locale>
<locale href="http://www.xyz.co.uk">United Kingdom</locale>
</office>
</company>
```

Extended links can point to one or more targets. In the example above, the href is stored in the child elements (<locale>) of the linking element (<office>). A simple link would store the target in a single href of the linking element.

Out-of-line Links

While extended links and simple links can be quite powerful, they are still inline links, meaning they are present in the documents. Thankfully, XLL is not limited to inline links and offers the XML author support of out-of-line links. Out-of-line links do not have to be stored in the documents, but instead can be stored in an external linking document. This model is similar to Cascading Style Sheets, where one CSS document can control the way all documents look.

Out-of-line links come in handy when a large number of documents are linked to each other in one or more ways. For example, if this book were posted on the Web, each item in the table of contents would be a link to the page containing that item, whether it was a chapter heading or a specific section. For simplicity, I would also provide a link to a subsection from both the table of contents and the top of each chapter. So, the particular subsection would have two links pointing to it.

Now, imagine if I were to move the page that had the particular subsection, or change its named anchor. I would have to go into each page and manually change the link or run the whole book site through a program that had a search-and-replace feature. With out-of-line links, I could change the link in one place, the link document, and it would affect every reference to that link in my entire site.

At the time of this writing, out-of-line links have not found much support in applications. That is sure to change as XML becomes more accepted and the importance and power of out-of-line links becomes apparent.

XPointers

When using HTML, a named anchor is used to link to a specific part of a a document. Just as HTML linking was improved in XML through XLinks, the concept of named anchors is improved in XML through XPointers.

XPointer, or XML Pointer Language, is defined by the W3C as a language that supports addressing into the internal structures of XML documents, [providing] for specific reference to elements, character strings, and other parts of XML documents.

An XPointer consists of a series of location terms, either absolute or relative. Each location term specifies a location, has a keyword, and can have arguments. For example, the location term child(4, CD) refers to the fourth child element whose type is CD.

Absolute Location Terms

Absolute location terms do not depend on the existence of a location source.

root

If an XPointer begins with root(), the location source is the root element of the containing resource. If an XPointer omits any leading absolute location term, it is assumed to have a leading root() absolute location term.

origin

The origin keyword produces a meaningful location source for any following location terms only if the XPointer is being processed by application software in response to a request for traversal such as defined in the XLink specification. If an XPointer begins with origin(), the location source is the sub-resource from which the user initiated traversal rather than the default root element. This allows XPointers to select abstract items such as the next chapter.

id

If an XPointer begins with id(Name), the location source is the element in the containing resource with an attribute having a declared type of ID and a value matching the given name.

html

If an XPointer begins with html(NAMEVALUE), the location source is the first element whose type is A and which has an attribute called NAME whose value is the same as the supplied NAMEVALUE. This is exactly the function performed by the "#" fragment identifier in the context of an HTML document.

Relative Location Terms

Relative location terms depend on the existence of a location source.

child

Identifies direct child nodes of the location source.

descendant

Identifies nodes appearing anywhere within the content of the location source.

ancestor

Identifies element nodes containing the location source.

preceding

Identifies nodes that appear before (preceding) the location source.

following

Identifies nodes that appear after (following) the location source.

psibling

Identifies sibling nodes (sharing their parent with the location source) that appear before (preceding) the location source.

fsibling

Identifies sibling nodes (sharing their parent with the location source) that appear after (following) the location source.

XPointer Support

As of the time of this writing, XPointers are not supported in any applications. That should change quickly, though, as more and more applications are created.

There's a lot more to XPointers than the location terms and general discussion offered here.

Consult http://www.w3.org/TR/1998/WD-xptr-19980303 for the latest on XPointers.

Advanced XML Features

There are currently recommendations for a number of auxiliary XML technologies that promise to help XML grow into more widespread use and meet the challenges set forth in the original XML recommendation.

Namespaces

An XML namespace is a collection of names, identified by a Uniform Resource Identifier (URI), that provides a simple method for uniquely identifying the element names and attributes in an XML document.

XML namespaces help the author avoid name collisions on elements that have the same name but are defined in separate vocabularies. For example, a bibliography may have a <cat> tag, shorthand for category, and <cat> exists only under <book>. At the same time, there could be a <cat> tag defined under the <pet> tag. Namespaces help make the distinction between two tags like these. With documents shared all over the Internet, XML namespaces can really make a difference.

If you are interested in learning more about this exciting technology, point your browser to http://www.w3.org/TR/REC-xml-names/.

Summary

This chapter offers a basic overview of XML. Specifically, we covered:

- ♦ What XML is

- ♦ Why you would want to use XML

- ♦ How XML works

- ♦ Structuring XML documents using DTDs and Schemas

- ◆ Displaying XML with XSL

- ◆ Linking with XML

- ◆ Namespaces, an advanced topic

In the next chapter, we will cover some tools you can use to create your own XML documents.

3

XML Tools

Although XML can easily be created using your favorite text editor, its power can be maximized by complementing it with other development tools. These tools can be third-party authoring tools, programming editors, or database systems, among others.

The goal of this chapter is to cover some of those tools and provide you with the information you need to determine what is required to develop your own XML applications. We start by covering the most basic XML tool, the parser.

Parsing Tools

A parser is a program that reads through an XML document for the purpose of generating output. Parsers do not necessarily render XML files, but are an important part of publishing your XML documents. A parser can be written in practically any language. At the time of this writing, a quick glance on the Web shows parsers written in Java, TCL, C, Visual Basic, Perl, Python, and C++. Parsers can be in the form of a command line tool, a GUI-based program, and even an ActiveX control.

Parsers vary in their capabilities. One parser merely generates a list of tags, another more powerful parser generates a document tree. Some parsers have validation built in, and some even have XSL processing capabilities. Parsers come in different shapes and sizes, as the saying goes, and when choosing one, it all comes down to what you need.

Choosing an XML parser also depends on what you want to do. Do you want a parser that simply parses your XML document and outputs a tree? Or do you want a parser that validates your document in addition to outputting a tree? Once you have these questions answered and you know what you want in a parser, you can begin evaluating the different choices out there and decide what best suits you and your organization.

xmlproc

xmlproc is an XML parser written in Python. xmlproc is a nearly complete validating parser, with minor deviations from the XML specification. It supports namespaces, and provides access to DTD information.

SAX drivers are provided with this parser, as is support for the SGML Open Catalog and XCatalog 0.1.

xmlproc deviates from the XML specification in that external parameter entities are not allowed inside markup declarations. xmlproc also does not attempt to deal with different character sets or encodings, and does not check for illegal characters below . Finally, the parser allows some syntactic constructs to cross entity boundaries in ways that are not allowed.

xmlproc can be used in two ways, as a command-line parser or in Python code. The command-line parser is discussed here; the Python code is discussed in Chapter 6.

Using the Command-Line

To use xmlproc from the command-line, you must have a Python interpreter installed and linked to the .py extension. Most flavors of Unix and Unix clones, such as Linux, come with Python built-in. There is a Python distribution for Windows that you can download from the Web.

xmlproc at the command-line offers two options: One command to parse the file and not break on errors, and the other command to parse and validate the document.

The first, xpcmd.py, continues parsing after fatal errors. Its usage is:

xpcmd.py [-l language] [-o format] [-n] doc

Where language is the ISO 3166 language code for language to use in error messages, format is the format to output parsed XML, and doc is the document to parse (or the URL of the document to parse).

The second, xvcmd.py, validates the XML document and provides more options:

xvcmd.py [-c catalog] [-l language] [-o format] [-n] [doc]

Where catalog is the path to the catalog file to use to resolve public identifiers, language is the ISO 3166 language code for language to use in error messages, format is the format to output parsed XML, and doc is the document to parse (or the URL of the document to parse). -n denotes reporting of qualified names as URI name for namespace processing.

Python is a very versatile language and is gaining in popularity. Python, like Perl, is Web enabled, which means a developer could very easily develop an XML application in Python and access it via CGI requests.

I particularly like xmlproc when I am in my Linux environment. xmlproc can be downloaded from http://www.xml.com.

Xparse

Xparse is an XML parser implemented in JavaScript. Xparse is one of my favorite parsers because it is so easy to use and it offers a graphical representation of my XML documents.

Xparse can be found at http://www.jeremie.com/Dev/XML/index.jer. To use it, click the Test link on Jeremie's site. You will be presented with a two-frame window. The left-hand frame contains your XML source code, or you can point to your XML document through a URL. The right-hand frame displays a tree diagram of your parsed source. See Figure 3-1.

Xparse has a lot of ingenuity behind it and it's a quick way to do some XML testing while surfing the Web. It isn't necessary to open a separate application. Xparse is also a good way to demonstrate how XML works to someone who doesn't have an XML parser on his machine.

Xparse is written in less than 5 kilobytes of JavaScript. Best of all, you can download and study the JavaScript code to see how it works.

DOMParser

DOMParser is an interesting parser; it does not read raw XML source code but instead obtains elements, attributes, and so on from an instance of the XML Document Object Model (XML DOM is covered in Chapter 6).

DOMParser is a SAX-compliant parser, with the difference being that DOMParser does not take its input from InputSource but rather from a method, parse(Document doc). DOMParser is my favorite parser when it comes to quick-and-dirty XML DOM work.

XML Authoring Tools

There is a variety of authoring tools that support XML, and there are some tools that are specifically designed for creating XML documents. These tools vary in price as much as they vary in capability.

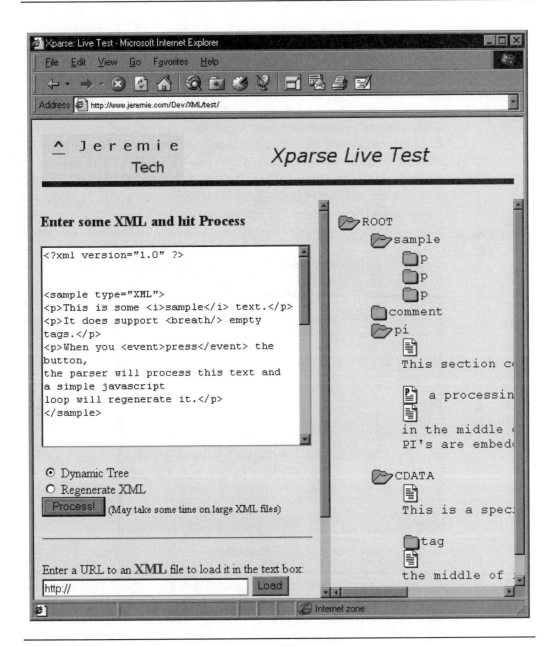

Figure 3-1: Screenshot of Xparse, the JavaScript XML parser

XML authoring tools are very popular right now. Some of the information may change by the time this book hits the press, so check each company's Web site for more information.

Macromedia Dreamweaver

Macromedia Dreamweaver, which can be downloaded from Macromedia's Web site at http://www.macromedia.com, offers a number of capabilities of interest to the XML developer, including XML parsing. I particularly like the feature that allows me to store XML tags in a tag database. I can also add XML objects to Dreamweaver's object palette and create property inspectors for editing XML. (See Figure 3-2.)

Figure 3-2: Screenshot of Macromedia Dreamweaver

Of course, Dreamweaver is a full-featured Web development tool that goes beyond XML editing. Dreamweaver offers Dynamic HTML capabilities, site management, Cascading Style Sheet support, and a plethora of other features. This is a lot of extra stuff for someone who only wishes to create and manipulate XML documents, and at $300, Dreamweaver may not be the most cost-effective tool for your XML needs.

Microsoft XML Notepad

There are a number of XML tools that are completely free. Microsoft XML Notepad, for example, is a free application that lets you create and manage XML through a tree paradigm. (See Figure 3-3.)

Microsoft XML Notepad is a good tool for creating XML files because it lets you visually lay out your tags. Although I prefer to create my tags and documents by hand, when I want to view a tree diagram of my XML documents I use Microsoft XML Notepad. The latest version of Microsoft XML Notepad is available on the Web at http://msdn.microsoft.com/xml.

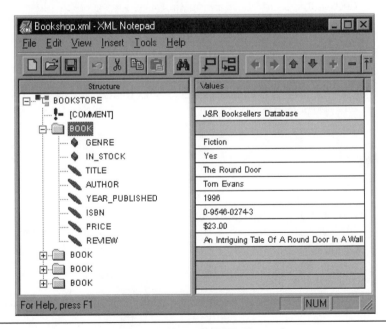

Figure 3-3: Screenshot of Microsoft XML Notepad

XMetaL

XMetaL is a product from SoftQuad, the creators of HoTMetaL, one of the very first HTML editors.

A cross between HoTMetaL and SoftQuad's SGML tool, Author/Editor, XMetaL is an extensible editor that offers the power of generic markup without the restrictions of a fixed DTD and without the complexity of an SGML editor.

XMetaL is a validating, structured editor, and includes an Attribute Inspector. The Attribute Inspector is a dialog for editing element attributes as well as context-sensitive tagging.

XMetaL is based on HoTMetaL, not Author/Editor, so it is as easy to use as the HoTMetaL editor. It includes the features of HoTMetaL, such as OLE authentication, docking toolbars, and a clean interface for editing documents while the tags are hidden.

XMetaL supports XLL, CSS, and XSL. The plan is to include graphic tools for mapping XSL to tags, since XMetaL does not require a DTD for development. XMetaL generates CSS styles to accompany the XML document when exported.

Visual XML

Another tool currently in development is Visual XML, written by Pierre Morel. Visual XML is written in Java and requires Sun's JDK v1.1.6. Visual XML is a generic structured editing application that lets you edit both documents and DTDs. Visual XML is a great tool for creating XML documents intended for Web searching.

One of the things I liked about Visual XML did not have anything to do with XML. The user can select one of three interfaces: Metal, Windows, or Motif. This made the application fun to use and the fact that it works very well for beta software is also heartening.

XML Pro

XML Pro is an interesting editor because it is data-centric versus document-centric. The XML Pro user interface puts a hierarchical view of the document in the primary workspace and has a full-time view of attributes and attribute values. This is quite different from the classic structured editor that emphasizes the text editing space and provides secondary window space for attribute editing and the like.

XML Pro is written in Java and requires the JDK 1.1.6 runtime. At $150, it is a tool most can afford to evaluate.

Adept Editor

Adept Editor 7.0, a descendant of ArborText's excellent validating SGML editor, is an XML authoring tool developed by ArborText that can save SGML documents as XML and XML documents as SGML, but requires a DTD for all documents. Adept provides a wealth of features to aid the XML author, including a composition module that displays a preview of the document, a customizable user interface, and schematized view of the document structure.

Adept Editor is an industrial strength tool not for the faint of heart. Arbor-Text has promised an end-user version of Adept that is simplified and quicker to set up. In the meantime, Adept Editor is not intended for the casual user intending to make well-formed XML, but is instead intended for professional document authors.

ArborText Adept Editor runs on Unix and Windows.

WordPerfect SGML

Back in the 1980s, WordPerfect ruled the word processing world. During the days of DOS, WordPerfect was the word processor of choice, with version 5.1 proving the most popular.

In the early 1990s, WordPerfect was purchased by Novell for a large sum of money. Unfortunately for Novell, Windows was gaining in popularity and WordPerfect 6.0 for Windows, facing stiff competition from Microsoft Word, was not doing too well in the marketplace.

Eventually, Novell sold the WordPerfect product to Corel for much less money. Corel, the makers of the popular CorelDraw program, saw an opportunity in WordPerfect to join the fray of desktop software.

Since then, WordPerfect has grown into a very good product. Corel decided to include SGML support in a special version of WordPerfect, called WordPerfect SGML 8.

WordPerfect SGML's support of SGML and XML is superb. Its implementation of SGML is excellent, the product is easy to use, and the integration of structure with style is second to none.

Support for real-time validation against arbitrary DTDs is provided in WordPerfect SGML 8, with promises of XSL support in a future version. This product also includes a legal copy of Microstar Near & Far Lite DTD viewer. WordPerfect SGML 8 runs on Windows and Unix.

Adobe FrameMaker+SGML

Adobe FrameMaker+SGML is an extension of Adobe FrameMaker, a popular book-oriented authoring tool. FrameMaker+SGML can create both structured and unstructured documents, and is best suited for authors who have to produce printed versions of their documents.

FrameMaker+SGML is a professional WYSIWYG (What You See Is What You Get) page makeup tool that outputs SGML, HTML, PDF, and XML, with localized support for English, German, Japanese, and French.

Adobe FrameMaker+SGML runs on Windows, Macintosh, Solaris, HP/UX, IBM AIX, SunOS, and SGI IRIX platforms.

Content Management Tools

The purpose of a content management tool is to provide a centralized location for management of content. The tools discussed here vary widely in price and functionality, and offer differing support for authoring tools.

Keep in mind that these are not the only tools out there. These are just a few of the tools that I have exposure to, and I think they serve as good examples of what is available. Be sure to check the individual companies' Web sites for more product information.

SGML Database Editorial System

SGML Database Editorial System, developed by Auto-Graphics Inc., is a system designed for database publishing. The product is based on Smart Editor, a record-oriented text editor that has built-in SGML functionality and is interfaced to a relational database.

The SGML Database Editorial System supports CD-ROM, print, and Web publishing, and offers integration with FrameMaker+SGML, Quark, and Xyvision software. It supports Microsoft SQL Server and Oracle database systems.

The server portion is supported under Windows NT, and the client is supported under Windows 98 and Windows NT.

Astoria

Astoria is an XML-aware document management system developed by San Diego-based Chrystal Software. Astoria works with authoring tools to improve access to and control over information.

Combined with an editor, Astoria supports editing, authoring, and searching, as well as translation and multimedia distribution.

Astoria works with Object Design's Object Store as the database solution, and supports Adobe FrameMaker+SGML, ArborText Editor, Adobe FrameMaker, and InContext 2 for authoring.

The Astoria server product runs under Solaris and Windows NT 4.0, with clients supported under Windows NT and Windows 95.

Oracle 8i

Oracle is the powerhouse of database systems, with a large market share and a large organization behind its products.

With Oracle's release of Oracle 8i, the company offers a database system with built-in XML support. Oracle 8i should prove to be an interesting platform for developing XML-enabled document management systems.

XML support in Oracle 8i takes shape in three key parts. The Oracle XML Parser, written in Java, is fully XML 1.0 compliant and is designed to programmatically process XML documents. Oracle 8i's database file system (iFS) supports XML to automate parsing and assembly of data. Oracle 8i also offers an XML-enabled section searching feature in the ConText search engine.

Remember that Oracle 8i is a database system, and not a document-management system. It is mentioned here because of its built-in support of XML.

Oracle 8i runs on Windows NT and several Unix platforms.

Object Store

ObjectStore is an object database management system (ODBMS) with XML capabilities. ObjectStore can index, serve, manage, and query XML documents.

ObjectStore has an interesting feature that lets one define a database schema with a DTD and manipulate the data through HTML tags. Object databases are well-suited to working with structured XML documents. Relational databases must map XML to relational tables and flatten the XML data into rows and columns, while an object database allows the data to be naturally stored and manipulated at an element level of granularity.

ObjectStore is currently available for various flavors of Unix, Windows NT (Alpha and Intel), Windows 95/98, and OS/2.

Summary

In this chapter, we covered some popular tools for authoring and managing XML, including shrinkwrapped products and programming libraries.

Specifically, we covered:

- ◆ Parsing tools implemented in various languages

- ◆ Popular authoring tools, varying in capabilities

- ◆ Popular content management tools, including databases

The next chapter covers some existing XML applications and how they can work for you.

4

Applications of XML

An "application of XML" denotes the use of XML for a specific application, as opposed to an "XML application," which is an application that is designed to produce XML. Either of these definitions can be argued, but they are presented here for clarification purposes.

Although XML is a relatively new technology, there already exists a number of recommendations to the W3C for new applications of XML. Four of these applications, Extensible Forms Description Language, Vector Markup Language, Mathematical Markup Language, and Channel Definition Format, are covered in this chapter to present to you an example of how XML can be used to create a separate markup language. However, it does not stop there. These four languages have very good uses and you may find them valuable to your organization.

Extensible Forms Description Language

During the years between 1993 and 1998, UWI.Com developed an Internet language to handle the difficult task of digitizing complex forms. This language was called the Universal Forms Description Language (UFDL).

When XML came onto the scene, UWI.Com saw an opportunity and took it. An XML syntax was created for UFDL, and XFDL was born.

XFDL was designed by UWI.Com and Tim Bray to meet the need of intelligent, legally binding, and secure business forms that are required by Internet sites that, for example, use electronic commerce or provide government forms.

An XFDL form consists of questions, or form templates, and answers, or input data. Without the questions, the answers have no meaning. Other Web-based forms do not create legally-binding records because they transmit and store only the answers. XFDL stores the form template, data, and internal logic in a single file. This file can be authorized and secured with a digital signature.

Basically, XFDL allows you to describe a form using XML. At the moment, there are not any tools that automatically generate XFDL. Neither is it possible to write a DTD for an XFDL form making it necessary to use a dedicated tool to validate an XFDL form.

Although this is a fairly technical discussion of XFDL, because it references things not yet discussed, I wanted it that way so you could jump right in, head first.

XFDL Form Structure

An XFDL form is an XML document whose root element is of the XFDL type. The root element requires the version attribute. The XFDL syntax is as follows:

```
<!ATTLIST XFDL version CDATA #REQUIRED>
```

An XFDL element contains zero or more option elements followed by one or more page elements. The option elements that occur before the first page are referred to as *form global options*. Typically, form global options contain information that applies to the whole form.

A page element contains zero or more global options, followed by zero or more item elements. Page global options usually contain information that applies to the whole page. Page global options take precedence over form global options.

Items

At its most basic level, an item is a single object in a page or form. Items can be used to transport information such as a digital signature or data requests. Items can also represent graphical user interface objects, like buttons and text fields. (See Figure 4-1.)

Item Type	Description
action	Performs the same tasks as a button (submit, print, etc.) at a set interval; action is non-visible.
box	Groups a set of GUI objects on a page
button	Can perform a variety of tasks when pressed by the user.
cell	Defines a single entry in a list, popup, or combobox.
check	Defines a single checkbox.
combobox	An editable field combined with a popup list.
data	Carries binary information, such as digital images.
field	Captures (and validates, if necessary) single- or multiline text input from the user.
help	Text that can be associated with other items that can provide contextual help.
label	Contains an image or text.
line	A graphic used as a separator, like a horizontal rule.

Figure 4-1: The prebuilt XFDL item types

Item Type	Description
list	A list box populated with user-specified cell items.
popup	Contextual display of text
radio	A single radio button
signature	The digital signature sent when a user presses a signature button.
spacer	A non-visible GUI object that provides relational positioning capability.
toolbar	Items in a toolbar appear in a separate window above the form page.

Figure 4-1: The prebuilt XFDL item types

Items can contain zero or more option elements. The options define the characteristics of the item, and any item that contains zero options is defined by the option defaults.

XFDL includes a prebuilt list of items that you can use in your forms, but also allows application-defined items. Application-defined items help the form developer break down a problem into separately solveable parts.

Options

Options define named attributes of items, pages, or forms. XFDL also supports application-defined options.

An option's content can be one of three formats: simple character data, a compute, or an array of XML elements. The content attribute identifies which type of content will appear. (See Figure 4-2.)

Option	Description
activated	Includes focused and mouseover; based on system events.
bgcolor	Includes fontcolor, labelcolor, labelbgcolor, and labelfontcolor; specifies color for an item.

Figure 4-2: Option types and descriptions

Option	Description
borderwidth	Includes labelborderwidth; specifies whether an item has a 3D border.
coordinates	The location of a mouse click on an image.
data	Includes datagroup; creates an association between data terms and the buttons that provide file enclosure.
delay	Specifies the timing and occurrence of the event in an action item.
editstate	Specifies read only, read/write, or write only.
filename	Includes mimetype; gives information about an enclosed document.
fontinfo	Includes labelfontinfo; defines the font, point size, and effects (bold, underline, italic, strikethrough, etc.).
format	Contains subelements that parameterize input validation.
group	Groups radio buttons together.
help	Identifies the help item associated with an item.
image	Defines the file containing an image for an item.
itemlocation	Includes size and thickness; defines the location and size of an item.
justify	Sets item text to left-aligned, right-aligned, or justified.
label	Links a text label with an item.
mimedata	Stores large binary data.
next	Includes previous; links an item to the tab order in a page.
printsettings	Sets the paper rendition of a form into parameters.
saveformat	Includes transmitformat; controls how the form is written (XFDL, HTML, etc.).

Figure 4-2: Option types and descriptions

Option	Description
scrollhoriz	Includes scrollvert; defines horizontal and vertical scrollbars for an item.
signature	Includes signdatagroups, signer, signformat, signgroups, signitemrefs, signitems, sinoptionrefs, and signoptions; provides a digital signature.
triggeritem	Identifies which action, button, or cell was pressed last.
type	Specifies whether the action, button, or cell item will perform a network operation, print, save, etc.
url	Provides the address for a page.
value	Holds the primary text associated with an item.
visible	Sets the visibility for an item.

Figure 4-2: Option types and descriptions

The default content format is simple. If the content format is simple, then the content attribute is not required. This situation dictates that the option must contain text with no child elements.

If the content is identified as a compute, then the option may contain a cval element. The cval element contains simple character data that represents the computed value of the option. If the cval element is not present, XFDL equates it to <cval></cval>.

The compute element requires the presence of a computational expression. Typically, the form performs the computes on the client and reports the results to the server. This means that an application can think of the compute as character data.

The third format for an option's content is an array of XML elements. The option must contain one or more array elements and the content attribute is required and should be set to "array."

The fontcolor option uses array elements. Here is an example:

```
<fontcolor content="array">
```

```
<ae>162</ae>
<ae>43</ae>
<ae>97</ae>
</fontcolor>
```

The array element takes the same content attribute that option elements do, and its contents are controlled by the value of the attribute in the same way.

Reproducing Documents

XFDL processors are expected to preserve the XML prolog and epilog, the comments within the XFDL element, and all element attributes appearing in start tags but not specifically defined by XFDL. The attributes must be associated with their respective start tags, and the comments must be associated with the respective pages, items, options, or array elements to which they apply. The XFDL processor must be able to reproduce these language components for digital signatures and for saving or transmitting the form.

XFDL Compute Structure

An XFDL compute can appear between <compute> and </compute>. Most XFDL processors preserve a compute as character data, but some must parse the text of a compute, creating a tree data structure to represent all computes in a form.

XFDL computes automatically support free-form text. Unlimited white space is supported, with the exception of quoted strings. So, all white space appearing outside of a quoted string is ignored.

Structure of Expressions

An XFDL compute can be either a conditional or mathematical expression. A conditional expression has three parts separated by the ? operator. The first part is a Decision, whose logic can apply logical-or (||), logical-negation (!), and logical-and (&&) to the results of logical comparisons. The logical operators are left associative, and the comparators cannot be chained.

A mathematical expression (Expr) can include addition, subtraction, multiplication, division, exponentiation, integer modulus, unary minus, and string concatenation. Proper order of operations is observed (remember My Dear Aunt Sally, M[ultiplication] D[ivision] A[ddition] S[ubtraction], from elementary school?) and parentheses can be used to override the order of operations.

Definition of Value

A value can be a compute in parantheses, which, as mentioned before, provides an override for the order of operations. A value can also be a quoted string, an XFDL reference to an element whose data is obtained when the compute is evaluated, and a result of a function call.

Quoted Strings

An XFDL quoted string must be surrounded by quotation marks (" "), and can be of arbitrary length. XFDL quoted strings can also be multiline to support readability.

White space is, of course, ignored. Double quotes are included by escaping them with a backslash (\). Tab and newline are represented by \t and \n, respectively. The backslash must be escaped as well, resulting in \\.

Function Call Syntax

Function calls run code that may be external to the XFDL form definition. XFDL includes a set of predefined functions for doing standard mathematical operations. The list is available at http://www.w3c.org.

Running XFDL Computes

When a form starts, it must run all computes to provide content for the current value tags. Each time an event causes a change to the simple data content or current value of an option or array element, a RunXFDLComputes() is called with a list containing only the element that changed. (See Figure 4.3.)

If a string of simple data is assigned to an element via a public API call, then the compute and its current value are destroyed.

```
Z = empty list
Do {
NewChangeList = empty list
For I = 1 to n(C) do
Pertinent = (E = nil) ? true : false
For J = 1 to n(E)
If C_I contains E_J' then Pertinent = true
If Pertinent
F_P = parent element containing C_I
If current value of F_P is not equal to eval(C_I)
NewChangeList+=F_P
Z += F_P
cval(F_P) = eval(C_I)
E = NewChangeList
} while (E is not empty)
return Z
```

Figure 4-3: RunXFDLComputes, reprinted from the XFDL 1.0 Draft

Sample XFDL Forms

These samples are taken directly from the W3C XFDL 1.0 Draft. I think they are excellent examples of how XFDL works.

The first example is designed to show a whole XFDL form. After the global options are declared, the page contains three fields. You may recognize this as the Pythagorean Theorem.

```
<?xml version="1.0"?>
<XFDL version="4.1.0">
<bgcolor content="array">
<ae>128</ae> <ae>128</ae> <ae>128</ae>
</bgcolor>

<page sid="Pythagorean Theorem">
<bgcolor content="array">
<ae>192</ae> <ae>192</ae> <ae>192</ae>
</bgcolor>
<label>Pythagorean Theorem Form</label>

<field sid="A">
<label>Enter A:</label>
<value>3</value>
```

```
</field>

<field sid="B">
<label>Enter B:</label>
<value>4</value>
</field>

<field sid="C">
<label>Hypotenuse Length C:</label>
<editstate>readonly</editstate>
<value content="compute">
<cval>5</cval>
<compute>sqrt(A.value^"2" + B.value^"2")</compute>
</value>
</field>

</page>
</XFDL>
```

The second example does not include the XML prolog, and is designed to show more computes than the form in the first example. This example could be used in a credit card payment application.

```
<field sid="PayNow">
<label>What portion of this bill do you want to pay now?</label>
<value>0</value>
<format content="array">
<type>dollar</type>
<ae>add_ds</ae>
<ae>mandatory</ae>
<range content="array">
<ae content="compute">
<cval>35</cval>
<compute>Balance.value * "0.05"</compute>
</ae>
<ae content="compute">
<cval>700</cval>
<compute>Balance.value</compute>
</ae>
</range>
</format>
</field>
<label sid="DemonstrateSuboptionReferencing">
<value content="compute">
```

```
<cval>dollar add_ds 35700</cval>
<compute>
PayNow.format[type] + " " + PayNow.format[1] + " " +
PayNow.format[range][0] + PayNow.format[range][1]
</compute>
</value>
</label>
```

XFDL is definitely not for everybody. For the author who isn't familiar with other document description languages, XFDL is complicated and difficult to grasp.

However, XFDL can be worth it. As we move toward a Web-based economy, secure and legally binding forms will prove invaluable.

Vector Markup Language

The Vector Markup Language is still in the note process, which means it is not a standard approved by the W3C. That disclaimer aside, VML is a very promising development in the XML world.

VML is an XML application that defines a format for encoding vector information with additional markup to describe how that information can be displayed and edited.

What Are Vector Graphics?

Vector graphics use geometrical formulas to represent images. By contrast, raster graphics, also known as bitmap graphics, use a pattern of dots to represent images. Vector graphics are more flexible than bitmap graphics because they can be stretched and resized. Vector-based images require less memory than raster-based images, and look better on monitors with higher resolution. Bitmap graphics always appear the same, regardless of a monitor's resolution.

Most monitors are raster devices, which means that vector objects are rasterized before they are displayed. So, the difference between vector graphics and bitmap graphics is that vector graphics are not converted into bitmaps until the last possible moment. Conceivably, vector graphics representations can be output on any device, including monitors and printers, at any resolution and size.

Programs that create and manipulate vector graphics are called *draw programs*. Animation tools and CAD programs, to name a couple of examples, use vector graphics. A list of common vector graphics file formats is in Figure 4-4.

Programs that create and manipulate bitmap graphics are called *paint programs*. Microsoft Paint and Adobe Photoshop are two popular programs that are used to create bitmap graphics.

CGM	Computer Graphics Metafile; standard format
DXF	Data Exchange File; created by AutoDesk for CAD
EPS	Encapsulated PostScript; created by Adobe
HPGL	Hewlett-Packard Graphics Language; old, but good support
IGES	Initial Graphics Exchange Specification; ANSI standard for three-dimensional wireframe models
PIC	Lotus Picture File; designed to represent graphs in Lotus 1-2-3
PICT	Developed by Apple Computer for storing and exchanging graphics files; supported by programs that run on MacOS
WMF	Windows Metafile; format for exchanging graphics files in Windows applications

Figure 4-4: Common vector graphics file formats

Vector Graphics and VML

Remember that VML supports the markup of vector graphic information in the same way that HTML supports the markup of textual information. VML was not designed to simply display prebuilt vector images (such as a .DXF) in the browser; instead, VML allows you to create vector images through VML markup. With location and related information for a vector path, VML renders related objects (such as raster images) using native operating system functionality.

VML describes editable objects. These objects are shapes (see Figure 4-5) or collections of shapes called *groups*. In HTML, the editable objects are paragraphs, forms, and tables. VML supports a wide variety of editors and will ensure that different editors can recognize and correctly handle each other's data.

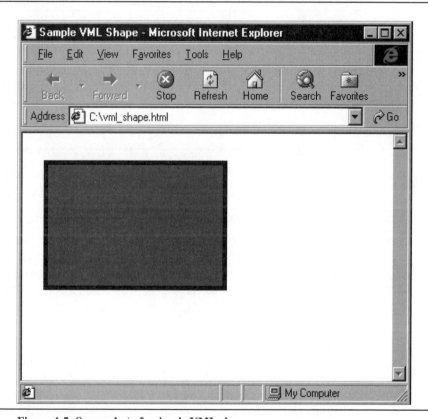

Figure 4-5: Screenshot of a simple VML shape

This code creates the vector graphic in Figure 4-5:

```
<html xmlns:v="urn:schemas-microsoft-com:vml">
<head>
<title>Sample VML Shape</title>
<object id="VMLRender" classid="CLSID:10072CEC-8CC1-11D1-986E
-00A0C955B42E">
</object>
<style>
v\:* { behavior: url(#VMLRender); }
</style>
</head>
<body>
<v:rect style='width:150pt;height:100pt' fillcolor="red"
strokecolor="black" strokeweight="3.5pt"/>
</body>
</html>
```

Benefits of VML

There are many benefits to using VML. First, it provides for the easy exchange of vector graphics between document authors. One need only cut-and-paste the VML code to get the vector image and put it on another page.

Second, VML graphics are very small. This makes for faster downloads and a more pleasant user experience. Try it out for yourself. Copy and paste the HTML code above into a file on your Webserver, and then browse to the Webserver with Internet Explorer 5.0. The image will instantly appear (I'm assuming your Webserver is a remote machine. Of course the image would load superfast if you are running the Webserver on your local machine.)

Third, VML is an open standard. This means that any application that supports VML *should* render VML the same as the next application. Since VML is based on XML, you know that VML is rooted in a strong markup language.

Finally, many organizations are embracing VML. You've already seen Internet Explorer 5.0's support in Figure 4-5. At the time of this writing, companies including Autodesk, VISIO, and Macromedia have pledged support for VML in their products.

Remember that VML does not replace GIF or JPG images. Instead, it complements them. The important distinction is that VML produces vector graphics, while GIF and JPG images are raster graphics.

VML Implementation

There are two types of VML implementations: A viewer type and an editor type. A viewer type will generally support the entire VML specification, save for the portions that are directly related to editing documents. An editor type will generally only support the specific features needed to output the data the editor manipulates. An editor type should also be able to correctly position VML produced by other applications (remember, it must be able to read the other editors data), but the ability to render shapes created by other applications is not required.

To avoid confusion, when I think of VML, I generally stay within the confines of the technical specification because I don't plan to develop a piece of software that views or edits VML. If I did need to develop that software, I would license a COM object or library to handle it for me. You may have a different requirement; I invite you to read the VML specification for further information.

VML Design Requirements

The VML specification lists eight crucial requirements that guided the design of VML. These eight items, listed below, give insight to how VML was designed to work and what the designers had in mind when they were putting VML together.

1. VML should retain the information required for further editing. In other words, VML must be extensible. This is so VML can meet the requirements of all editing applications. This forces the possibility for every application to add its own editing data.

2. VML should support the interchange of data between applications. Applications must be able to read and edit the information of another application, even if each application adds its own data.

3. VML must use the existing mechanisms of HTML and CSS (Cascading Style Sheets). This ensures that VML implementations can reuse code and mechanisms.

4. VML must be backward compatible with existing user agents. In this context, a user agent is a program that interprets marked-up languages. This can include a Web browser or a spider program, among others. To support backward compability, VML has built-in provisions to allow alternate bitmap representations.

5. VML must provide efficient representations of vector graphics. One way VML addresses the verbosity of textual descriptions is by following a design principle of using concise names for frequently used attributes.

6. VML should allow the implementation of subsets. This is important for developers who want to create applications that don't require all of VML's functionality.

7. VML should support hand-editing. Have you ever known an HTML author who does his or her coding in Windows Notepad, BBedit, or emacs? Some people prefer to do their HTML coding by hand. The VML designers realized that, since HTML is so simple, hand-editing is an option. So, they decided that VML should be simple enough to support hand-editing.

8. VML should support scripting and the requirements of animation. This has many ramifications, including leading to a desire for the structure of VML to match the structure of the graphic it's defining, as well as leading to the use of types of VML attributes that are applicable to animation.

VML is currently supported in Microsoft Internet Explorer 5.0. The VML support in Internet Explorer 5.0 is pretty good; you might notice in the screenshots that the rendering user-agent is indeed Internet Explorer 5.0.

Mathematical Markup Language

HTML does not provide native tags for marking up mathematical expressions. If you want to display this demonstration-purposes-only fake mathematical expression

$$\frac{(x\phi + y\phi)}{y!}$$

in your Web browser, you would have to create it as an image and reference it with the $<$IMG SRC$>$ tag. What's worse, you have to first create the image in a mathematics program, such as Mathematica, and then get your equation into a graphics format of some kind.

The Mathematical Markup Language (MathML) is meant to alleviate the pain of displaying mathematical content on the Web. MathML is the foundation of using mathematical expressions in Web pages. MathML supports markup for presenting mathematical equations in a display, and semantic markup for mathematical content, which is vital to scientific applications.

One of the interesting aspects of MathML is that it is meant to be created by a program, or as the W3C Recommendation puts it, "a machine." MathML is a low-level format for describing mathematics, and is designed to be handled by equation editors or other mathematics packages.

Semantic and Presentational Tags

Let's consider another mathematical expression, a bit simpler and more realistic than the previous example:

$$2x^2 - 8 = 0$$

This example can be presented in two ways: using semantic tags and using presentational tags.

Semantic Tags

Semantic tags in MathML are designed to describe your content. Here is the equation using semantic tags:

```
<apply>
<minus/>
<apply>
<times/>
<cn>2</cn>
</apply>
<apply>
<power/>
<ci>x</ci>
<cn>2</cn>
</apply>
<apply>
<cn>8</cn>
</apply>
```

From the code, you can see the equation represented in English, and if you follow the structure, you can see how the equation works.

Presentational tags

Presentational tags in MathML are more like the presentation tags in HTML, such as <B> or (gasp) <BLINK>. Here is the equation using presentational tags:

```
<mrow>
<mrow>
<mn>2</mn><mo>&invisibletimes;</mo>
<msup><mi>x</mi><mn>2</mn>
<mo>-</mo>
<mn>8</mn>
<mrow>
```

Presentational tags generally start with "m" and then use "n" for number, "i" for identifier, "o" for operator, and so on. The `<mrow>` are there for structuring into horizontal groups.

MathML Implementations

MathML is not directly supported by the two major browsers, but there are numerous plug-ins and Java applets out there that display MathML content in a browser.

The W3C MathML recommendation lists some applications that support MathML. (See Figure 4-6.).

Amaya	W3C's browser and authoring tool for Web pages
EzMath	Convenient way to author MathML
IBM techexplorer	Technical/scientific document viewer and renderer
Maple	Computer algebra system that can import and export MathML
Mathematica	High-quality mathematical typesetting and editing; renders and exports MathML
MathType	An intelligent equation editor
Publicon	Full-featured publishing system designed for producing professional-quality technical documents
WebEQ	Java-based collection of tools for authoring and rendering MathML

Figure 4-6: MathML software

MathML has a very bright future and serves as an excellent example of XML's capabilities.

Channel Definition Format

When push technology debuted, it promised to change the way people surfed the Net forever. The concept of push technology was that the user would subscribe to data services (such as a newspaper) and the data from that service would be "pushed" down to the user's machine, rather than having the user "pull" data down by requesting it himself.

Push technology operates under the assumption that the user specify his or her data requirements, whether they be sports scores, news articles, stock tickers, or practically anything else you can imagine that is accessible via a Web server.

Channel Definition Format (CDF) is an XML-based solution for push technology. CDF allows a Web author to push data from frequently updated data sources, called channels, to programs that are capable of receiving this data. When you subscribe to a CDF channel, the downloading of data is automatic, meaning it will happen without you telling it to.

Microsoft's implementation of CDF is called Active Channel. Active Channel is supported by Internet Explorer 4.0 and above. In this discussion, we will cover Active Channel since it is the most widespread implementation of CDF.

Netscape does not support CDF.

How Active Channel Works

An Active Channel basically consists of one or more Web pages and its associated files (i.e., images) and a CDF file. The Web pages make up the content for the channel, and the CDF file gives the developer the tools he needs to build a channel that allows subscribers to access the information.

In other words, the CDF file gives the channel its structure by describing the navigation hierarchy for the channel.

A CDF file contains no content of its own. Remember, the CDF file is the file that describes the structure for an Active Channel. The CDF file is a sort of site map that is meant to aid the subscriber in navigating the channel. The CDF file uses XML to control the deployment and information refreshing of the Active Channel.

When a subscriber visits an Active Channel, Internet Explorer downloads all of the information contained in that channel so the subscriber can view it offline. This "offline browsing" capability is valuable to people who pay a per-hour charge for Internet access, like ISDN users. Of course, browsing information that is stored locally is much faster than browsing content on a Web server.

It should be noted that Active Channels are *meant* to be viewed offline. This means that CGI or Active Server Pages cannot be used in Active Channel content because it will not work offline. If you can figure out some way to do what you want in client-side script (such as JavaScript), that would definitely be the better way to go.

Implementing Active Channel

One of the best things about CDF is that only a Web server is needed to use it. Even better, only a text editor is needed to create a CDF file! I like to use Microsoft CDF Generator, which can be downloaded from the MSDN site at http://msdn.microsoft.com.

Implementing an Active Channel takes three basic steps. In this discussion, we will use a text editor to create an Active Channel, since not everyone runs Windows.

Create the CDF File

We'll go through the process of creating a CDF file one step at a time. This will help you better understand how CDF works and it should help you determine if CDF is something you want to throw resources at.

Create an XML Document

The first thing you do is open a new, blank text file and insert the text that identifies the XML character set and version number. This text should be the first line of your document.

```
<?XML ENCODING="UTF-8" VERSION="1.0"?>
```

The ?XML element, as you know, identifies this file as an XML document. The ENCODING and VERSION attributes in this example are not necessary because the default values are used, but it is a good idea to specify this information anyway.

Save the Document as a CDF File

It's probably a good idea to go ahead and save the document as a CDF file now. The file extension must be .CDF or Internet Explorer won't know what to do with the file. With the .CDF file extension, the server returns the correct MIME type to the browser and the browser understands that it must treat the file as a CDF channel. Without this MIME type, the CDF file is displayed in the browser as text.

Create the CHANNEL Element

Next, put in the CHANNEL element. Everything you put in the CDF file will be inserted between the open (<CHANNEL>) and close (</CHANNEL>) tags. The CHANNEL element defines the top level of the CDF's hierarchy, with its HREF attribute pointing to the top-level Web page in the CDF file.

```
<CHANNEL BASE ="http://www.DVDmdb.com/"
HREF="/channels/CDF.htm"
LASTMOD="1999-04-24T20:22"
PRECACHE="YES"
LEVEL="1"> </CHANNEL>
```

The LASTMOD attribute specifies the date the page was last modified. The PRECACHE attribute specifies whether or not the browser should precache the site. The LEVEL attribute specifies the number of levels deep the browser should "go." The BASE attribute allows the author to use relative paths, such as "/file.htm".

In this example, Internet Explorer is going to precache the CDF.html file and all of the pages linked to it. When you don't want to precache every page, simply set the LEVEL attribute to 0.

Insert the TITLE and ABSTRACT Elements

The TITLE and ABSTRACT elements are important to a channel because the text contained in these elements will represent the channel in the Windows Media Showcase on users' desktops, as well as in the Channel bar in Internet Explorer 4.0. These elements are ignored by the offline Favorites feature in Internet Explorer 5.0; thus, the title appearing in the HEAD section of the channel will represent offline Favorites in the Favorites bar in Internet Explorer 5.0.

```
<TITLE>DVDmdb Channel</TITLE>
<ABSTRACT>Provides updates for DVDmdb information</ABSTRACT>
```

The TITLE element specifies the title of the channel. The ABSTRACT element attaches a description of the channel.

Create the Update SCHEDULE

The SCHEDULE element is ignored by the offline Favorites feature in Internet Explorer 5.0, but still works in channels. With the SCHEDULE element, one can choose to update a channel's content daily, weekly, monthly, or when he or she chooses Update All Subscriptions from the Favorites menu (Synchronize from the Tools menu in Internet Explorer 5.0).

```
<SCHEDULE>
<INTERVALTIME DAY="7"/>
</SCHEDULE>
```

In this example, the channel's content is updated weekly. The channel developer can also use the EARLIESTTIME and LATESTTIME elements to specify a range of valid update times. This would help in managing server loads.

Add LOGO Images

This step is optional. The images specified in the LOGO element will represent the channel in the same places as the <TITLE> and <ABSTRACT>

elements discussed above. Default images are provided when necessary.

```
<LOGO HREF="http://www.DVDmdb.com/channel/image1.gif"
STYLE="IMAGE-WIDE"/>
<LOGO HREF="http://www.DVDmdb.com/channel/image2.gif"
STYLE="IMAGE"/>
<LOGO HREF="http://www.DVDmdb.com/channel/image3.gif"
STYLE="ICON"/>
```

Any image format supported by Internet Explorer 4.0 or 5.0 (depending on your target browser) can be used in the LOGO element.

Specify Pages with the ITEM Element

Before Internet Explorer 5.0, browsers only gave the option to cache all or none of a page's links. With Internet Explorer 5.0, authors can choose which pages are cached when users add pages to Favorites.

```
<ITEM HREF="http://www.DVDmdb.com/channel/next.htm"
LASTMOD="1999-04-28T23:13"
PRECACHE="YES"
LEVEL="1">
<TITLE>DVDmdb Executives</TITLE>
<ABSTRACT>Profiles the executive team at DVDmdb</ABSTRACT>
<LOGO HREF="/images/logo.jpg" STYLE="IMAGE"/>
</ITEM>
```

Since PRECACHE is set to "YES" and the LEVEL attribute is set to "1", *next.htm* will be cached, as well as all pages linked to *next.htm*.

Be sure to save your CDF file at this point. Be sure to add the .CDF extension if you haven't already.

Link the Web Page to the CDF

When you create a channel, you have to link your Web page to the CDF file. There are two separate ways to do this: one for the Active Channel and one for an offline Favorite (remember that offline Favorites are supported in Internet Explorer 5.0 only).

First, add the "Add Active Channel" button to your Web server. Microsoft used to require Active Channel developers to sign up and accept the terms of the Active Channel Logo agreement, but at the time of this writing, Microsoft had relaxed the qualifications.

Here's what the Add Active Channel image looks like:

Microsoft has a whole section of its Microsoft Developer Network (MSDN) site devoted to Active Channel. It seems that Microsoft changes their site constantly, so where it is today could be different from where it is six months from now. I would recommend cruising over to the MSDN Web Workshop site at http://msdn.microsoft.com.

Once you have that image on your HTML Web page, Microsoft recommends you add some browser check code to the <HEAD></HEAD> section of your page. Here's the browser check code reprinted from their Web site:

```
<SCRIPT LANGUAGE="JavaScript">
function isMsie4orGreater(){
var ua = window.navigator.userAgent; var msie = ua.indexOf ("MSIE");
if (msie > 0) {
return (parseInt (ua.substring (msie+5, ua.indexOf(".", msie))) >= 4)
&& (ua.indexOf ("MSIE 4.0b") <0); }
else { return false; }}
</SCRIPT>
```

If you have something simpler that does the same thing, go for it. For adding browser check code to my pages, I use Macromedia Dreamweaver's built-in JavaScript library.

Now that you have the Add Active Channel button, the CDF file on the Web server, and the browser check code, the next thing to do is add the code to link to theCDF file from your Web page. Here's the code I used for the DVDmdb channel:

```
<A NAME="DVDmdb"
HREF="http://www.microsoft.com/ie">
<IMG SRC="/images/activebutton.gif border=0 width=136
```

```
    height=20></A>
<SCRIPT LANGUAGE="JavaScript">
if ( isMsie4orGreater()) {DVDmdb.href = "/DVDmdb.cdf"}
</SCRIPT>
```

This is the way Microsoft recommends you implement Active Channel in a Web page. It works pretty well, but you're invited to find your own methods. I used ASP on the DVDmdb server, but I can't reprint that code here. Here's a hint: Use the MSWC.BrowserType object.

Making an offline Favorite is very easy. Here's the code:

```
<LINK REL="Offline" HREF="/channel/DVDmdb.cdf">
```

For offline Favorites the REL attribute of the LINK element (which is built into HTML) is set to "Offline."

CDF Element Definitions

Let me warn you ahead of time: this section is technical, like the breakdown of XFDL earlier in this chapter. With VML and MathML, this chapter offers a topical discussion of how the languages work. With XFDL, CDF, and RDF (discussed briefly below), we're diving deeper into how it works because these three XML technologies will probably prove the most useful in an enterprise environment. My aim is to help you figure out if you want to take the time to learn this stuff or spend the money to send someone to class.

CDF consists of seven major elements, listed in Figure 4-7.

Element	Description
Channel	Defines a channel.
Item	Defines a channel item.

Figure 4-7: CDF's major elements

Element	Description
UserSchedule	Reference to a user-specified schedule
Schedule	Defines a particular schedule.
Logo	Defines an image to represent a channel or channel item.
Tracking	Defines user-tracking parameters of a channel.
CategoryDef	Defines a category.

Figure 4-7: CDF's major elements

Each of these major elements has its own set of child elements. The best way to show how the major elements and their child elements relate is by showing you the XML DTD for each element.

Common Child Elements of Channel and Item

The elements listed in Figure 4-8 are child elements common to Channel and Item. I like to think of it as more of a "share" kind of relationship, where they share characteristics.

Element	Description
Title	Defines the title of the parent element.
LastMod	Defines last modified date.
Abstract	Brief description of the channel.
Author	Defines the author of the channel.
Publisher	Defines the publisher of the channel.
Copyright	Defines the copyright for the channel.
PublicationDate	Notes the channel's date of publication.
Logo	Graphical representation of the channel.

Figure 4-8: Child elements shared by Channel and Item

Element	Description
Keywords	List of keywords that describe the channel.
Category	Category in which this channel belongs.
Ratings	Rating of the channel, usually by PICS.
Schedule	Schedule for keeping channel up-to-date.
UserSchedule	Reference to a user-specified schedule.

Figure 4-8: Child elements shared by Channel and Item

Each individual attribute is pretty self-explanatory. The XML DTD clarifies how each attribute works:

```
<!ELEMENT Title EMPTY>
<!ATTLIST Title VALUE CDATA #REQUIRED>
<!ELEMENT LastMod EMPTY>
<!ATTLIST LastMod VALUE CDATA #REQUIRED>
<!ELEMENT Abstract EMPTY>
<!ATTLIST Abstract VALUE CDATA #REQUIRED>
<!ELEMENT Author EMPTY>
<!ATTLIST Author VALUE CDATA #REQUIRED>
<!ELEMENT Publisher EMPTY>
<!ATTLIST Publisher VALUE CDATA #REQUIRED>
<!ELEMENT Copyright EMPTY>
<!ATTLIST Copyright VALUE CDATA #REQUIRED>
<!ELEMENT PublicationDate EMPTY>
<!ATTLIST PublicationDate VALUE CDATA #REQUIRED>
<!ELEMENT Keywords EMPTY>
<!ATTLIST Keywords VALUE CDATA #REQUIRED>
<!ELEMENT Category EMPTY>
<!ATTLIST Category VALUE CDATA #REQUIRED>
<!ELEMENT Ratings EMPTY>
<!ATTLIST Ratings PICS-Label CDATA #REQUIRED>
```

Hopefully, you know how to read XML DTDs. If this seems confusing to you, refer to Chapter 2 for a little help.

Channel Element

This is the Channel element XML DTD:

```
<!ELEMENT Channel (LastMod | Title | Abstract | Author | Publisher |
Copyright | PublicationDate | Keywords | Category | Rating | Channel |
Item | Schedule | IntroURL | Authorization | IsClonable | MinStorage |
Tracking )*>
```

The Channel has six explicit elements, shown in Figure 4-9.

Element	Description
Channel	One or more subchannels of the channel
Item	One or more article profiles
IntroURI	URI to introductory Web page of channel.
Authorization	Authenticode for channels.
MinStorage	Minimum Storage size required, in kilobytes
Tracking	Provides information on how channel should track users.

Figure 4-9: Channel element's explicit child elements

The XML DTD for the minor elements:

```
<!ELEMENT IntroURI EMPTY>
<!ATTLIST IntroURI VALUE CDATA #REQUIRED>
<!ELEMENT Authorization EMPTY>
<!ATTLIST Authorization VALUE CDATA #REQUIRED>
<!ELEMENT MinStorage EMPTY>
<!ATTLIST MinStorage VALUE CDATA "0">
```

The Channel element shares LastMod, Title, Abstract, Author, Publisher, Copyright, PublicationDate, Logo, Keywords, Category, Ratings and Schedule with the Item element.

The Channel element also has two explicit *children*, HREF and IsClonable. HREF defines the URI for the next updated version, and IsClonable describes if the channel can be copied or moved within the channel changer hierarchy.

Item Element

The Item element defines a unit of information for the user, such as an article, that usually corresponds to a Web page. The XML DTD for the Item element:

```
<!ELEMENT Item (LastMod, Title, Abstract, Author, Publisher,
Copyright, PublicationDate, Keywords, Category, Rating, Schedule,
    Usage )*>
```

The Item element has five explicit, unshared attributes:

Attribute	Description
HREF	URI of article contents
MIMEType	MIME Type of article contents
IsVisible	Defines the visibility of the item as YES or NO.
Priority	HI, NORMAL, or LOW priority
Precache	YES caches retrieved documents, NO does not cache retrieved documents, and DEFAULT is whatever the user sets.

Figure 4-10: The Item element's explicit attributes

The XML DTD for these child elements:

```
<!ATTLIST Item HREF CDATA #REQUIRED>
<!ATTLIST Item MIMEType CDATA #IMPLIED>
<!ATTLIST Item IsVisible (YES, NO) "YES">
<!ATTLIST Item Priority (HI, NORMAL, LOW) "NORMAL">
<!ATTLIST Item Precache (YES, NO, DEFAULT) "DEFAULT">
```

Refer to the previous figures for the elements shared between Channel and Item.

Item has one explicit child element, Usage, which indicates how an item should be used.

UserSchedule Element

The UserSchedule element specifies a client-side user defined schedule.

```
<!ELEMENT UserSchedule EMPTY>
<!ATTLIST UserSchedule VALUE (DAILY, WEEKLY, HOURLY)
#REQUIRED>
```

The UserSchedule element does not share attributes with any other element.

Schedule Element

The Schedule element defines a repeating interval of time.

```
<!ELEMENT Schedule (StartDate?, EndDate?, IntervalTime?,
EarliestTime?, LatestTime?)>
```

The Schedule element has five child elements, shown in Figure 4-11.

Child Element	Description
Start	The day on which the schedule will begin.
End	The day on which the schedule will expire.
IntervalTime	Defines the interval for repeition of the schedule.
EarliestTime	Defines the earliest time during the schedule.
LatestTime	Defines the latest time during the schedule.

Figure 4-11: Schedule element's child elements

The XML DTD for the child elements:

```
<!ELEMENT StartDate EMPTY>
<!ATTLIST StartDate VALUE CDATA #REQUIRED>
<!ELEMENT EndDate EMPTY>
<!ATTLIST EndDate VALUE CDATA #REQUIRED>
<!ELEMENT IntervalTime EMPTY>
<!ATTLIST IntervalTime DAY CDATA "0">
```

```
<!ATTLIST IntervalTime HOUR CDATA "0">
<!ATTLIST IntervalTime MIN CDATA "0">
<!ATTLIST IntervalTime SEC CDATA "0">
<!ELEMENT EarliestTime EMPTY>
<!ATTLIST EarliestTime DAY CDATA "0">
<!ATTLIST EarliestTime HOUR CDATA "0">
<!ATTLIST EarliestTime MIN CDATA "0">
<!ATTLIST EarliestTime SEC CDATA "0">
<!ELEMENT LatestTime EMPTY>
<!ATTLIST LatestTime DAY CDATA "0">
<!ATTLIST LatestTime HOUR CDATA "0">
<!ATTLIST LatestTime MIN CDATA "0">
<!ATTLIST LatestTime SEC CDATA "0">
```

The Schedule element does not share child elements or attributes with any other elements.

Logo Element

The Logo element defines an image that can be used to represent a channel or channel item.

The DTD for the Logo element is very simple:

```
<!ELEMENT Logo EMPTY>
<!ATTLIST Logo HREF CDATA #REQUIRED>
<!ATTLIST Logo TYPE (BIG WIDE SMALL REGULAR)
"REGULAR">
```

The Logo element has two attributes: HREF, which is the URL to the image for the logo, and Type, which indicates which context image should be used.

Tracking Element

The Tracking element indicates how a channel should implement user tracking. Like the Logo element, the Tracking element is simple.

```
<!ELEMENT Tracking (PostURL?)>
<!ELEMENT PostURL EMPTY>
<!ATTLIST PostURL HREF CDATA #REQUIRED>
```

The Tracking element has one attribute, PostURL, which defines the URL to which tracking results are posted to.

Active Channel Example

This is a sample channel I built for a satirical news site that I worked on in 1997. Feel free to take the code and manipulate it to your liking.

```
<!DOCTYPE Channel SYSTEM "http://www.w3c.org/Channel.dtd">
<Channel BASE="http://www.spygame.com/"
HREF="news.cdf">
<IntroUrl VALUE="http://www.spygame.com/cdf-setup.html" />
<LastMod VALUE="1997.03.31T09:30-0600" />
<Title VALUE="Spy Game" />
<Abstract VALUE="Finding news and making fun of it." />
<Author VALUE="Robert Standefer" />
<Schedule>
<EndDate VALUE="1997.04.30T09:30-0500"/>
<IntervalTime DAY=30 />
<EarliestTime HOUR=12 />
<LatestTime HOUR=18 />
<Logo HREF="/images/spy-news.gif" Type="REGULAR" />

<ITEM HREF="/news/0401.html">
<LastMod VALUE="1997.03.31T09:30-0600"/>
<Title VALUE="Man Finds Third Gear" />
<Abstract VALUE="A Dallas man finally found third gear in his new
    sports
car, effectively adding years of life to his transmission. Get the full story
here." />
<Author VALUE="Robert Standefer" />
</ITEM>

<ITEM HREF="/news/0402.html">
<LastMod VALUE="1997.04.02T11:30-0600"/>
<Title VALUE="Local Hero Gives Up" />
<Abstract VALUE="Town hero James Schmidt decided today to stop
trying to save the atmosphere of downtown buildings, citing 'progress'
for his decision."/>
<Author VALUE="Robert Standefer/">
</ITEM>

<ITEM HREF="/news/0403.html">
```

```
<LastMod VALUE="1997.04.03T11:30-0600"/>
<Title VALUE="Postal Service Calls Number Three"/>
<Abstract VALUE="Bluebonnet Postal Station officially called ticket
holder number three during normal operations today. Ticket holders four
through eighty await their turn."/>
<Author VALUE="Robert Standefer/">
</ITEM>

<ITEM HREF="/wait/scrnsaver.html">
<USAGE VALUE="Screensaver"/>
</ITEM>
</CHANNEL>
```

This snippet of code from the channel definition of Spy Game basically shows you how a channel works. For this channel, I designed an application that generated the CDF file from article data in a database.

If you want to jump into XML right now, an Active Channel could be the best place for you to start. They are easy to create and maintain, and the results are immediate. Just remember that Active Channels only work with Internet Explorer.

Resource Description Framework

Resource Description Framework, or RDF for short, is an implementation of XML similar to Active Channel, with one major difference: RDF works in Netscape, not in Internet Explorer.

RDF deserves a section all its own, so I included its specification in Appendix B.

Summary

This chapter covered some applications of XML. For some, a real-world application of XML can mean the difference between giving XML a passing thought and getting XML training for developers. The applications of XML covered in this chapter were:

- ◆ The Extensible Forms Description Language

- ◆ The Vector Markup Language

- ◆ The Mathematics Markup Language

- ◆ Channel Definition Format

The next chapter covers "real-world" XML. Some of the topics discussed in the next chapter include requirements for using XML, how to tackle some implementation issues, and XML middleware.

5

Real-World XML

The technical aspects of XML are intriguing and the future of the technology is definitely bright; however, many IT managers are asking themselves, "How do I use XML *now*? Where do I start?"

This chapter covers XML in the "real world." This includes a discussion of how XML can be viewed in a Web browser, as well as how XML can be stored on a server and delivered using Active Server Pages or an XML server-side delivery mechanism. Finally, a discussion of popular XML middleware is provided to show some of the options in that area.

This chapter will prove to be the most useful for the IT manager considering integrating XML into his or her enterprise, while not knowing exactly how he or she is going to do it.

XML in the Web Browser

Generally speaking, XML can be viewed in two sources: the client and the server. By *viewed*, I mean the physical display of an XML document after it has been parsed.

The client side of this equation can be met by the use of a Web browser. Since a Web browser is required to browse the Web, it is logical to assume that the Web browser would be the primary choice of users who wish to view Web-based XML documents. For those who prefer XML processing to be performed on the server, that discussion is offered in the next section.

For the purpose of this chapter, we will operate under the assumption that a user wishes to view XML documents that are stored on a server and delivered over the Web, whether internal (intranet) or external. There are certainly some client applications that offer inherent XML support, but they are not as ubiquitous as the Web browser. So while you are reading this chapter, remember that we're thinking Web.

XML in the Web browser proposes some interesting caveats. As it is with most other technologies in the Web world, different browsers offer varying levels of support of XML.

Currently, XML is supported in differing levels in two major browsers: Internet Explorer 4.0 and Internet Explorer 5.0. At the time of writing, Internet Explorer 5.0 is in widespread release, Mozilla is in limbo, and Netscape 6 is in beta. Thus, I touch on XML support in Navigator 6.0, but keep in mind that things may change before the browser is released.

The 3.0 Browsers

I uncovered two solutions for displaying XML in Internet Explorer 3.0 and Netscape Navigator 3.0. One is a JavaScript at http://www.jeremie.com. The other is a Java applet that I couldn't find, although I'm sure exists.

Internet Explorer 4.0

Microsoft Internet Explorer 4.0 offers some support of XML. To be fair, XML was far from release when Internet Explorer 4.0 came out. Internet Explorer 4.0 does not fully support XML, but it does offer a decent set of features.

Generalized XML Parser

To parse XML files, Internet Explorer 4.0 provides two options. The first, the XML Parser in Java, is a validating XML parser in the form of Java source code, which Microsoft recently integrated into its new Java Virtual Machine (VM).

The other option, Microsoft XML Parser in C++, is an XML parser written in C++. It sacrifices validation capability for high performance. Unless you know C++, though, this parser will not help you much.

XML Object Model

The XML Object Model (XOM) included with Internet Explorer 4.0 is designed to provide a means by which one can navigate and manipulate an XML document.

The XOM provides access to structured data through XML parsers, giving developers the capability of working with the data.

The XOM is based on the W3C recommendation for the XML Document Object Model, which is covered in Chapter 6 of this book.

XML Data Source Object

Finally, Internet Explorer 4.0 provides a means for viewing XML documents through the XML Data Source Object. The XML DSO uses Dynamic HTML's data binding capabilities to connect to the structured data and display it as a HTML page.

XML support in Internet Explorer 4.0 becomes less and less important as the release dates for the 5.0 browsers approach. Microsoft's Web site is currently phasing out their Internet Explorer 4.0/XML content and replacing it with Internet Explorer 5.0-related content. If you would like more information on this topic, consult http://www.microsoft.com/xml.

Internet Explorer 5.0

Microsoft Internet Explorer 5.0 provides our first glimpse into the power of XML on the Internet. Internet Explorer 5.0 provides significantly more XML support than Internet Explorer 4.0.

Direct Viewing of XML

Internet Explorer 5.0 lets the user directly view XML documents in the Web browser, without requiring any conversion performed beforehand.

Internet Explorer 5.0 treats XML files the same as it treats HTML files. This means that the user can add an XML file to the Favorites folder, and the XML files are represented in the History list.

When a user browses to an XML file, Internet Explorer 5.0 renders the document based on the rules defined in the corresponding XSL or CSS file. When Internet Explorer 5.0 encounters an XML document that does not reference a style sheet, it renders the document with a default style sheet, and this can have varying results. An example of viewing an XML file with no XSL in Internet Explorer 5.0 is in Figure 5-1.

Internet Explorer 5.0 depends on correct notation as specified in the W3C recommendation when it renders XML documents. For example, when Internet Explorer 5.0 encounters the following code:

```
<?xml version="1.0"?>
<?xml stylesheet type="text/xsl" href="cdcoll.xsl">
```

it knows that it should grab a stylesheet of type XSL, called cdcoll.xsl, from the current directory.

When Internet Explorer 5.0 encounters an error, such as invalid or non-well-formed document, it reports that error. This is a great feature that allows the XML author to capture problems and display error messages that

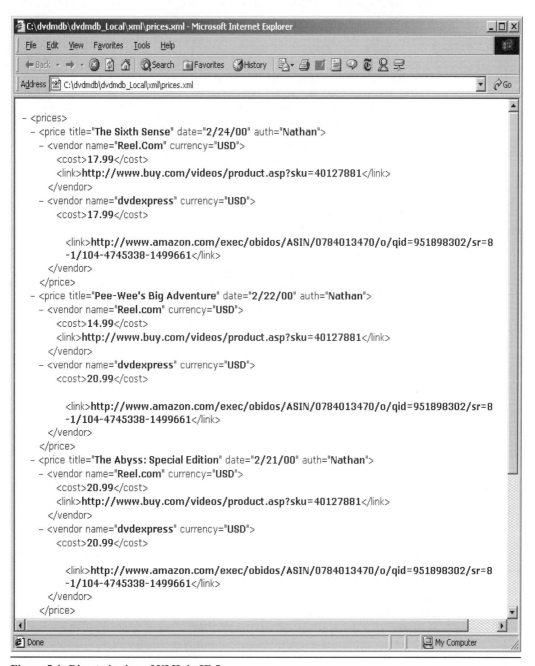

Figure 5-1: Direct viewing of XML in IE 5

make sense to the user, rather than just letting the user sit and wonder about what he did wrong.

Processing XSL

To successfully view an XML document that has a linked XSL sheet in Intnernet Explorer 5.0, the style sheet must be from the same protocol and domain as the XML document. For example, if your XML document is at http://www.xmlplace.net/files/doc.xml, then your XSL style sheet should be stored at http://www.xmlplace.net as well. It does not necessarily have to exist in the same directory. This is an interesting security feature; when Internet Explorer 5.0 finds that the linked XSL file is stored elsewhere, it reports an access violation.

High-performance, Validating Engine

Unlike Internet Explorer 4.0, which included two separate parsers (one validating and one not), Internet Explorer 5.0 includes a single engine that is both validating and fast. The parsing engine in Internet Explorer 5.0 also supports XML namespaces. Namespace support is integrated into the direct viewing capability, XSL, and the XML DOM programming interfaces.

XSL Support

As noted above, Internet Explorer 5.0 supports XSL. Internet Explorer supports XSL as of the latest W3C Working Draft, and it includes support for programmatic access to information within an XML data set on the client or server.

XML Data Islands

XML Data Islands are "chunks" of XML data embedded in an HTML document. An XML data island can be embedded in an HTML document using the XML tag or by overloading the HTML SCRIPT tag.

To use the XML tag in an HTML document, your code looks something like this:

```
<HTML>
<BODY>
<XML ID=XMLID>
```

```
<XMLDATA>
<DATA> Text goes here ... </DATA>
</XMLDATA>
</XML>
</BODY>
</HTML>
```

This is an example of how XML data can be embedded in an HTML document. Since it is part of the HTML document, the XML data is scriptable via the HTML Document Object Model.

To overload the SCRIPT tag, you write code like this:

```
<SCRIPT ID="XMLID" LANGUAGE="XML">
<XMLDATA>
<DATA>Your text goes here ... </DATA>
</XMLDATA>
</SCRIPT>
```

This method and the <XML> tag work equally well for me, but I prefer to use the <XML> tag.

C++ XML Data Source Object

This XML DSO allows the developer to bind HTML elements directly to an XML data island.

XML Schemas

Schemas, as mentioned in Chapter Two, define rules of an XML document. Remember that a DTD is a schema. Internet Explorer 5.0 includes support for the XML-Data note submitted to the W3C. XML-Data is discussed in Chapter 7.

XML Document Object Model

The XML Document Object Model is a standard object model offering programmatic control of XML document structure, content, and more. Internet Explorer 5.0 includes full support of the XML DOM and makes it accessible from scripts, Visual Basic, and other languages. The XML Document Object Model is discussed in detail in Chapter 6.

Microsoft's Pledge of Support

Microsoft has pledged their support of XML in their products, and the capabilities in Internet Explorer 5.0 shows their confidence. Microsoft hosts a great site offering a ton of information at http://www.microsoft.com/xml.

Netscape Navigator 6.0

Netscape says it supports XML in its Navigator 6.0 product. XML support in Navigator 6.0 comes in the form of a delivery component called Aurora. Aurora utilizes Resource Description Framework (RDF). The RDF specification can be found in Appendix B.

Aurora seeks out and explores information across desktops, databases, and networks. Aurora also manages this information, giving the user a "one stop shopping" experience for his or her XML needs.

Aurora will appear on the desktop as a "windowpane" interface element that groups together pointers to resources. RDF lets the Aurora navigation element point to local files of different types, such as spreadsheets, database fields, and word processing documents.

Viewing the same document in Netscape Navigator 6.0 that we viewed in Internet Explorer 5.0 yields entirely different results, as seen in Figure 5-2.

Interestingly enough, when you view the source of the XML document, something interesting happens. (See in Figure 5-3.)

What the future holds for Netscape Navigator 6.0 is unclear at this time. My searches on Netscape's site turned up much less than what Microsoft presented about XML on its site. This is disappointing, as Netscape 6.0 is the premiere choice for browsing on UNIX systems, and therefore those users are left out in the cold when it comes to an XML browser solution. However, perhaps details will arise as time goes by.

Figure 5-2: Direct viewing of an XML file in Navigator 6.0

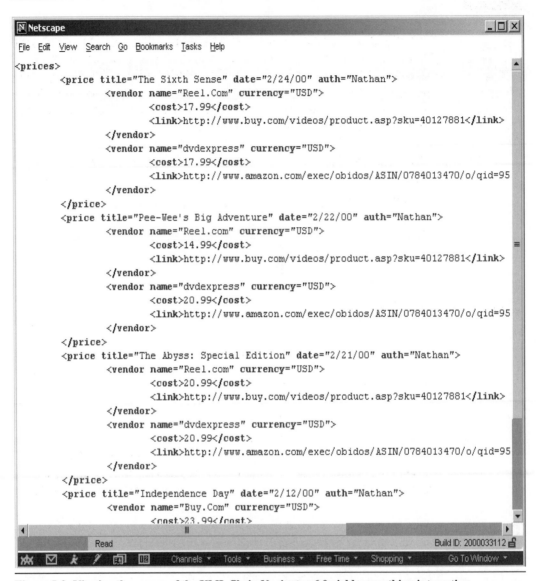

Figure 5-3: Viewing the source of the XML file in Navigator 6.0 yields something interesting

Mozilla

Mozilla should not be confused with Netscape 6.0, even though they both come from the same parent. Mozilla is the free source version of Netscape's browser, and development of Mozilla is proliferated by independent software developers. My discovery has been that the Mozilla developers acknowledge the power and usefulness of XML and have plans to fully integrate it into the Mozilla browser.

According to http://www.mozilla.org, Mozilla's support of XML comes in the form of RDF. For your convenience, the RDF specification is reprinted in Appendix B.

At the time of this update, April 2000, Mozilla is in limbo. We'll have to wait and see what happens to it.

XML on the Server

XML on the server is a touchy subject these days. I've seen many battles going on in the newsgroups about which server-side delivery mechanism is best for delivering XML.

There are many choices when delivering XML from the server. CGI applications written in Perl, Java servlets, Java Server Pages, Active Server Pages, C, C++, and Python code can all be written to deliver XML. Database choices are equally open, allowing for practically any database system available, including Oracle, Microsoft Access, Informix, and Sybase.

This section covers two different technologies that essentially perform the same function: parsing XML on the server and delivering it to the client. Whether the XML comes from a database or a directory tree, something has to handle the conversion before the data gets to the client.

But before we get to that, we should examine the pros and cons of server-side XML. The advantage to server-side is that all of the XML files are converted at one place and served to the client.

The disadvantage to server-side conversion of XML documents is the load the conversion places on the server. You should examine both options, client-side or server-side, and make your own determination.

XML Enabler

The XML Enabler is a Java servlet developed by IBM that can successfully implement stylesheets such as the LotusXSL technology. Using the XML Enabler, any browser can send requests to the servlet. The servlet responds by formatting the data using different XSL stylesheets. The system administrator can configure which stylesheets go with which browser types.

So, if your browser supports HTML 3.2, the XML Enabler will send down HTML that conforms to the HTML 3.2 specification. If your browser supports HTML 4.0, the XML Enabler will send down documents that conform to the HTML 4.0 specification.

XML Enabler supports any browser that can read HTML. With the XML Enabler, developers need not be concerned with what browser the client is running. The XML Enabler technology allows the developer to concentrate on intelligently using XML-tagged data, without worrying about what kind of browser the client is using to view the data.

To use XML Enabler, the system administrator defines the mapping between browser types and XSL stylesheets. When that is done, the servlet gets XML data from a data source, and then formats that data using an XSL stylesheet.

When XML Enabler gets a request, it gets the XML document requested by the client, as the URL of that document is passed as a parameter. The servlet then looks at the the user-agent field of the HTTP header and selects the XSL stylesheet that corresponds to that browser type.

When the XML document and the XSL stylesheet are selected, the two are combined by the Lotus XSL Processor, and the output is served to the client.

XML-based Middleware

It can be argued that XML itself is a kind of middleware. It exists between the client and the server and provides its own core set of services. In some cases, XML can be the mechanism that resides between the client and data services.

The two particular pieces of software I chose to cover offer differing levels of XML support. One is a content management and personalization tool, the other is an XML server. By no means the only products out there, these two represent the goings-on in the XML middleware world.

Vignette StoryServer

Vignette bills their StoryServer product as "the industry's leading Web application system for managing relationships throughout the online customer lifecycle." This basically means that StoryServer is a Web middleware product that helps organizations manage content and build sites that maintain customer relationships.

StoryServer's XML support can be found throughout the product. At its core, StoryServer provides an XML implementation for building, managing, and delivering XML-based documents. This support allows for the access of static content through dynamic applications.

StoryServer provides a full XML parser that includes support for validation against DTDs, persistent storage of parsed XML documents in a relational database, transformation of XML documents, cross-document indexing and querying, and a natural-language query mechanism.

That's a lot of stuff, but StoryServer is a large product. Let's examine one feature at a time.

XML Parser

This is important. Whether or not a product offers a slew of great features is irrelevant if its parser is no good. StoryServer's parser offers full parsing capabilities, including the ability to validate documents against arbitrary DTDs.

Persistent Storage of XML Documents

Parsing the same static document over and over consumes system resources and lengthens the user's wait time. StoryServer does something interesting to overcome this: once it parses a document, it stores that document's tree in a relational database for reuse. This significantly speeds up document access since the database itself can be queried rather than the document. Imagine parsing a 310-page book each time you want to search for *Vignette* in its content.

XML Document Transformation

StoryServer provides the all-important functionality of converting XML documents to HTML before serving them to the client. A lack of this functionality would severely limit the product to serving only those clients that support direct viewing of XML, such as Internet Explorer 5.0. Vignette made sure this wouldn't happen with its flagship product, so server-side document transformation is provided.

Cross-Document Indexing and Querying

This feature is directly related to StoryServer's persistent storage feature. Since the documents are stored in a relational database, StoryServer can query an entire database of documents rather than having to search one document at a time. In my opinion, this is one of the product's best selling points to e-commerce ventures.

Natural-Language Query Mechanism

A natural-language query mechanism is a fancy name for a replacement for SQL. In other words, StoryServer doesn't require the use of complex SQL commands when performing queries, but rather supports natural language, similar to the search mechanism at http://www.deja.com.

System Requirements

StoryServer supports Sybase, Oracle, Informix, and Microsoft SQL Server databases, and Netscape, Apache, and Microsoft IIS Web servers.

Vignette can be found on the Web at http://www.vignette.com.

Bluestone XML Suite

According to Bluestone's product documentation, XML Suite "provides everything you need to develop and deploy robust and flexible applications for maximum competitive advantage." From this, we can gather that Bluestone XML Suite is a complete environment for developing and deploying XML applications.

Bluestone takes a two-pronged approach to this by offering two core parts of XML Suite, a GUI development tool called Visual-XML and XML-Server for hosting dynamic XML applications.

At face value, Bluestone XML Suite seems like a lot like the Web Application Servers that are currently available, such as HAHTsite or Active Server Pages/Visual Interdev. But rather than offer a comparison of Bluestone XML Suite to these other products, let's concentrate on what Bluestone offers in the realm of XML.

XML-Server

Bluestone XML-Server offers some very powerful capabilities. First and foremost, XML-Server is capable of simultaneously generating, receiving, and interpreting XML documents. Written entirely in Java, XML-Server hosts XML applications as well as the services required to run those applications.

XML-Server is a platform designed for business-to-business e-commerce, supply chain integration, EDI communications, and thin-client Internet-enabled device communications.

XML-Server offers native connectivity with most enterprise-class database systems, including Oracle, Sybase, Microsoft SQL Server, Informix, and DB2. It also supports ODBC and JDBC.

Bluestone XML-Server also offers support of key open standards, including XSL, XQL, JavaBeans, COM, and CORBA.

This stuff is all really cool, but it's meaningless if you don't know how the product is supposed to help you run your business better. Let's imagine that you run a large electronic commerce site that sells digital video discs

(DVD). Your business sources its DVDs from three different distributors, all of whom are running XML servers. Your entire stock is stored in an Oracle database. Your DBA has written a trigger that fires off when the database detects that fewer than 100 copies of a particular DVD (let's say *Star Wars*) remain in stock. When the trigger executes, XML-Server automatically creates an XML purchase order and electronically sends it to the supplier that has *Star Wars* in its trading stock. The supplier's XML server automatically processes your XML purchase order and retrieves your shipping and billing information from the supplier's database, which effectively fulfills your order. An XML document sends you a confirmation and tells your server a delivery date, so if you are backordered, your customers will know when you expect stock to arrive.

Sounds cool, doesn't it? The really neat thing is that, if the documents conform to a DTD specified by you and your suppliers, they can be running any XML server, Bluestone or not. You are running Oracle, they're running Informix, and the XML document lets the two database systems "talk" to each other with no confusion. Basically, your computers and their computers speak the same language: XML.

Visual-XML

Simply put, Visual-XML is an XML rapid application development (RAD) tool. Think of Visual Interdev with XML as its output language and you have Visual-XML.

Visual-XML shortens development cycles by offering a fast, flexible tool for creating XML and DTD documents and Java document handlers on XML-Server.

The cool thing about Visual-XML is that it lets you bind data elements to XML, DTD, and DOM trees in a drag-and-drop environment. The development environment also provides database browsing capabilities, as well as a facility to create and execute SQL statements. Visual-XML also includes a neat set of wizards that help speed the process of creating XML applications.

I like Visual-XML. In no time at all, I was able to build a nice little XML application that categorized my Spy Game stories by keywords, rather than by date, so I can later write my own XML searching engine to scan through my Spy Game stories and return headlines that are related to my visitor's search criteria. XML searching is covered more in-depth in Chapter Eight.

I want to point out that Bluestone XML-Suite is a *server-side application*, and does not require the use of any specific browser. Any client application that supports the W3C XML specification should work with Bluestone XML documents.

Bluestone can be found on the Web at http://www.bluestone.com.

Summary

This chapter provided your first glimpse into how XML can work for your enterprise. We covered a number of topics pertaining to this, including:

- ◆ Viewing XML in your Web browser

- ◆ Using XML on the Server

- ◆ XML applications as middleware

- ◆ Two examples of XML-based middleware and their benefits

The next chapter gets a little more technical, as we discuss XML development concepts. We'll cover some development tools and the all-important XML Document Object Model.

6

Developing XML-Enabled Applications

This chapter covers developing applications that support XML. We call these applications *XML-Enabled Applications* because they offer inherent support and manipulation of XML documents.

This support is added programmatically to our applications. As such, this chapter discusses using specific programming languages that are good for developing XML-enabled applications. Before it jumps into that, however, the chapter offers an overview of a key XML technology that is important to application developers who wish to add XML support to their software. This key technology is called the Document Object Model.

The Document Object Model

XML offers a flexible and intuitive way to structure data. However, as powerful as XML is, it does not process data. Fortunately, we have a technology that can process XML data for us.

The Document Object Model (DOM) offers programmatic access to the components of an XML document. Using a DOM-supporting scripting language, such as JavaScript or VBScript, you can move around inside the XML data and execute queries, process data, or modify data.

The DOM exposes a set of objects for use in authoring and developing XML documents and applications. XML DOM objects have properties and methods that are specific to working with XML.

With the XML DOM you can load and parse XML files, gather information about those files, and navigate and manipulate those files.

DOM Requirements

In its Working Draft for the DOM, the W3C sets forth a list of requirements for the DOM. This list identifies what the DOM should be able to do, giving insight into the capabilities and functionality of the DOM.

The requirements are broken up into 11 sections: General, Structure Navigation, Document Manipulation, Content Manipulation, Event Model, Stylesheet Object Model, DTD Manipulation, Error Reporting, Document Meta Information, UA Information, and Security, Validity, and Privacy.

Understanding each of these requirements is important to understanding the whole of the DOM.

General Requirements

1. The Object Model is language neutral and platform independent. This means that the object model should work with any language and on any operating system.

2. There will be a core DOM that is applicable to HTML, CSS, and XML documents. This one is particularly interesting because it says that there will be one DOM for all three technologies, rather than a separate DOM for each.

3. The Object model can be used to construct and deconstruct the document. You can use the object model to build a document and you can use the object model to take a document apart.

4. The Object Model will not preclude use by either agents external to the document content, or scripts embedded within the document. This means the object model will make itself available to external programs and embedded scripts, like JavaScript.

5. Consistent naming conventions must be used through all levels of the Object Model. The obvious benefit of this is simplicity among implementations.

6. A visual UI component will not be required for a conforming implementation of the Object Model. In other words, the object model will not require a visual apparatus for an implementation.

7. The specific HTML, CSS, or XML document object models will be driven by the underlying constructs of those languages.

8. It must be possible to read in a document and write out a structurally identical document to disk.

9. The Object Model will not expose the user to problems with security, validity, or privacy. Why bother the user with such information? Your application should have sufficient error handling code.

10. The Object Model will not preclude other mechanisms for manipulating documents. In other words, the object model won't force you to use a specific method or program to manipulate documents.

Structure Navigation Requirements

> 1. All document content, including elements and attributes, will be programmatically accessible and manipulable. This opens up the document to scripting languages and the like.

> 2. Navigation from any element to any other element will be possible, except where such navigation would compromise security.

> 3. There will be a way to uniquely and reproducibly enumerate the structure of static documents.

> 4. There will be a way to query for elements and attributes, subject to security and privacy considerations. This is important for developers creating DOM-enabled applications.

> 5. Basic low-level functions will be provided, along with convenience functions that build upon them, but have a consistent access method.

Document Manipulation Requirements

> 1. There will be a way to add, remove, and change elements and/or tags in the document structure.

> 2. There will be a way to add, remove, and change attributes in the document structure.

> 3. Operations must restore consistency before they return.

> 4. A valid static document acted upon by the DOM will deliver a consistent reproducible document structure.

Content Manipulation Requirements

> 1. There will be a way to determine the containing element from any text part of the document.

> 2. There will be a way to manipulate content.

> 3. There will be a way to navigate content.

Event Model Requirements

> 1. All elements will be capable of generating events. These events can be managed programmatically with event handlers, provided by the parser.
>
> 2. There will be interaction events, update events, and change events.
>
> 3. The event model will allow responses to user interactions.
>
> 4. The event delivery mechanism will allow for overriding of default behavior.
>
> 5. Events will bubble through the structural hierarchy of the document.
>
> 6. Events are synchronous.
>
> 7. Events will be defined in a platform-independent and language-neutral way.
>
> 8. There will be an interface for binding to events.

Stylesheet Object Model Requirements

> 1. All style sheets will be represented in the object model.
>
> 2. There will be a CSS stylesheet model.
>
> 3. Selectors, rules, and properties of individual style sheets can be added, removed, and changed.
>
> 4. All elements of a CSS style can be added, removed, and changed in the object model.
>
> 5. All properties as defined in the CSS specification.

DTD Manipulation Requirements

> 1. There will be a way to determine the presence of a DTD.
>
> 2. There will be a way to query declarations in the underlying DTD.

3. There will be a way to add, remove, and change declarations in the underlying DTD.

4. There will be a way to test conformance of all or part of the given document against a DTD.

Error Reporting Requirements

1. The DOM will provide a document-wide error logging and reporting mechanism.

2. Error reporting will be primarily via exceptions.

3. The DOM error state can be queried.

Document Meta Information Requirements

There will be information about the document and its embedded objects such as cookies.

UA Information Requirements

There will be a way of obtaining relevant information about the display environment, including the UA brand information and version number, and the HTTP header (where appropriate).

Security, Validity, and Privacy Requirements

1. Each object must be responsible for maintaining its own internal consistency.

2. It must be safe to have multiple threads operating on the same object.

3. Object locking must be incorporated to ensure consistent results.

4. It must be possible to prevent scripts on one page from accessing another page.

5. Firewall boundaries must be respected.

6. It must be possible to restrict access and navigation to specific elements.

7. An external security API will be provided.

That sums up the requirements. A good understanding of these require-ments will prepare you for further study of the DOM. When it comes to ac-tually sitting down and writing code, having this list handy will benefit you immensely.

Nodes in a Tree

The document object model adds a layer of abstraction to working with XML documents. Rather than looking at the XML document as a series of start and end tags, we can use the DOM to instead look at the XML docu-ment as a tree, with parent and child elements and attributes represented as nodes on this tree.

Thus, a DOM representation of an XML document consists of a tree that in turn consists of a set of a nodes. Nodes can be one of 12 types. These are shown in Figure 6-1.

Node Type	Description
Document	A document tree has precisely one Document node, which is the root of the tree.
DocumentFragment	Holds portions of a document.
Element	Represents each element in a document.
Attr	Represents an attribute of an element in a docu-ment.
ProcessingInstruction	Represents a processing instruction in a document.
Text	Represents text in a document that has no markup. Text nodes are never allowed to contain markup.
Comment	Represents a comment in a document.
CDATASection	Represents a CDATA section in a document.
EntityReference	Represents entity references in a document.

Figure 6-1: Node Types provided by the DOM

Node Type	Description
Entity	Represents parsed or unparsed entities in a document, but not entity declarations.
Notation	Represents a notation in a document.
DocumentType	Represents the document type of a document.

Figure 6-1: Node Types provided by the DOM

Each of the twelve node types exposes its own methods and attributes. For example, take the Document object. It exposes three attributes: doctype, implementation, and documentElement.

The doctype attribute denotes the DTD associated with the document. Doctype is read-only.

The implementation attribute is a reference of the DOMImplementation object that handles the document. A DOM application can use objects from multiple implementations.

Finally, the documentElement attribute allows direct access to the child node that is the root element of the document.

The Document object exposes nine methods: createElement, createDocumentFragment, createTextNode, createComment, createCDATASection, createProcessingInstructions, createAttribute, createEntityReference, and getElementByTagName.

Each of these objects has its own parameters and raises its own exceptions. Let's take a look at each one.

The createElement method creates an element of a specified type. It takes tagName as a parameter, with tagName representing the name of the element type to instantiate. This parameter is case-sensitive in XML. createElement returns a new Element object and throws a DOMException when it encounters an error.

The createDocumentFragment method simply creates an empty DocumentFragment object. Its return value is that new DocumentFragment, and it has no parameters nor does it raise an exception.

The createTextNode method creates a Text node based on the data passed as the parameter. Its return value is the new Text object and the method raises no exceptions.

createComment simply creates a Comment node based on the string passed as the parameter. It raises no exceptions and returns the new Comment object.

The createCDATASection method creates a CDATASection node based on the data parameter, and it returns the new CDATASection object and it raises the DOMException.

createProcessingInstruction creates a ProcessingInstruction node given the target part of the processing instruction as a parameter, and the data for the node as another parameter. It returns the new ProcessingInstruction object and it raises the DOMException.

The createAttribute method creates an instance of Attr of the given name, which can then be set on an Element using the SetAttribute method. createAttribute takes the name of the attribute as a parameter and returns the Attr object. It raises DOMException.

createEntityReference simply creates an EntityReference object, taking the name of the entity as a parameter and returning the new EntityReference object. It raises DOMException when it encounters an error.

getElementsByTagName returns a NodeList of all the Elements with a given tag name. It takes the tagname as a parameter, with * matching all tags, and returns a new NodeList object containing all of the matched Elements. This method raises no exceptions.

An understanding of the inner workings of the DOM can help the XML developer overcome technical challenges when dealing with a specific implementation of the DOM.

Programming XML

So you have your data structured in XML documents. What do you do with it? How do you get it out? We touched on it briefly in Chapter 5, but in this section we'll discuss using programming languages to crack open the XML document shell and get to the meaty data that exists inside.

We will cover adding XML support to applications written in Visual Basic, Perl, and PHP. Visual Basic development is limited to Windows-based computers. Perl exists for just about every Web server out there. PHP runs on most Web servers.

If you are using another language, such as C++, Python, or Java, there are books in your favorite bookstore that offer want you want to know.

We're going to discuss development of an application that uses XML to store configuration data in text files, sort of like a flat file database. This XML database will store information a particular collection. I use this model again because it is a simple way to understand XML. In this case, we'll store our DVD collection.

Based on that, we can formulate an idea of how our XML documents will look. For example:

```
<collection-file>
<collection name="DVD">
<item name="title">DVDtitle</item>
</collection>
</collection-file>
```

From this, we can create our schema:

```
<?xml version="1.0" ?>
<schema xmlns="urn:W3C.org:xmlschema"
```

```
xmlns:dt="urn:W3C.org:xmldatatypes">
<elementType id="collection-file">
<element type="#collection" occurs="REQUIRED"/>
</elementType>
<elementType id="collection">
<element type="#item" occurs="REQUIRED"/>
</elementType>
</schema>
```

We're not going to force our documents to adhere to the schema. The schema, in this case, will simply serve as a reference point when creating our documents. We'll assume for this exercise that our collection files will be well-formed XML documents.

Keep in mind that we're not going to develop a complete application here. We just want to see how each programming language deals with our problem. You can make the decision on your own as to which method and approach you wish to take.

Visual Basic and XML

Visual Basic is a great tool for quickly building Windows-based applications. But Visual Basic's real power is in its COM-creation ability, and when combined with the power of Microsoft Transaction Server, Visual Basic can be a formidable tool for creating middleware applications.

Since XML functions well at the middleware level, it is a natural relationship between Visual Basic and XML. In this section, we'll look at creating a function in Visual Basic that will parse our document and give us the information we want to extract.

Internet Explorer 5.0 provides an object for COM-enabled languages, such as Visual Basic, called Microsoft.XMLDOM. We'll use this COM object for the XML processing in our application.

To use the DOM in Visual Basic, create an instance of the XMLDOM object. Before you can do this, however, you have to set a reference to the XML type library (MSXML.dll) through the Project References dialog box in Visual Basic.

Once the reference is set, you can then create an instance of the XMLDOM object:

```
Dim xDoc As MSXML.DOMDocument
Set xDoc = New MSXML.DOMDocument
```

By the way, if the MSXML.dll file is not on your computer, you can get it by installing Microsoft Internet Explorer 5.0 or you can download a version of the Microsoft XML Parser from Microsoft's Web site.

In this discussion, we'll be using two parts of the XMLDOM object: The DOMDocument class and the IXMLDOMNode interface. The DOMDocument class gives us access to our XML document, and the IXMLDOMNode interface gives us access to individual nodes of our document tree.

So we already have our DOMDocument, and now we want to load a document. This is achieved through a simple method, Load.

The Load method can load documents from a local disk, via a URL, or over the network via a UNC pathname. We'll load our document from a local disk using this code:

```
If xDoc.Load("d:\xmldocs\dvds.xml") Then
'Do stuff with the document
Else
'Error handling
End If
```

To load a document from a URL, you must specify the entire URL, including the http:// directive.

```
If xDoc.Load("http://www.dvdmdb.com/dvds.xml") Then
'Do stuff
Else
'Error
End If
```

The parser loads the file asynchronously by default. You can change this by setting the Async property of your document to false. If you set it to false, the parser will not relinquish control to your program until the document is completely loaded and parsed. Otherwise, you will need to use the document's `ReadyState` property.

Before you start looking at a document, you need to examine its `ReadyState` property to ensure the document is ready for your perusal. The `ReadyState` property returns one of five values, shown in Figure 6-2.

State	Value
Uninitialized; loading has not started	0
Loading; while the load method is executing	1
Loaded; load method is complete	2
Interactive; data has only been partially parsed	3
Completed; data is loaded, parsed, and ready for action	4

Figure 6-2: ReadyState property values

So now our XML document is loaded. The next step is to look inside the document and get the information we want. This is where the IXMLDOM-Node interface comes in handy. The IXMLDOMNode interface is what allows your program to read and write to individual node elements.

The IXMLDOMNode interface exposes two methods for accessing the nodes: the NodeType property and the NodeTypeString property. NodeType provides an enumeration of DOMNodeType items, and NodeTypeString allows for the retrieval of a textual string for the node type.

There are 13 DOMNodeType items, but we're only going to use one for this example, NODE_TEXT. This item lets us get to what is between our tags, as you'll see in some code later on.

Once the document is loaded, we can start moving down the node hierarchy. This can be handled through the ChildNodes property of the DOMDocument instance. ChildNodes gives you an entry point to all of the nodes in your document tree, from the top down.

ChildNodes exposes two properties, Level and IXMLDOMNodeList. Level returns the number of existing child nodes, and IXMLDOMNodeList returns an enumerated list of all of the individual nodes of the ChildNodes property.

With all of this information, it should be relatively easy to put together the Visual Basic code to handle our needs.

```
Private Sub cmdGoNodes_Click()
Dim xmlDoc as MSXML.DOMDocument
Dim xmlNode as MSXML.IXMLDOMNode
set xmlDoc = New MSXML.DOMDocument
xmlDoc.validateOnParse = False
If xmlDoc.Load("http://www.dvdmdb.com/dvds.xml") Then
'Document loaded
For Each xmlNode In xmlDoc.ChildNodes
If xmlNode.NodeType = NODE_TEXT Then
If xmlNode.ParentNode.NodeName = "item" Then
MsgBox "DVD Title: " & xmlNode.NodeValue
End If
End If
Else
MsgBox "Error!"
End If
End Sub
```

Of course, this sample is assuming that we don't need any real error-checking. However, when dealing with XML documents, it's always a good idea to have some kind of apparatus to handle your errors. Unless you are a perfect programmer who never makes a typo, you will make errors.

Error Handling

MSXML.XMLDOM exposes the ParseError object to help you on your way. Using the IXMLDOMParseError interface, which exposes seven properties of the ParseError object, you can figure out what went wrong in your document.

Here is our code with error handling built in:

```
Private Sub cmdGoNodes_Click()
'Document objects
```

```
Dim xmlDoc As MSXML.DOMDocument
Dim xmlNode As MSXML.IXMLDOMNode
set xmlDoc = New MSXML.DOMDocument

'ParseError objects
Dim xmlParseError as MSXML.IXMLDOMParseError
Dim sError As String
Set xmlParseError = xmlDoc.ParseError

xmlDoc.validateOnParse = False
If xmlDoc.Load("http://www.dvdmdb.com/dvds.xml") Then
'Document loaded
For Each xmlNode In xmlDoc.ChildNodes
If xmlNode.NodeType = NODE_TEXT Then
If xmlNode.ParentNode.NodeName = "item" Then
MsgBox "DVD Title: " & xmlNode.NodeValue
End If
End If
Else
'Error handling
sError = "The following error(s) caused your document to fail:" & vbCrLf
sError = sError & "Error number: " & xmlParseError.errorCode & vbCrLf
sError = sError & "Reason: " & xmlParseError.reason & vbCrLf
End If
End Sub
```

Remember to follow good practice and destroy your DOMDocument object when you are finished with it. It does not expose a close method, so simply setting it to Nothing will do the trick.

This code should serve as a jumping-off point for you or your developers. There is a wealth of information on the Web about Visual Basic and XML. Don't let anything hold you back!

Perl and XML

Most people involved in the Web programming business know what Perl is. Developed by Larry Wall as an alternative to C's complications, Perl, which stands for Practical Extraction and Reporting Language, has grown into its own as a good programming language for string processing and regular expressions. For a few years, Perl dominated the CGI scripting scene.

That being said, how can we use Perl to develop our XML collection program? Perl has its own set of considerations, and its own set of conveniences. It also has support of an amazing XML parser called XML::Parser, by Clark Cooper.

For this exercise we'll use Cooper's XML::Parser module. We could use regular expressions to parse our document, but why would we want to? With XML::Parser you simply tell the parser what you want and it will do the work; each time it finds what you told it you wanted, it makes calls which your code can understand.

This code instantiates the XML parser so we can parse our document and get what we want:

```perl
use XML::Parser;

my $tgt_collection; #tgt_ prefix indicates target
my $tgt_item;
my $cur_collection; #cur_ prefix indicates current
my $item_value;

sub getCollectionData {
my($xmlfile, $coll, $item, $default_value) = @_;
my $parser = new XML::Parser(ErrorContext => 2);
$parser->setHandlers(Start => \&entry);

$tgt_collection = $coll
$tgt_item = $item;
$cur_collection = "";
$item_value = $default_value

$parser->parsefile($xmlfile);

return $item_value;
}

sub entry {
my $parser_context = shift;
my $element = shift;
my %attr = @_;

if($element eq 'collection') {
$cur_collection = $attr{'name'};
```

```
} elseif ($element eq 'item' && $cur_collection eq $tgt_collection) {
if ($attr{'name'} eq $tgt_item) {
$item_value = attr{'value'};
$parser_context->finish();
}
}
}
```

This code essentially uses some package-global variables and exposes the XML::Parser module as an object. Then we tell the parser what events we're interested in, and in this case we're exclusively handling start tags. The parser runs and parses the entire document, which is loaded into memory. Each time it encounters a start tag, it runs the entry function.

This way works fine, but it's not the best way. Enter the Document Object Model. The DOM exposes a whole new set of capabilities for playing around with our XML document.

Using XML::DOM is pretty simple compared to XML::Parser and, to a greater extent, regular expressions. Parsing a file with XML::DOM is done like this:

```
use XML::DOM;
$parser = new XML::DOM::Parser (NoExpand => 1);
$doc = $parser->parsefile ($xmlfile);
```

A bit simpler than the other way, right? So using the XML::DOM module, we can go over the tree and find a specific tag.

```
sub findChild{
my $parent = shift;
my $name = shift;
my$node = $parent->getFirstChild();

while ($node) {
if ($node->getNodeType() == XML::DOM::ELEMENT_NODE
&& $node->getTagName() eq "collection"
&& $node->getAttribute("item") eq $item) {
return $node;
}
$node = $node->getNextSibling();
}
```

```
return undef;
}
```

So there we have it. This code is so much simpler than the other code, and we're using functions built in to the XML::DOM module that simplify our code.

Perl is a very powerful language, and its support of XML through modules is excellent. If you are a Perl developer, you should not have very much difficulty integrating XML into your applications.

Active Server Pages

I chose to discuss ASP (Active Server Pages) for this discussion because it is the server-side language that I know best. Although the syntax and methods are different from other languages, the concepts are the same so you should be able to apply them to your CGI language of choice.

As mentioned above, Microsoft Internet Explorer 5.0 fully supports the the XML Document Object Model and its programming interfaces, as well as some other XML technologies including XSL, namespaces, and schemas. The XML DOM (also known as the XOM) allows authors to easily parse XML documents, and exposes those documents as tree structures that are easy to navigate.

In order to programmatically use the XML DOM on the server you must install Internet Explorer 5.0 on the server. This is necessary because IE5 installs a number of supporting components. Installing IE5 on the server also opens up a few other server-side capabilities that are not related to XML, but are valuable nonetheless. Knowing this should help you deal with the requirement of installing 30 megabytes of browser files on a computer that is customarily not used for Internet browsing. Make sure you install the latest and greatest version of IE5, available at Microsoft's Web site.

With that out of the way, we concentrate on server-side XML with the XML DOM that is provided by the installation of Internet Explorer 5.0. First of all, there are two groups of DOM programming interfaces: one that defines interfaces that are needed to write applications that support XML, and one that defines interfaces to make it easier for developers and authors to use XML.

Using Microsoft.XMLDOM

Microsoft provides a COM object with Internet Explorer 5.0 called XMLDOM. This object exposes the XML DOM to developers creating server-side applications.

Creating an instance of the XML DOM object on the server using ASP is simple using this code:

```
<% Set oXML = Server.CreateObject("Microsoft.XMLDOM") %>
```

Once the object is instantiated on the server, there is a choice of either building an XML document or loading an existing one. Typically, developers use the XMLDOM object to load an existing XML document, so that's what we'll do for this discussion. When you opt to load an existing document, you can either load a string of XML text or open the XML document and load its contents. Again, for this discussion we will concentrate on the second option and load our entire XML document.

Before going further into this topic, we should establish our XML document. I created this document for my satirical news site, Spy Game:

```
<?xml version="1.0"?>
<!DOCTYPE SpyGame SYSTEM
"http://www.spygame.com/news/xml/SpyGame.dtd">
<issue>
<masthead>
<date-published>10 March 1999</date-published>
<copyright>Copyright 1999 Robert Standefer</copyright>
<disclaimer>All representations contained herein are
    satirical.</disclaimer>
</masthead>
<news-item>
<headline>
Schoolteacher Does Not Enjoy Student-Provided Apple
</headline>
<subhead>
"It was kind of mealy," schoolteacher says.
```

```
</subhead>
<story-link>
http://www.spygame.com/news/03101999/article.asp?id=5425
</story-link>
</news-item>
<news-item>
<headline>
Universe Series Finale Most-Watched Ever
</headline>
<subhead>
Billions worldwide witness collapse of life as they know it
</subhead>
<story-link>
http://www.spygame.com/news/03101999/article.asp?id=4033
</story-link>
</news-item>
</issue>
```

You should be able to tell from the document how Spy Game is structured, and what kind of "services" it provides. The document also tells you that this document must be valid, as a DTD is referenced in the <!DOCTYPE>.

To feed the document into Microsoft.XMLDOM, we use this code:

```
<% Set oXML = Server.CreateObject("Microsoft.XMLDOM")
oXML.async = False
oXML.Load "SpyGameStories-03101999.xml"%>
```

This code demonstrates use of the async property. I set this property to False because I don't want the DOM object to perform an asynchronous download of my XML document, which is important because I want to use the document's contents immediately after the document is loaded.

Looking at the Contents

So now we have an XML document stored in our DOM object. What do we do with it now? Remember that the DOM exposes the contents of an XML document in a tree of nodes, with a node consisting of an element and nested sub-elements. This means that we are going to have to create a series of node objects to handle the data and expose it to us so we can manipulate its contents.

The DOM exposes some methods to help us figure out what's in an XML document. One of these methods is getElementsByTagName() method, which we will use to get a list of nodes in the document.

One of the most important parts of my XML document is the copyright. This shows my ownership of the stories contained on my site. So I want to extract this information from my document. The copyright information is stored in the <copyright> node in my document. To get the text, I'm going to loop through a list of all of the nodes within my XML document. To do this, I have to create a node list object to store the list of nodes. A quick look at my DTD shows that the <copyright> element cannot contain any sub-elements, so I know that whatever's between <copyright> and </copyright> is what I want. I can get this information with the text property. Here's the code:

```
<% set oXML = Server.CreateObject("Microsoft.XMLDOM")
'The asterisk is a wildcard
oXML.async = False
oXML.Load "SpyGameStories-03101999.xml"
set oNodeList = oXML.getElementsByTagName("*")
for iCount = 0 to (oNodeList.Length - 1)
if oNodeList.item(iCount).nodeName = "copyright" then
sCopyright = oNodeList.item(iCount).text
Exit For
end if
Next %>
```

So now we have the text of my copyright message. Notice the asterisk, and where I mention that it is a wildcard. We'll come back to that a little later.

Retrieving Multiple Pieces of Data

The copyright message is one piece of data, and the looping method works fine for that, but what about the headlines? There are two headlines in my XML document, and each is handled a little differently.

Like <copyright>, <headline> does not have any sub-elements. This means that we can simply count the number of instances of the <headline> tag, and that will let us know how many headlines exist in the document. Rather than loop through the nodes list, we can simply use the length property.

```
<% set oNodeList = oXML.getElementsByTagName("headline")
iHeadlines = oNodeList.Length %>
```

Now we can print out each headline, like so:

```
<% set oXML = Server.CreateObject("Microsoft.XMLDOM")
oXML.async = False
oXML.Load "SpyGameStories-03101999.xml"
set oNodeList = oXML.getElementsByTagName("headline")
iHeadlines = oNodeList.Length
%>
<HTML>
<HEAD>
<TITLE>
List of Headlines
</TITLE>
</HEAD>
<BODY>
<% for iCount = 0 to (iHeadlines - 1)
set oHeadline = oNodeList.item(iCount)
Response.Write oHeadline.childNodes(0).text & "<BR>"
Next %>
</BODY>
</HTML>
```

Did you notice that I specified "headline" instead of "*"? This tells the DOM object that I want a specific node returned. Like SQL queries, specifying the criteria you want returned speeds up your code, but you have the option to return all nodes should you want them.

Error Handling

Remember that my document uses a DTD, which forces validation. What happens if my document doesn't conform to the DTD? What about well-formedness? What happens when the XML DOM encounters an error in my XML document?

Thankfully, the XML DOM object exposes an object called parseError, which contains information about the last parsing error. This object is provided to handle your debugging and error handling needs. Using parseError is simple:

```
<% If oXML.parseError.errorCode <> 0 Then
'handle the error
End If %>
```

I always write code that checks the value of `parseError.errorCode` after loading my XML documents. As a matter of fact, it's in a function that I include in every ASP page I write that uses XML documents. It's your decision on how you want to handle errors, and you have at least one option.(See Figure 6-3.)

Property	Description
errorCode	The error code
line	The line number in the XML document where the error occurred.
linepos	The character position in the line containing the error.
filepos	The absolute file position in the XML document containing the error.
reason	The cause of the error.
url	The URL of the XML document containing the error.
srcText	The data where the error occurred.

Figure 6-3: **parseError** Properties

PHP and XML

PHP is a server-side, cross-platform, HTML embedded scripting language. It's very similar to ASP in function, meaning you add PHP script to HTML pages and run them on a server, but the similarities stop there.

PHP's scripting language more closely resembles Perl than VBScript. As such, the implementation of XML in PHP looks a lot like the implementation of XML in Perl. As a matter of fact, PHP uses James Clark's expat parser, originally developed for Perl, for its XML functionality.

Unfortunately for PHP users, it's a lot harder to get started with XML than it is for Visual Basic or Perl users. You have to use a make rule in the PHP makefile, and download the expat RPM package, and run configure with the --with-xml option. Then you have to build PHP, not to mention many other steps before PHP is ready to work.

In this section, we'll assume you are using an ISP that has already set up with PHP and has the XML option turned on.

Jim Clark's expat parser toolkit will parse XML documents, but will not validate them. The toolkit (hereafter called the *extension*) lets the programmer create XML parsers and then subsequently define handlers for XML events. That's a little different from the simplicity of the DOM, but it will work.

There are seven XML event handlers. Each one is prefaced by xml_. Events are issued whenever the XML parser encounters start or end tags.

The seven XML event handlers are:
- xml_set_element_handler()
- xml_set_character_data_handler()
- xml_set_processing_instruction_handler()
- xml_set_default_handler()
- xml_set_unparsed_entity_decl_handler()
- xml_set_notation_decl_handler()
- xml_set_external_entity_ref_handler()

Each one of these event handlers has a specific function. For example, xml_set_notation_decl_handler()is called for declaration of a notation.

This code, reprinted from http://www.php.net, shows how to use PHP to parse XML:

```
$file = "dvds.xml";
$depth = array();

function startElement($parser, $name, $attributes) {
global $depth;
for ($int = 0; $int < $depth[$parser]; $int++ {
```

```
print " ";
}
print "$name\n";
$depth[$parser];
}

function endElement($parser, $name) {
global $depth;
$depth[$parser]--;
}
$xml_parser = xml_parser_create();
xml_set_element_handler($xml_parser, "startElement",
    "endElement");
if(!($fp = fopen($file, "r"))){
die("Could not open XML input");
}
while ($data = fread($fp, 4096)) {
if(!xml_parse($xml_parser, $data, feof($fp))) {
die(sprintf("XML error: %s at line %d",
xml_error_string(xml_get_error_code($xml_parser)),
xml_get_current_line_number($xml_parser)));
}
}
xml_parser_free($xml_parser);
```

Although documentation is scarce, I hope this gives you a small taste of how XML works with PHP. I should note that PHP with expat does not support combining an XML document with an XSL stylesheet.

Summary

In this chapter, we covered a great deal of material. The objective was to introduce you to some concepts of XML development, as well as some specific programmatic approaches to adding support for XML to your applications.

Specifically, we covered:

- ◆ Requirements for the XML DOM

- Specific capabilities of the DOM

- Technical intricacies of the DOM

- Programming XML in Visual Basic

- Programming XML in Perl

- Programming XML in ASP

- Programming XML in PHP

I hope this information has proven useful to you and has whetted your appetite. Ultimately, I hope this chapter has helped you get a better grasp on the technical aspects of working with XML.

7

XML in the Data Tier

An important part of considering XML in the enterprise is database integration. You may ask yourself questions such as, "How does XML work with SQL?" and "Will XML mesh well with my existing databases?" These questions have answers, and those answers are explored in this chapter.

XML is a language that describes data and can function as a data format. This chapter explores XML in the data tier, both as a format and as a delivery mechanism.

This chapter offers a discussion of XML's relationship with two of the most popular database systems, Microsoft SQL Server 2000 and Oracle 8i. Both of these products offer support of XML, but in varying degrees. It should help you gain an understanding of how well XML will work with your current installation.

The XML-Data Schema

We briefly mentioned the XML Schema language in Chapter 2. Now, we can start to examine it more closely and figure out how it can benefit you. I want to mention before we get started that schemas are optional.

The XML Schema language is based on the XML-Data note submitted to the W3C, which corresponds to the feature set proposed for Document Content Definition (DCD). For the purposes of this book, I use the terms XML-Data, XML schemas, and XML Schema language interchangeably.

Remember that XML schemas offer the advantage over DTDs in that schemas are written in XML, so there is no unique syntax to learn. This flexibility makes schemas very attractive to XML authors. Basically, XML schemas allow you to define the rules governing relationships between elements and attributes. Schemas can be parsed and managed just like "regular" XML documents.

I chose to cover XML schemas in this chapter because they provide insight into how to use XML as a data format. One more thing of interest: Schemas are supported in Internet Explorer 5.0.

Defining Schemas

Defining a schema means you have to adhere to a set of guidelines for schema syntax. It's much simpler than creating DTDs, and it's very intuitive.

Let's take a look at what makes up a schema. Our code from Chapter 2 is reprinted here:

```
<?xml version="1.0" ?>
<Schema name="schema_example" xmlns="urn:schemas-microsoft-
    com:xml-data">
<ElementType name="Sample1" content="textOnly">
<ElementType name="Sample2" content="textOnly">
</Schema>
```

The definitions in an XML schema are contained within the top-level Schema document element. The Schema document element definition must come from the namespace, specified by xmlns. The Schema document element should also contain namespace declarations for any other schemas to which it will adhere, such as the data type namespace. When referring to this particular namespace, you can use dt:type to specify data types for your elements and attributes. Adding in the code for that namespace gives us this:

```
<?xml version="1.0" ?>
<Schema name="schema_example"
    xmlns="urn:schemas-microsoft-com:xml-data"
    xmlns="urn:schemas-microsoft-com:datatypes">
<ElementType name="Sample1" content="textOnly">
<ElementType name="Sample2" content="textOnly">
</Schema>
```

If you take a close look at the Schema element, you will see I have added another namespace prefixed by xmlns. This namespace, hosted by Microsoft, makes data typing available to my documents.

The Schema element can contain as many top-level declarations as you desire. These top-level declarations include the principal XML schema elements ElementType and AttributeType. These elements require a name attribute that is explicit and unique within the schema. The content of the schema begins with the AttributeType and ElementType declarations of the innermost elements, and must precede their corresponding attribute and element content declarations.

An ElementType can contain other ElementType elements. You can use the order and group attributes to add further definition, and minOccurs and maxOccurs to define the number of occurrences for a group or element.

There are four categories to define the content type for an element: empty (empty), text only (textOnly), subelements only (eltOnly), or a combination of text and subelements (mixed). Empty indicates no content at all. These categories are specified in the content attribute of ElementType using the values noted in parantheses above.

Schema Information Access

Schemas can be accessed via two methods. You can load the schema directly using its URL or you can access the type declarations through the definition property. Loading it directly gives you the familiar tree-view, while loading it through the definition property returns the XMLDOMNode representing the type declaration for the instance node. Since the XMLDOMNode is part of the tree created when the schema was parsed, it is possible to traverse the schema using the object model.

To get the XMLDOMDocument, which would reprsent the entire schema, simply reference the ownerDocument property on the XMLDOMNode returned by the definition property. Considering our schema defined above:

```
'Sample1Elem is the first sample1 element.
Set Sample1Elem = XMLDoc.selectSingleNode("//sample1")
'Sample1Type is the ElementType declaration for Sample1
Set Sample1Type = Sample1Elem.definition
'Sample1Schema is the in-memory representation of the schema
Set Sample1Schema = Sample1Type.ownerDocument
```

The schema representation acquired through ownerDocument is by default read-only. To get a read-write version, you have two options: Load the document using the load method (and pass it Sample1Schema, since the Load method can take an XMLDOMDocument node as its parameter), or add the documentElement of the node to an empty XMLDOMDocument.

Using the Load method for this purpose is relatively straightforward:

```
xmlDocument.Load(Sample1Schema)
```

Adding the documentElement of the node to an empty XMLDOMDocument is also pretty simple:

```
xmlEmptyDocument.appendChild(Sample1Schema.documentElement)
```

Either one of these methods should work fine. I haven't discovered a performance benefit with one over the other, although my guess would be that the second method is more efficient than the first.

I hope I have successfully conveyed how schemas work and how to work with them. As we delve further into programming concepts and the idea of XML as an integral part of an application, schemas will prove to be even more valuable.

XML as a Data Source

Creating XML data sources using existing data is very simple. It's also very handy because you can create a bunch of XML documents using the results of an SQL query and use these XML files individually from the server. That means you can use XML as a data format.

First, assume that you already have data. For this example, we'll use my DVD data. I have a table called tblDVD that has an entry for every DVD I own. It's an Access database with an interface on my Windows CE palmtop so I always know what I want to know about my DVD collection. (See Figure 7-1.)

tblDVD		
ID	Integer	not null
TITLE	Text(75)	null
ANAMORPHIC	YesNo	null
STUDIO	Text(75)	null

Figure 7-1: tblDVD, which stores all of my DVD information

It is a simple table design, to say the least. Basically, my need for storing this data stems from owning a television that supports anamorphic video. This table stores the name of every DVD released, or on a release date list. That way, I will always know if a DVD is anamorphic or not.

The data in tblDVD is represented in Figure 7.2.

ID	TITLE	16x9	STUDIO
1	The Sixth Sense	Yes	Buena Vista
2	The Last Starfighter	Yes	Live
3	The Abyss: Special Edition	No	Fox

Figure 7-2: The data represented in tblDVD

ID represents a unique identifier. TITLE is the title of the movie on DVD. 16X9 is shorthand for ANAMORPHIC, which is an identifier for whether or not the DVD is presented enhanced for widescreen televisions. Finally, STUDIO is simply the name of the studio that put out the DVD.

This data is accessible via ADO and ODBC, since it is stored in an Access database. Once we get the data into an XML data source, we will be able to get to the data through a simple script. This will make my data available to anyone on the Web.

We have to write ASP code to do the dirty work of transforming the data in the tables into an XML data source. The end result will still be an ASP file, but rather than output HTML, it will output accessible XML.

There are two advantages to this. First, the data is still generated dynamically from the Access table, so I'm still able to use Access to update my data and keep my XML data source updated automatically. Second, I can populate my XML data source using a script which greatly simplifies entering large blocks of data, for example, release lists.

Before we get into the particulars of the code, let's build an XML document for our data. I imagine the XML document as being structured like so:

```
<?xml version="1.0">
<dvd>
<disc>
<id></id>
<title></title>
```

```
<anamorphic></anamorphic>
<studio></studio>
</disc>
</dvd>
```

DVD is the top-level element of the document, and it contains one or more disc elements.

Writing the ASP file that will output populated XML documents is very simple. The ASP page should start with the default scripting language and, if it is your style, Option Explicit. Then output the first two lines of the XML document, which are the XML declaration and the top level element.

```
<%@LANGUAGE="VBScript"%>
<% Option Explicit %>
<?xml version="1.0">
<dvd>
```

At this point we want to construct an iterative loop to output all of the data between the corresponding tags. In pseudocode, this is what we are trying to build:

```
<%@LANGUAGE="VBScript"%>
<% Option Explicit %>
<?xml version="1.0">
<dvd>
'do
'tag info
'loop
</dvd>
```

The first thing we have to do to accomplish this is create a connection to the database. We will then loop through the ADO recordset to output our data:

```
<%
Dim oConn
Dim oDVD
Dim sSQL
Set oConn = Server.CreateObject("ADODB.Connection")
oConn.Open "tblDVD"
sSQL = "SELECT id, title, anamorphic, studio FROM tblDVD"
```

```
Set oDVD = oConn.Execute(sSQL)
Do While Not oDVD.EOF
%>
```

Since we have already defined the structure for our XML document, we can just plug it into the ASP code:

```
<disc>
<id><%=oDVD("id")%></id>
<title><%=oDVD("title")%></title>
<anamorphic><%=oDVD("anamorphic")%></anamorphic>
<studio><%=oDVD("studio")%></studio>
</disc>
```

This is the code that builds our XML documents for us. To complete the project, simply close the loop and the XML document:

```
<% oDVD.MoveNext
Loop
%>
</dvd>
```

Just close the database connection, destroy the objects, and it's all done. The ASP code all put together looks like this:

```
<%@LANGUAGE="VBScript"%>
<% Option Explicit %>
<?xml version="1.0">
<dvd>
<%
Dim oConn
Dim oDVD
Dim sSQL

Set oConn = Server.CreateObject("ADODB.Connection")
oConn.Open "tblDVD"
sSQL = "SELECT id, title, anamorphic, studio FROM tblDVD"
Set oDVD = oConn.Execute(sSQL)

Do While Not oDVD.EOF
%>

<disc>
<id><%=oDVD("id")%></id>
```

```
<title><%=oDVD("title")%></title>
<anamorphic><%=oDVD("anamorphic")%></anamorphic>
<studio><%=oDVD("studio")%></studio>
</disc>

<% oDVD.MoveNext
Loop
%>
</dvd>

<% oDVD.Close
Set oDVD = Nothing
oConn.Close
Set oConn = Nothing
%>
```

When you execute the ASP page, you get this:

```
<?xml version="1.0">
<dvd>
<disc>
<id>1</id>
<title>The Sixth Sense</title>
<anamorphic>Yes</anamorphic>
<studio>Buena Vista</studio>
</disc>
<disc>
<id>2</id>
<title>The Last Starfighter</title>
<anamorphic>Yes</anamorphic>
<studio>Live</studio>
</disc>
<disc>
<id>3</id>
<title>The Abyss: Special Edition</title>
<anamorphic>No</anamorphic>
<studio>Fox</studio>
</disc>
</dvd>
```

So there you have it, a quick way to get your database data into XML form. The output from the ASP page can be saved as an XML document from the browser, or you can write script code to output everything to a specified file using the FileSystemObject.

We won't get into the details on how to access the data source via script. I'll save that for a second edition.

Oracle 8i and XML

It's no secret that Oracle 8i is a powerful and popular database system. Oracle says their product is the leading solution for information management on the Internet. It's no surprise that Oracle introduced XML support to their product line with Oracle 8i.

Oracle's Web site says their XML strategy is, "Deliver the best platform for developers to productively build and cost-effectively deploy reliable and scalable Internet applications exploiting XML." Oracle is attempting to make this strategy come alive with a host of XML capabilities built into and around the Oracle 8i product. Oracle 8i offers XML support across a broad range, such as in the database server, in packaged applications, and in Core XML support built in Java and running on the Oracle 8i Platform for Java.

Oracle 8i XML Support

Oracle 8i offers what they call Core XML Support. Core XML Support promises several things for the developer. For instance, it promises to make developers more productive by simplifying the tight integration of XML with database data and extending the power of database queries to XML documents. It also promises to make applications more stable by exploiting the speed of the Oracle 8i query engine and server-optimized Java VM, as well as by processing database data and XML together in the same server, eliminating network traffic for data access. Finally, it promises to make applications more cost-effective to deply by providing a reliable, scalable, and manageable server platform supporting industry standards, and it will run on current and future hardware from NT & Linux PCs to parallel clusters of mainframe-class machines.

The Core XML Support is comprised of three facilities:

♦ Oracle XML Parser, for programmatic processing of XML documents

♦ XML support in iFS to automate parsing and rendering of data between the database and XML

♦ XML-enabled section searching in ConText for more precise searches over structured documents

Each of these facilities has its own strengths. We'll examine each individually to get a better feel for just what they have to offer.

Oracle XML Parser

Implemented in Java, the Oracle XML Parser can run on the Oracle 8i Java VM, discussed below. With support of XML 1.0, and the goal of being 100% compliant, the Oracle XML Parser can be used as both a validating and non-validating parser. It also provides two common APIs for developers, the DOM and Simple API for XML (SAX), which is not discussed in this book.

The standards-compliant XML parser is part of the Oracle 8i platform and is available on any system to which Oracle 8i has been ported. This means that any system that is running Oracle 8i has an XML parser available. In the future, the parser will include a PL/SQL interface, and using one of these APIs to process XML documents in Oracle 8i will be that much simpler.

XML Support in iFS

iFS refers to the Oracle Internet File System. The iFS allows a developer to define new file types provides built-in support for defining, parsing, and rendering those file types that are XML documents.

When the developer registers an XML file type, he supplies a document descriptor (an XML-based syntax to describe the schema of its XML-based file types) that defines the file type's XML structure (or schema), as well as how it should be stored in the database.

When a file is saved or sent to iFS, it recognizes the document as one of the defined file types, parses its XML, and stores the data in tables as the developer has indicated in the document descriptor. The same information is used to render the XML document when a particular instance of the file type is requested through any of the iFS-supported protocols.

There are two ways to store the highly structured XML data: Store into and render from a series of related tables, or load the entire XML document into a text blob (a blob in a database typically stores entire files). Occasionally, one may want to have a hodgepodge of structured data and structured text markup. This requirement can be met by combining the two approaches.

For example, consider our DVD data. A "DiscInfo" filetype might point to PubDate and Studio tables. A DiscReview file type, which would mix structured text markup for a review with structured data about the disc, would store the data in tables and the structured markup as text fragments in text blobs. Consider this XML document:

```
<?xml version="1.0"?>
<DiscReview>
<ReviewID>1405</ReviewID>
<ReviewCat>Horror</ReviewCat>
<DiscInfo>
<PubDate>3-27-2000</PubDate>
<Studio>Buena Vista</Studio>
</DiscInfo>
<ReviewText>
The Sixth Sense is a beautifully crafted film starring Bruce Willis. The
    disc has a <VideoQuality>beautiful</VideoQuality> transfer. Sound
    is <SoundQuality>excellent</SoundQuality> but does not show off
    a 5.1 sound system. The disc earns <Rating>5</Rating> stars.
</ReviewText>
...
</DiscReview>
```

Once the iFS file types are stored in the database, their content can be searched using SQL queries and the files can be browsed and organized via a tool like Windows Explorer. This means I can browse reviews by filename while all of the disc information is stored in the database.

XML-enabled Section Searches in ConText

XML documents or document fragments stored as text blobs in the database can be indexed by the ConText text-based search engine. ConText allows developers to pinpoint their searches to a specific section of a document, where sections are defined by the XML tags in the document, or document fragment. ConText is integrated into the database and SQL, so developers can perform queries that involve both structured data and indexed document fragments. Consider this query, which is from Oracle documentation:

```
SELECT * FROM
DVDInfo di, DVDReview dr
WHERE dr.Author='rob'
AND CONTAINS (ReviewText, 'beautiful WITHIN VideoQuality') >0
AND CONTAINS (ReviewText, '5 WITHIN Rating') >0
AND . . . /* Join Clauses */
```

This capability greatly expands the control a developer can have over the data. When the data is loaded into the database, the developer can take advantage of this powerful searching tool.

Oracle 8i Platform for Java

Oracle 8i offers a JDK 1.1.6-compatible Java Virtual Machine in the database server. Written from scratch, the VM is optimized to run in a highly scalable server environment. In addition to the new VM, Oracle 8i ships with a JDBC implementation designed to make any database access performed by Java code executing in the database very fast. Anything running on the Oracle 8i Java VM, as well as the VM itself, will run anywhere Oracle 8i runs.

A set of *platform services* run on top of the Java VM, enabling developers to build database-driven applications in Java and PL/SQL. These services include:

◆ Enterprise JavaBeans 1.0 Server for transaction components

♦ Java Stored Procedures for integrating Java code with SQL and PL/SQL

♦ Web Server to enable invoking Java Servlets running in the database from a browser over HTTP

♦ Object Request Broker based on VisiBroker for Java for distributed object communications

♦ Internet File System (iFS) for organizing and accessing documents and data using a file/folder-based metaphor through standard Windows and Internet protocols

Using these platform services allows developers to create custom Internet applications that integrate Java and the database in any way they want.

An in-depth discussion of Java, Oracle 8i, and XML is outside the scope of this book. However, there are excellent books on the market that cover this subject, and I invite you to take a look at one.

Microsoft SQL Server 2000 and XML

Microsoft SQL Server 2000, codenamed "Shiloh," promises a considerable amount of support for XML. For example, you can query SQL over HTTP with a URL, bring the data down to the browser, and manipulate it on the client machine. Going further, you could use XSL to handle the sorting and convert the XML to HTML.

Along with expanding on SQL Server 7.0 in the areas of scalability, manageability, availability, and data warehousing, SQL Server 2000 introduces cool new functionality focused on e-commerce. SQL Server 2000 will be completely XML-enabled.

SQL Server 2000 allows you to pass a SQL query on the end of a querystring. For example:

```
http://localhost/data_base?sql=SELECT+*+FROM+table
    +FOR+XML+AUTO
```

It will also allow you to keep prebuilt queries and stored procedures on your IIS server. These queries (and procedures) can be executed by POSTing a form or calling it in the URL (GET would work too).

The data can be returned in an XML format you specify (including by schema) or you can use AUTO to return the results in an automatically formatted structure.

Unfortunately, the information on SQL Server 2000 is somewhat scant, at least it is at the time of this writing. At the very least, it should whet your appetite and give you a rough feel for what SQL Server 2000 has in store for XML developers.

The XML support in SQL Server 2000 can be best summed up in three core features, which make SQL Server 2000 an XML-enabled database server:

♦ The data in a SQL Server database can be updated through an XML-based gram

♦ SQL Server can be accessed through HTTP using a SQL-compliant URL

♦ The Select statement has a new FOR XML clause that supports retrieving data in XML format

These features should considerably simplify building Web pages.

If SQL Server 2000 is not released when this book is in your hands, you can download a Technology Preview from Microsoft's Web site. The link, which may change by the time you read this, is http://msdn.microsoft.com/workshop/xml/articles/xmlsql/.

The Technology Preview is an IIS ISAPI filter that will demonstrate the XML capabilities of SQL Server 2000. It provides http access to SQL Server, as well as XML formatting capabilities. It also allows XML updating.

Continuing with our use of our tblDVD database and all of its columns, let's examine how this all works. Since this is SQL Server, and tblDVD is a table, we need a database, DVDdb. A sample query would be:

```
http://localhost/DVDdb?sql=SELECT+*+FROM+
tblDVD+FOR+XML+AUTO
```

To pass a query in a URL, you simply pass a root argument, SQL, and set it equal to a valid SQL statement. Be sure to substitute + for a space, and use escape sequences for other characters, such as &, %, and .

If you execute the URL listed above, you get back something like this:

```
<?xml version="1.0" encoding="UTF-8" ?>
<root>
<row id="1" title="The Sixth Sense" anamorphic="Yes" studio="Buena
    Vista/>
<row id="2" title="The Last Starfighter" anamorphic="Yes"
    studio="Live"/>
<row id="3" title="The Abyss: Special Edition" anamorphic="No"
    studio="Fox"/>
</root>
```

All of the data is generated by SQL Server, then the ISAPI module returns it in XML format, all on the fly.

FOR XML Calls

Let's continue to use the DVD database, but flesh it out a little more. If you remember, tblDVD stored the id, title, anamorphic boolean, and studio. I mentioned a little later a DVDInfo table and a DVDReview table, with some sample XML.

Let's split up tblDVD into two tables for our SQL Server exercise. The two tables roll up into the DVD_DB database. The two tables we'll use for this discussion are outlined in Figure 7-3.

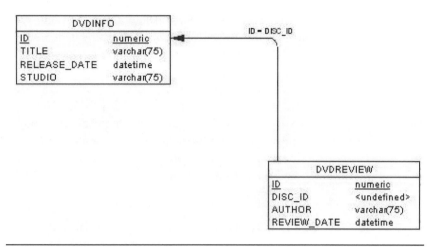

Figure 7-3: DVD_DB model

Noting that XML statements are currently only available through a URL via http, let's construct a simple SQL statement:

```
SELECT id, title, studio FROM DVDINFO WHERE id = 3
```

This query simply returns the record with ID of 3 (in this case, it's *The Abyss: Special Edition*). If you run this on regular old SQL Server, you get row-based results. Ho hum.

However, you can run this query in a browser through the URL, and retrieve the data directly into the browser in XML format. Simply reconstruct the query by escaping reserved characters and spaces, and then indicate you want your output as raw XML with the RAW XML specifier:

```
SELECT+id,title,studio,+FROM+DVDINFO+WHERE+ID+=+3
    +FOR+XML+RAW
```

Construct your URL by appending this query onto your querystring, like so:

```
http://localhost/DVD_DB?sql=SELECT+id,title,studio,
    +FROM+DVDINFO+WHERE+ID+=+3
```

```
+FOR+XML+RAW
```

If everything works out ok, you should get your data output in the browser. If you noticed, we specified FOR XML RAW in that query, yet we specified FOR XML AUTO in the query preceding it.

Well, there are three XML formats you can specify for your data: XML RAW, XML AUTO, and XML EXPLICIT. XML RAW returns your data in raw XML format with the row attribute the default for all data. XML AUTO returns your data with the database table name as an attribute instead of the generic row attribute. Finally, XML EXPLICIT lets you specify how the XML will be structured when returned from a query. It's a little more complicated than the other two.

Basically, you can define a template for your XML and specify XML EXPLICIT to have all of your data returned in that template. That's a pretty complex discussion that we probably shouldn't go into here. Once SQL Server 2000 is out, there will be plenty of useful information on how to specify templates for using with SQL queries.

So that's SQL Server 2000's XML support in a nutshell. Hopefully, by the time this is published (or shortly thereafter), Microsoft will have released SQL Server 2000 and there will be books available on how to exploit all of its capabilities.

For now, try out the Technology Preview I mentioned in the beginning of this section. Its documentation is not very forthcoming, and you'll get more information in this section, but the preview itself should give you everything you need to get excited about XML in SQL Server 2000.

Summary

In this chapter, we covered the relationship between XML and databases. We looked at schemas, XML as a data format and the varying levels of support for XML in two major database systems, SQL Server 2000 and Oracle 8i. Specifically, we covered:

- The XML-Data Schema and schemas in general

- Using XML as a data source

- XML support in Oracle 8i

- XML support in SQL Server 2000

The next, and final, chapter in this book examines a case study that demonstrates how XML and corresponding technologies were used to create a successful Web site.

8

Case Study: DVDmdb.com

In 1999, DVDmdb.com, a site dedicated to the discussion of the DVD format and all it has to offer, was launched. The site grew out of a passion for home theater. DVD-related Web sites have been very successful and it is quite a lot of fun running one.

This chapter shows you what was done to make XML work for DVDmdb.com. It includes a discussion of the server setup, applications, databases, and methods, and provides a good idea of one approach to creating an XML-enabled site.

The Objective

We knew when we set out to create DVDmdb.com that it was going to be difficult to categorize and maintain a large bulk of content, especially since we had so much content at launch. Brian Roberts designed the entire site, and I found myself in charge of developing some kind of content management system that would allow for easy publishing and automatic retrieval.

DVDmdb.com is structured similarly to a newspaper. Figure 8-1 is a screenshot of the site. The main page is made of up three columns. The first column contains linked headlines, and under each headline there is a teaser that links to the full story, if a full story is available. The second column contains the list of DVD reviews. Under the title of the newest review is a line of text that is pulled from the actual review. So when a reader comes to the site and sees we have uploaded a review of *The Iron Giant*, he can read the text beneath the DVD title and get the summary of our review. For example, "This is the best DVD I've ever seen." Finally, the third column contains a list of the latest preorder deals offered by our affiliates.

Considering the different types of data, DVDmdb.com offers up some unique challenges. I had to make sure that the data could easily be shared between pages without making repetitive database calls. I also had to define the relationships between documents; for example, the line of text from a review that is displayed on the main page. I didn't want to write complicated code that would do this for us.

After careful consideration and hours in front of a whiteboard, it was determined that XML would serve our needs very well. Sharing data among XML documents is a breeze, and XML would also benefit us by making our site more scalable. Ultimately, XML would ensure us the flexibility in sharing data with other sites, and that was very important to us.

Approaching XML from the standpoint of application developer opened a few challenges to us. First, we had to determine what the best method was for manipulating our XML documents. We knew we wanted to take advantage of the Microsoft XMLDOM since that is what we knew best.

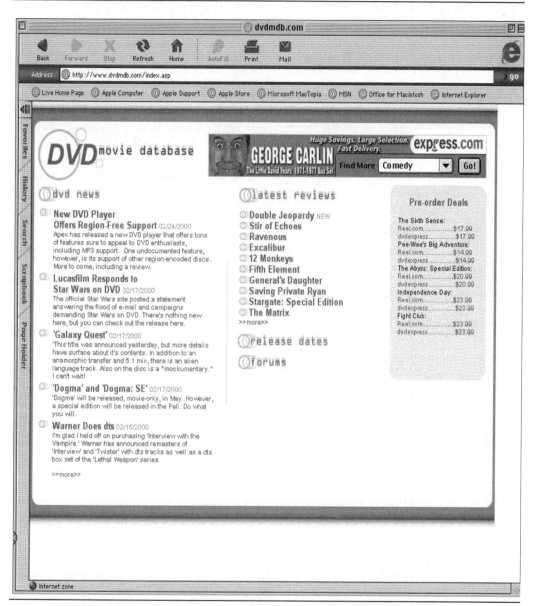

Figure 8-1: The dvdmdb.com Web site

We decided to use ASP to get to and manipulate our data, and to use COM to handle the spidering process that generated XML pages.

Unfortunately, I can't divulge the details of the COM-based spidering process. I have to keep something secret and the COM has the most original stuff in it. I'll make reference to the spider but you won't see any of its source or details about how it works.

After we made the decision of what tool we were going to use to develop our site, we sat down and talked about the database. We decided to go with a Microsoft Access database for the soft launch, and we would move to SQL Server 2000 when it became available.

Everything is mapped out nicely in the diagram in Figure 8-2.

Please keep in mind as you are reading that our solution was not necessarily the best, nor would it apply to all situations. Thus, you shouldn't think of this as the definitive way to develop an XML-enabled site; you should examine your own needs and come up with your own answers.

The Database

The database in this application serves as a repository for the wealth of information that is DVDmdb.com. I have discovered that there are basically two ways to approach a design for a database that will be used with XML. First, you can store all of your documents as text files and have pointers to the text files in your database, or you can store the XML data in the database directly. We chose the latter method for DVDmdb.com.

The Data Model

Constructing the data model for DVDmdb proved to be a very comfortable task. I already had my data logically structured in my brain; all it took was constructing an entity relationship diagram and then generating the database, and it would all be ready to go. Right?

I created the entity-relationship diagram in PowerDesigner, which is my tool of choice for data modeling. The data model is in Figure 8-3.

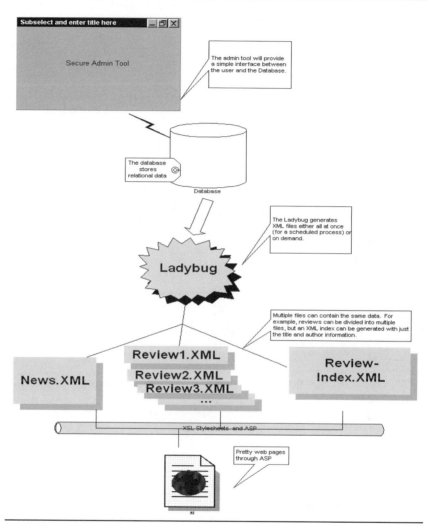

Figure 8-2: DVDmdb data flow

When designing the model, I had simplicity in mind. There are only six tables, and only four of them have relationships. News and Reviews are separate entities because their data is different from the data in DVD, DVD_Values, DVD_Features, and DVD_Feature_Values.

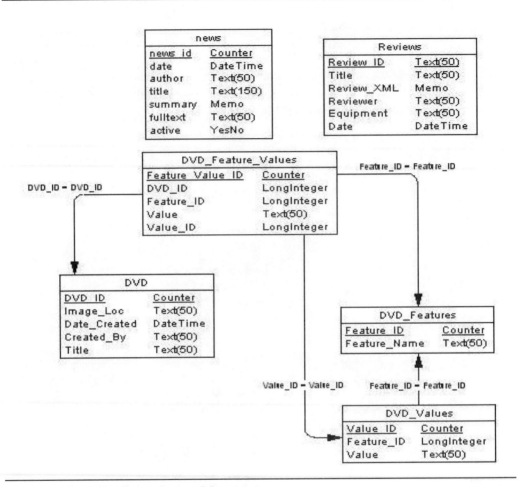

Figure 8-3: The DVDmdb.com data model

As I mentioned earlier, we chose to store our XML information directly in the database. Ultimately, this decision was made because it affected our scalability; in other words, it would simplify our move to SQL Server 2000. In fact, it would be possible in SQL Server 2000 to store the entire DVDmdb.com Web site and retrieve the whole thing with a single http URL query.

Sample Data

If you take a look at the data model, you'll see that we have six tables, and four of those tables have relationships. Looking at the table names should give you a clear idea of what they store, but just in case they don't, I'll provide some sample data from the database. Figures 8-4, 8-5, and 8-6 are screenshots straight from Microsoft Access.

DVD : Table

DVD_ID	Image_Loc	Date_Created	Created_By	Title
1		12/21/1999	Nathan	Stir of Echoes
2		1/3/2000	Brian	Double Jeopardy
3		1/4/2000	Rob	Ravenous
(AutoNumber)				

Record: 1 of 3

Figure 8-4: The DVD table

news : Table

news_id	date	author	title	summary	fulltext	active
1	2/24/2000	Brian	New DVD Player	Apex has released a new DVD player that offers tons of		☑
2	2/17/2000	Brian	Lucasfilm Responds	The official Star Wars site posted a statement answering		☑
3	2/17/2000	Brian	'Galaxy Quest'	This title was announced yesterday, but more details		☑
4	2/17/2000	Brian	'Dogma' and 'Dogma: SE'	'Dogma' will be released, movie-only, in May. However,		☑
5	2/15/2000	Brian	Warner does DTS	I'm glad I held off on purchasing 'Interview with the		☑
6	2/15/2000	Brian	Fight Club Delayed	'Fight Club' has been delayed until 6/6. Whatever. As long as		☑
7	2/14/2000	Brian	Bond	The second installment of the Bond box set is due out 5/16.		☑
8	2/7/2000	Brian	'House on Haunted Hill'	Warner announced a release date for a feature rich transfer		☑
10	2/7/2000	Brian	'Abyss' Problems?	According to The Digital Bits' rumor mill, there could be		☑
(AutoNumber)						☐

Record: 1 of 9

Figure 8-5: The News table

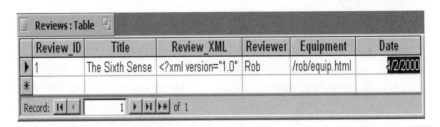

Figure 8-6: The Reviews table

These are the three main tables for the DVDmdb site. The auxiliary tables are not shown here because they are not paramount to an understanding of how DVDmdb.com works.

Now that you have seen the database design and implementation, as well as some data, we're ready to move on to the meat of our discussion: the XML.

The XML Documents

The development of the XML side of DVDmdb.com required a bit more time and thought than the development of the database. It was not too difficult to lay out the structure of news.xml and review.xml (for News and Reviews, respectively); rather, the difficulty was deciding what tags to include and not to include, and when to make something an attribute versus when to make it a tag.

We sat down and churned out the XML structure, which is reprinted later in this chapter. We also churned out the XSL, which was not fun at all.

In keeping with the design intention of XML, I wanted to keep the architecture simple. There is only one schema, for Reviews. I made the decision to use only one schema, for reviews, because I figured we would be importing other people's data as news, and then in that case we would need to adhere to their schema, not our own (BizTalk). In the case of reviews, however, they are all our own and could benefit from the structure provided by a defined schema.

Structuring Documents

We covered schemas and how to use them in Chapter 7. You'll probably remember that schemas are good because they are easier to maintain, easier to read, and are basically a replacement for DTDs. They also offer simplified integration with other XML-based sites, and schema repositories like BizTalk.

As I previously mentioned, there is only one schema, Review.xml. I decided to adhere to the XML-Data schema hosted by Microsoft.

Let's take a look at the Review schema:

```
<?xml version="1.0" ?>
<Schema name="Review" xmlns="urn:schemas-microsoft-com:xml-
    data" xmlns:dt="urn:schemas-microsoft-com:datatypes">
<ElementType name="dvd" content="eltOnly">
<element type="title" minOccurs="1" maxOccurs="1"/>
<element type="imageURL" minOccurs="1" maxOccurs="1"/>
<element type="director" minOccurs="1" maxOccurs="1"/>
<element type="rating" minOccurs="1" maxOccurs="1"/>
<element type="copyright" minOccurs="1" maxOccurs="1"/>
<element type="special" minOccurs="1" maxOccurs="1"/>
<element type="format" minOccurs="1" maxOccurs="1"/>
<element type="anamorphic" minOccurs="1" maxOccurs="1"/>
<element type="sound" minOccurs="1" maxOccurs="1"/>
<element type="other" minOccurs="1" maxOccurs="1"/>
<element type="review" minOccurs="1" maxOccurs="1"/>
</ElementType>

<ElementType name="title" content="textOnly" dt:type="string"/>
<ElementType name="imageURL" content="textOnly"
    dt:type="string"/>
<ElementType name="director" content="textOnly" dt:type="string"/>
<ElementType name="rating" content="textOnly" dt:type="string"/>
<ElementType name="copyright" content="textOnly"
    dt:type="string"/>
<ElementType name="special" content="textOnly" dt:type="string"/>
<ElementType name="format" content="textOnly" dt:type="string"/>
<ElementType name="anamorphic" content="textOnly"
    dt:type="string"/>
<ElementType name="sound" content="textOnly" dt:type="string"/>
<ElementType name="other" content="textOnly" dt:type="string"/>
```

```
<ElementType name="review" content="eltOnly">
<element type="synopsis" minOccurs="1" maxOccurs="1"/>
<element type="video" minOccurs="1" maxOccurs="1"/>
<element type="audio" minOccurs="1" maxOccurs="1"/>
<element type="features" minOccurs="1" maxOccurs="1"/>
<element type="verdict" minOccurs="1" maxOccurs="1"/>
<attribute type="author"/>
</ElementType>
<ElementType name="synopsis" content="textOnly"
    dt:type="string"/>
<ElementType name="video" content="textOnly" dt:type="string"/>
<ElementType name="audio" content="textOnly" dt:type="string"/>
<ElementType name="features" content="textOnly"
    dt:type="string"/>
<ElementType name="verdict" content="textOnly" dt:type="string"/>
<AttributeType name="author" required="yes" dt:type="string"/>
```

This schema should be easy to understand. If not, please consult Chapter 7, where we talk more about the XML-Data schema.

Reviews

The review XML file is fairly straightforward. Take a look at this review of the film *Double Jeopardy* and see how it coincides with the schema printed above:

```
<?xml version="1.0" ?>
<dvd>
<Schema xmlns="urn:www-dvdmdb-com:review"/>
<imageURL>http://www.dvdmdb.com/images/doublejeopardy.jpg
</imageURL>
<director>Bruce Beresford</director>
<rated>R</rated>
<copyright>1999, Paramount</copyright>
<special>Scene access, Theatrical trailer</special>
<format>Widescreen 2.35:1</format>
<anamorphic>Yes</anamorphic>
<sound>English Dolby Digital 5.1</sound>
<other>Produced by Leonard Goldberg; Written by Douglas S. Cook;
    DVD released on 02/22/2000; running time of 105 minutes; Closed
    Captioned.</other>
<review author="Brian Roberts">
<film>"Murder isn't always a crime," but it should be a crime for films
    this mediocre to gross well over $100 million. This movie is
    extremely predictable and demands that your disbelief be
```

suspended more than usual so that the story might work. The suspense scenes were botched, save one, and I was teased with character depth that was never explored. Tommy Lee Jones is wasted as a result, but still manages to dominate a scene with what little he's given. Ashley Judd is good as always, but I can't help but wonder if more could have been brought out of her with better direction. I just wasn't convinced of her determination.</film>
<video>Paramount has made another excellent 16:9 enhanced transfer. The flesh tones were great and there was plenty of detail while staying true to the look of film. Blacks were great and colors were dead on. There was an unfortunate amount of dirt and scratches on the print used for the transfer, however. It is only noticeable because of the bright outdoor scenes that are frequent in this film, but it is pretty unforgivable since this is a brand new film and they should have had access to pure film elements for the transfer. Compression was clean without any artifacting.</video>
<audio>The sound was fine. There really isn't a whole lot here to impress your friends with surround sound. What is there is clean and balanced. I really liked the surround effects in the cabin of the boat. Creaking of wood and the sound of water against the hull is convincingly engulfing. My S530D had some synch problems in the last chapter.</audio>
<features>We get a trailer and a "featurette" for the special features on this disc. The cool thing about the trailer is that it shows you the entire movie. So, you could pretty much see this film in about 2 minutes if you were in a hurry. I'm being sarcastic, but I hate these trailers that show you everything. The featurette is just quick snippets of the cast and director talking about their characters or the weak plot. Boo!</features>
<verdict>Sound and picture is up to the standards that Paramount has been setting for itself lately, though I was really disappointed with the dirty print and the special features weren't very special. If you are still dying to see this film, this disc is a renter. There is nothing spectacular enough to make this film worth purchasing.</verdict>
</review>
</dvd>

The reviews are indexed in a single XML file, called review_index.xml. This file is created dynamically as each review is uploaded to the server. We'll discuss the uploading process later on in this chapter.

This is the XML for a review index:

```
<review-index>
<review-link date="2/29/00">
```

```
<title>Double Jeopardy</title>
<link>doublejeopardy</link>
</review-link>
<review-link date="2/24/00">
<title>Stir Of Echoes</title>
<link>stirofechoes</link>
</review-link>
<review-link>
<title>Ravenous</title>
<link>ravenous</link>
</review-link>
<review-link>
<title>Excalibur</title>
<link>excalibur</link>
</review-link>
<review-link>
<title>12 Monkeys</title>
<link>12monkeys</link>
</review-link>
<review-link>
<title>Fifth Element </title>
<link>fifthelement</link>
</review-link>
<review-link>
<title>General's Daughter</title>
<link>generalsdaughter</link>
</review-link>
<review-link>
<title>Saving Private Ryan</title>
<link>spr</link>
</review-link>
<review-link>
<title>Stargate: Special Edition</title>
<link>stargate</link>
</review-link>
<review-link>
<title>The Matrix</title>
<link>matrix</link>
</review-link>
</review-index>
```

So the review documents are pretty well-mapped out. Unfortunately, due
to the proprietary nature of the Web site, I can't divulge how the review
files are actually generated. To satiate you, however, I will show you how
we built the front page of the Web site from three different XML files. This

should help you on your way to figuring out how you want to do it on your own.

I'll go one step further and show you how we administer the news section of the Web site later on.

News

To continue with our discussion of the XML structure, consider this XML file, which contains the news for DVDmdb.com. This file, called news.xml, is used to build the front page of the site. The news is updated by the admins using a custom tool, which we'll discuss a little later. Here's news.xml:

```
<?xml version="1.0" ?>
<news>
  <articles align="left">
<article date="2/24/00" auth="Rob">
<title>New DVD Player Offers Region-Free Support</title>
<summary>Apex has released a new DVD player that
offers tons of features sure to
appeal to DVD enthusiasts, including MP3 support.
One undocumented feature, however, is its
support of other region-encoded discs.
More to come, including a review.
</summary>
</article>
<article date="2/17/00" auth="Brian">
<title>Lucasfilm Responds to Star Wars on DVD</title>
<summary>The official Star Wars site posted a statement
answering the flood of e-mail and campaigns demanding
 Star Wars on DVD. There's nothing new here,
 but you can check out the release
 <link href="http://www.starwars.com/episode-
    i/news/2000/07/news4b.html">here</link>.
</summary>
</article>
<article date="2/17/00" auth="Brian">
<title>'Galaxy Quest'</title>
<summary>'This title was announced yesterday,
 but more details have surface about it's contents.
 In addition to an anamorphic transfer
 and 5.1 mix, there is an alien language track.
  Also on the disc is a "mockumentary." I can't wait!
```

```
</summary>
</article>
 </articles>
 <articles align="right">
<article date="2/17/00" auth="Brian">
<title>Lucasfilm Responds to Star Wars on DVD</title>
<summary>The official Star Wars site posted a statement
answering the flood of e-mail and campaigns demanding
 Star Wars on DVD. There's nothing new here,
 but you can check out the release
 <link href="http://www.starwars.com/episode-
     i/news/2000/07/news4b.html">here</link>.
</summary>
</article>
<article date="2/17/00" auth="Brian">
<title>Lucasfilm Responds to Star Wars on DVD</title>
<summary>The official Star Wars site posted a statement
answering the flood of e-mail and campaigns demanding
 Star Wars on DVD. There's nothing new here,
 but you can check out the release
 <link href="http://www.starwars.com/episode-
     i/news/2000/07/news4b.html">here</link>.
</summary>
</article>
<article date="2/17/00" auth="Brian">
<title>Lucasfilm Responds to Star Wars on DVD</title>
<summary>The official Star Wars site posted a statement
answering the flood of e-mail and campaigns demanding
 Star Wars on DVD. There's nothing new here,
 but you can check out the release
 <link href="http://www.starwars.com/episode-
     i/news/2000/07/news4b.html">here</link>.
</summary>
</article>
<article date="2/17/00" auth="Brian">
<title>Lucasfilm Responds to Star Wars on DVD</title>
<summary>The official Star Wars site posted a statement
answering the flood of e-mail and campaigns demanding
 Star Wars on DVD. There's nothing new here,
 but you can check out the release
 <link href="http://www.starwars.com/episode-
     i/news/2000/07/news4b.html">here</link>.
</summary>
</article>
 </articles>
</news>
```

Notice the structure in this document. Each news item is in an article tag. The article contains a date and author. Subelements include the title and a summary, as well as an optional link to a full-text article.

Prices

Finally, there's the pricelist. This is the list of current hot deals that appears on the front page of DVDmdb.com every day. These deals are hand chosen by the administrators of the site and, in a way, reflect our personal tastes in films. Prices.xml is:

```
<prices>
<price title="The Sixth Sense" date="2/24/00" auth="Robert">
<vendor name="Reel.Com" currency="USD">
<cost>17.99</cost>

    <link>http://www.buy.com/videos/product.asp?sku=40127881</l
    ink>
</vendor>
<vendor name="dvdexpress" currency="USD">
<cost>17.99</cost>

    <link>http://www.amazon.com/exec/obidos/ASIN/0784013470/o/
    qid=951898302/sr=8-1/104-4745338-1499661</link>
</vendor>
</price>
<price title="Pee-Wee's Big Adventure" date="2/22/00"
    auth="Robert">
<vendor name="Reel.com" currency="USD">
<cost>14.99</cost>

    <link>http://www.buy.com/videos/product.asp?sku=40127881</l
    ink>
</vendor>
<vendor name="dvdexpress" currency="USD">
<cost>20.99</cost>

    <link>http://www.amazon.com/exec/obidos/ASIN/0784013470/o/
    qid=951898302/sr=8-1/104-4745338-1499661</link>
</vendor>
</price>
<price title="The Abyss: Special Edition" date="2/21/00"
    auth="Robert">
<vendor name="Reel.com" currency="USD">
<cost>20.99</cost>
```

```
<link>http://www.buy.com/videos/product.asp?sku=40127881</l
ink>
</vendor>
<vendor name="dvdexpress" currency="USD">
<cost>20.99</cost>

    <link>http://www.amazon.com/exec/obidos/ASIN/0784013470/o/
    qid=951898302/sr=8-1/104-4745338-1499661</link>
</vendor>
</price>
<price title="Independence Day" date="2/12/00" auth="Robert">
<vendor name="Buy.Com" currency="USD">
<cost>23.99</cost>

    <link>http://www.buy.com/videos/product.asp?sku=40127881</l
    ink>
</vendor>
<vendor name="Amazon" currency="USD">
<cost>23.99</cost>

    <link>http://www.amazon.com/exec/obidos/ASIN/0784013470/o/
    qid=951898302/sr=8-1/104-4745338-1499661</link>
</vendor>
</price>
</prices>
```

Notice the interesting structure of this document. There is a prices top-level element, with a price element for each DVD. Each price element contains the title, date, and author (in this case, who picked the deal) as attributes, and has the subelements vendor (with its own attributes), cost, and a link.

Building the Front Page

Like every other document except review.xml, the front page, default.asp, does not have a schema attached to it. In fact, the front page is an interesting animal in that it is built from three separate XML files: Review_index.xml, prices.xml, and news.xml.

Let's begin by looking at the source of index.asp, the index file for DVD-mdb.com:

```
<%@ Language=VBScript %>
<% Response.buffer = true %>

<%
'do the xml/xsl transformation
  ' Set the source and style sheet locations here
sourceFile ="index_data.asp"
styleFile =  "default.xsl"

' Load the XML
  set source = Server.CreateObject("Microsoft.XMLDOM")
  source.async = false
  source.load sourceFile
  if source.parseerror.errorcode <> 0 then
response.write "Error parsing source: " & source.parseerror.errorcode
  end if
  ' Load the XSL
  set style = Server.CreateObject("Microsoft.XMLDOM")
  style.async = false
  style.load styleFile
  if style.parseerror.errorcode <> 0 then
response.write style.parseerror.errorcode
  end if
  source.transformNodeToObject style, Response

%>
```

Ignore that XSL part for now. The XMLDOM object is parsing a file called index_data.asp. Why not index_data.xml? Well, let's take a look at the file and see why it's an ASP:

```
<?xml version='1.0'?>
<index-data>
<!-- #include file="news.xml" -->
<!-- #include file="review_index.xml" -->
<!-- #include file="prices.xml" -->
</index-data>
```

The ASP file is in fact an XML file, just with an ASP extension so it can include the three XML files I showed you above: news.xml, review_index.xml, and prices.xml. Essentially the parser is going through all three of these files as one big file.

We could have declared a schema for each of the files, and then one big schema that referenced the other smaller schemas. That's something we still may do in the future, and I certainly don't want to discourage you from doing it. In our case, we just didn't have time to do schemas, unfortunately.

Back to our file. Once we have parsed the mammoth file, we parse an XSL file called default.xsl. This file contains the XSL formatting tags for the index page.

Creating the XSL

As you have already seen, after we parsed index_data.asp we parsed and applied default.xsl. This handles the necessary transformations so our document can be properly displayed in any browser.

This is the source for default.xsl:

```
<?xml version="1.0"?>
<xsl:stylesheet xmlns:xsl="http://www.w3.org/TR/WD-xsl">
  <xsl:template match="/">
<html>
<head>
<title>dvdmdb.com</title>
<META NAME="keywords" CONTENT="dvd, forums, news, release,
    player, home, theater, software, dvd-rom, guide, database,
    anamorphic, 16:9, discussion, info, information, buyer" />
<META NAME="description" CONTENT="dvdmdb.com is your source for
    all things DVD" />
<meta http-equiv="Content-Type" content="text/html; charset=iso-
    8859-1" />
<STYLE type="text/css">BODY {
FONT-FAMILY: arial,helvetica; MARGIN-LEFT: 0px; MARGIN-TOP: 0px
}
P {
FONT-FAMILY: arial,helvetica; FONT-SIZE: 8pt
}
DIV {
FONT-FAMILY: arial,helvetica; FONT-SIZE: 8pt
```

```
}
TD {
FONT-FAMILY: arial,helvetica
}
A {
COLOR: #486C98; TEXT-DECORATION: none
}
A:hover {
COLOR: #0066ff; TEXT-DECORATION: underline
}
A:active {
COLOR: #0066ff; TEXT-DECORATION: underline
}
</STYLE>
<link rel="stylesheet" href="brmargin.css" /></head>

<body bgcolor="#ffffff">
<table width="743" border="0" cellspacing="0" cellpadding="0">
  <tr>
    <td><IMG height="35" src="/images/dvdtop.gif" width="763"
    /></td>
    <td><IMG height="35" src="images/dvdtop2.gif" width="18"
    /></td>
  </tr>
  <tr>
    <td height="394">
    <table width="100%" border="0" cellspacing="0" cellpadding="0">
      <tr>
        <td width="1%"
    background="/images/dvdside.gif"> </td>
        <td width="99%" valign="top" align="middle">
          <table width="100%" border="0" cellspacing="0"
    cellpadding="0">
          <tr>
            <td width="33%"><IMG height="77"
    src="/images/dvdlogo.gif" width="268" /></td>
            <td width="67%" align="right"><a
    href="http://click.linksynergy.com/fs-
    bin/stat?id=bbbU2zsALQU&amp;offerid=7845&amp;subid=0"
            ><IMG alt="DVD EXPRESS" border="0" width="468"
    height="60" src="http://ad.linksynergy.com/fs-
    bin/show?id=bbbU2zsALQU&amp;bids=7845&amp;gridnum=1&am
    p;catid=-1&amp;subid=0" />
            </a></td>
          </tr>
          </table>
```

```
            <table width="100%" border="0" cellspacing="0"
        cellpadding="0">
             <tr>
              <td width="39%" height="323" valign="top">
                <table width="300" border="0" cellpadding="2">
                 <tr>
                 <td width="291"><a href="news.asp"><IMG border="0"
        height="23" src="/images/news.gif" width="105" /></a></td>
                  </tr>
                  <tr valign="top">
                   <td height="96" width="291">
                     <table width="300" border="0">
                       <xsl:for-each select="index-
        data/news/articles[@align='left']/article">
<TR>
  <TD height="25" vAlign="top" width="21"><FONT
   color="#486c98" face="Arial, Helvetica, sans-serif"
   size="-1"><B><IMG height="10" src="/images/discs.gif"
   width="16" /></B></FONT></TD>
  <TD height="25" vAlign="top" width="262"><FONT
   color="#486c98" face="Arial, Helvetica, sans-serif"
   size="-2"><B><FONT size="-1"><a href="news.asp">
<xsl:value-of select="title" />
   <BR />
   Offers Region-Free Support</a> </FONT><FONT color="#9999ff"
   face="Arial, Helvetica, sans-serif"
   size="-2"><xsl:value-of select="@date" /></FONT><FONT
   size="-1"><BR />
   </FONT><FONT size="-2"><xsl:value-of select="summary" />
   </FONT></B></FONT></TD>
</TR>
                       </xsl:for-each>
                       <tr>
                        <td width="21" valign="top"> </td>
                        <td width="262" valign="bottom"><font face="Arial,
        Helvetica, sans-serif" size="-2" color="#486c98"><b><a
        href="news.asp">&gt;&gt;more&gt;&gt;</a></b></font></td>
                       </tr>
                     </table>
                   </td>
                 </tr>
                </table>
              </td>
              <td width="7%" height="323" valign="center"
        align="middle"><IMG height="200" src="images/divider.gif"
        width="6" /></td>
```

```
          <td width="33%" height="323" valign="top">
            <table width="250" border="0" cellpadding="2">
              <tr>
                <td height="20" width="262"><a
href="reviews.asp"><IMG border="0" height="23"
src="/images/latest.gif" width="166" /></a></td>
              </tr>
              <tr valign="top">
                <td height="96" width="262">
                  <table width="250" border="0">
                    <tr>
                      <td width="254" valign="top">
                  <xsl:for-each select="index-data/review-index/review-
link">
<font face="Arial, Helvetica, sans-serif" size="-2" color="#486c98">
<b>
<img src="/images/discs.gif" width="16" height="10" />
<font size="-1">
<a>
<xsl:attribute name="href">reviews/<xsl:value-of select="link"
    />.asp</xsl:attribute>
<xsl:value-of select="title" /></a>
</font>
</b>
</font>
<BR />
</xsl:for-each>
</td>
                    </tr>
                  </table>
                </td>
              </tr>
              <tr valign="top">
                <td height="19" width="262"><a
href="release_dates.asp"><IMG border="0" height="23"
src="/images/release.gif" width="154" /></a>
                </td>
              </tr>
              <tr valign="top">
                <td height="2" width="262"><a href="/forums"><IMG
border="0" height="23" src="/images/forums.gif" width="88"
/></a>
                </td>
              </tr>
            </table>
          </td>
```

```
            <td width="21%" height="323" valign="top">
              <table width="100%" border="0" cellspacing="0"
cellpadding="0">
                <tr>
                <td height="8"><IMG height="10" src="/images/box1.gif"
width="162" /></td>
                </tr>
                <tr bgcolor="#f0f0f0" valign="top">
                 <td height="250">
                   <table width="93%" border="0" cellpadding="5"
align="center">
                    <tr align="middle">
                    <td> <font face="Arial, Helvetica, sans-serif" size="-
1" color="#486c98"><b>Pre-order
                       Deals</b></font></td>
                    </tr>
                    <tr align="left" valign="top">
                     <td height="165">
                     <xsl:for-each select="index-data/prices/price">
<font face="Arial, Helvetica, sans-serif" size="-2">
<xsl:value-of select="@title" />:<BR />
<font color="#486c98">
<xsl:for-each select="vendor">
<a target="_blank">
<xsl:attribute name="href"><xsl:value-of select="link"
   /></xsl:attribute>
<xsl:value-of select="@name" /></a>................$<xsl:value-of
   select="cost" />
<BR />
</xsl:for-each>
 </font>
</font><BR />
</xsl:for-each>

                 </td>
                  </tr>
                 </table>
                </td>
              </tr>
              <tr>
              <td height="7"><IMG height="11" src="/images/box2.gif"
width="162" /></td>
               </tr>
              </table>
            </td>
          </tr>
```

```
        </table>
        <table width="100%" border="0" cellspacing="0"
    cellpadding="0">
            <tr align="center">
              <td height="20">
              <font face="Arial, Helvetica, sans-serif" size="-1"
    color="#507098"><a href="/index.asp">main</a></font><font
    face="Arial, Helvetica, sans-serif" size="-1" color="#C8D4E8">
|</font> <font face="Arial, Helvetica, sans-serif" size="-1"
    color="#507098"><a href="/news.asp">news</a></font><font
    face="Arial, Helvetica, sans-serif" size="-1" color="#C8D4E8">
|</font> <font face="Arial, Helvetica, sans-serif" size="-1"
    color="#507098"><a href="/contact.asp">
</a></font><font face="Arial, Helvetica, sans-serif" size="-1"
    color="#507098"><a href="/reviews.asp">
reviews</a></font><font face="Arial, Helvetica, sans-serif" size="-1"
    color="#C8D4E8">
| </font><font face="Arial, Helvetica, sans-serif" size="-1"
    color="#507098"><a href="/release_dates.asp">release
dates</a></font><font face="Arial, Helvetica, sans-serif" size="-1"
    color="#C8D4E8">
|</font> <font face="Arial, Helvetica, sans-serif" size="-1"
    color="#507098"><a href="/forums">forums</a></font><font
    face="Arial, Helvetica, sans-serif" size="-1" color="#C8D4E8">
| </font><font face="Arial, Helvetica, sans-serif" size="-1"
    color="#507098"><a href="/contact.asp">contact
information</a></font>
              </td>
            </tr>
          </table>
        </td>
      </tr>
    </table>
  </td>
  <td height="394"
    background="/images/dvdside2.gif"> </td>
 </tr>
 <tr>
  <td height="2"><IMG height="37" src="/images/dvdbottom.gif"
    width="763" /></td>
  <td height="2"><IMG height="37" src="images/dvdbottom2.gif"
    width="18" /></td>
 </tr>
</table>
</body>
</html>
```

```
  </xsl:template>

  <xsl:template match="review-link">

  </xsl:template>

  <xsl:template match="article">
<tr>
  <td width="3%" valign="top"><font face="Arial, Helvetica, sans-
    serif" size="-1" color="#486C98"><b><img
    src="/images/discs.gif" width="16" height="10"
    /></b></font></td>
  <td width="97%" valign="top"><font face="Arial, Helvetica, sans-
    serif" size="-2" color="#486C98"><b><font size="-1"><a
    href="news.xml">
<xsl:value-of select="title" />
</a></font><font face="Arial, Helvetica, sans-serif" size="-2"
    color="#9999FF"><xsl:value-of select="@date" /></font><font
    size="-1"><br />
    </font>
<font size="-2">
<xsl:value-of select="summary" />
</font>
</b></font></td>
</tr>
  </xsl:template>

  <xsl:template match="link">
<a>
  <xsl:attribute name="href"><xsl:value-of select="@href"
    /></xsl:attribute>
<xsl:value-of />
</a>
  </xsl:template>

</xsl:stylesheet>
```

The output of this XSL stylesheet when combined with the XML file gives
us the front page that you saw in the screenshot earlier in this chapter.

The News information can be accessed separately from the front page. As
such, news.xml has its own XSL file to handle its transformation. This is

the XSL for news.xml:

```
<?xml version="1.0"?>
<xsl:stylesheet xmlns:xsl="http://www.w3.org/TR/WD-xsl">
  <xsl:template match="/">
    <html>
<head>
<title>dvdmdb.com - Review Index</title>
<META NAME="keywords" CONTENT="dvd, forums, news, release,
    player, home, theater, software, dvd-rom, guide, database,
    anamorphic, 16:9, discussion, info, information, buyer" />
<META NAME="description" CONTENT="dvdmdb.com is your source for
    all things DVD" />
<meta http-equiv="Content-Type" content="text/html; charset=iso-
    8859-1" />
<STYLE type="text/css">BODY {
FONT-FAMILY: arial,helvetica; MARGIN-LEFT: 0px; MARGIN-TOP: 0px
}
P {
FONT-FAMILY: arial,helvetica; FONT-SIZE: 8pt
}
DIV {
FONT-FAMILY: arial,helvetica; FONT-SIZE: 8pt
}
TD {
FONT-FAMILY: arial,helvetica
}
A {
COLOR: #486C98; TEXT-DECORATION: none
}
A:hover {
COLOR: #0066ff; TEXT-DECORATION: underline
}
A:active {
COLOR: #0066ff; TEXT-DECORATION: underline
}
</STYLE>
<link rel="stylesheet" href="file:///C%7C/dvdmdb/brmargin.css"
    /></head>

<body bgcolor="#FFFFFF">
<table width="744" border="0" cellspacing="0" cellpadding="0">
  <tr>
    <td height="33" width="767"><img src="images/dvdtop.gif"
    width="763" height="35" /></td>
    <td height="33" width="27"><img src="images/dvdtop2.gif"
```

```
                                     width="18" height="35" /></td>
</tr>
<tr>
 <td height="420" width="767">
  <table width="100%" border="0" cellspacing="0" cellpadding="0">
    <tr>
      <td width="1%"
background="/images/dvdside.gif"> </td>
      <td width="99%" valign="top" align="center">
        <table width="100%" border="0" cellspacing="0"
cellpadding="0">
          <tr>
            <td width="33%"><img src="images/dvdlogo.gif"
width="268" height="77" /></td>
            <td width="67%" align="right"> </td>
          </tr>
        </table>
        <table width="100%" border="0" cellspacing="0"
cellpadding="0">
          <tr>
            <td width="8%" height="323" valign="top">  </td>
            <td width="85%" height="323" valign="top">
             <table width="100%" border="0" cellpadding="5">
              <tr>
               <td><font face="Arial, Helvetica, sans-serif" size="-1"
color="#C8D4E8"><font color="#507098"><a
href="index.asp">main</a>
               </font>|<font color="#507098"><a href="reviews.asp">
reviews
                </a></font><font color="#507098"> </font>|<font
face="Arial, Helvetica, sans-serif" size="-1" color="#507098"><a
href="forums.asp">
                  forums</a></font></font></td>
              </tr>
              <tr valign="top">
               <td height="257">
                <table width="100%" border="0" cellspacing="0"
cellpadding="0">
                  <tr>
                    <td valign="top" width="49%">
                      <table width="100%" border="0">

                  <xsl:apply-templates
select="news/articles[@align='left']/article" />

                      </table>
```

```
                    </td>
                    <td valign="top" width="51%">
                      <table width="100%" border="0">
<xsl:apply-templates select="news/articles[@align='right']/article" />
                      </table>
                    </td>
                  </tr>
                </table>
                <p> </p>
              </td>
            </tr>
          </table>
        </td>
        <td width="7%" height="323" valign="top"> </td>
      </tr>
    </table>
    <table width="100%" border="0" cellspacing="0"
  cellpadding="0">
        <tr valign="middle" align="center">
        <td height="20"><font face="Arial, Helvetica, sans-serif"
  size="-1" color="#507098"><a
  href="index.asp">main</a></font><font face="Arial, Helvetica,
  sans-serif" size="-1" color="#C8D4E8">
|</font> <font face="Arial, Helvetica, sans-serif" size="-1"
  color="#507098"><a href="news.xml">news</a></font><font
  face="Arial, Helvetica, sans-serif" size="-1" color="#C8D4E8">
|</font> <font face="Arial, Helvetica, sans-serif" size="-1"
  color="#507098"><a href="contact.asp">
</a></font><font face="Arial, Helvetica, sans-serif" size="-1"
  color="#507098"><a href="reviews.asp">
reviews</a></font><font face="Arial, Helvetica, sans-serif" size="-1"
  color="#C8D4E8">
| </font><font face="Arial, Helvetica, sans-serif" size="-1"
  color="#507098"><a href="release_dates.asp">release
dates</a></font><font face="Arial, Helvetica, sans-serif" size="-1"
  color="#C8D4E8">
|</font> <font face="Arial, Helvetica, sans-serif" size="-1"
  color="#507098"><a href="/forums">forums</a></font><font
  face="Arial, Helvetica, sans-serif" size="-1" color="#C8D4E8">
| </font><font face="Arial, Helvetica, sans-serif" size="-1"
  color="#507098"><a href="contact.asp">contact
information</a></font></td>
        </tr>
      </table>
    </td>
  </tr>
```

```
      </table>
    </td>
    <td height="420" width="27"
    background="/images/dvdside2.gif"> </td>
  </tr>
  <tr>
    <td height="2" width="767"><img src="images/dvdbottom.gif"
    width="763" height="37" /></td>
    <td height="2" width="27"><img src="images/dvdbottom2.gif"
    width="18" height="37" /></td>
  </tr>
</table>
</body>
</html>
  </xsl:template>

  <xsl:template match="article">
<tr>
  <td width="3%" valign="top"><font face="Arial, Helvetica, sans-
    serif" size="-1" color="#486C98"><b><img
    src="/images/discs.gif" width="16" height="10"
    /></b></font></td>
  <td width="97%" valign="top"><font face="Arial, Helvetica, sans-
    serif" size="-2" color="#486C98"><b><font size="-1"><a
    href="news.xml">
<xsl:value-of select="title" />
</a></font><font face="Arial, Helvetica, sans-serif" size="-2"
    color="#9999FF"><xsl:value-of select="@date" /></font><font
    size="-1"><br />
    </font>
<font size="-2">
<xsl:value-of select="summary" />
</font>
</b></font></td>
</tr>
  </xsl:template>

</xsl:stylesheet>
```

Viewing the transformed document in our browser shows us the basic
DVDmdb.com page with only the news information.

Now that you know how the database works, how the XML works, and
how the XML is transformed to HTML, we're ready to move on to the next
parts of our application. In the next section I'll show you how we upload

stories and how we deliver stories. Although I can't divulge everything about the delivery mechanism, I will, however, bend a little and show you some code from the COM that builds news.xml.

Publishing the Stories

The publishing system is in two parts: the uploading mechanism, written in ASP, and the downloading system, written in COM.

Uploading

The uploading mechanism functions basically same for all three sections of the site (features, news, and reviews, with prices falling under features). For this discussion, I'll cover the news part. Later, I will show you how the news page is built in the COM component.

The uploading mechanism takes the form of three pages. The first page is an index page listing all of the current news items by title (headline). You can see this page in Figure 8-7. The second page, shown in Figure 8-8, is the editing page. The editing page also acts as our "add a new article" page, since it is can provide a blank form for our new articles. The third page is news_process.asp, which handles the actual uploading

There is a fourth page, common_dbtools.asp, that is shared among all the pages on the site. These three pages, along with common_dbtools.asp, work in unison and provide us with our core ability to manage the site. Let's look at the code for each.

Common_dbtools.asp

This consists of a few functions to handle our database functions.

```
<%
'global variables
sRemConn = application("Connection1_ConnectionString")
'utility functions
function OpenRecs(sSql,sConnStr)
```

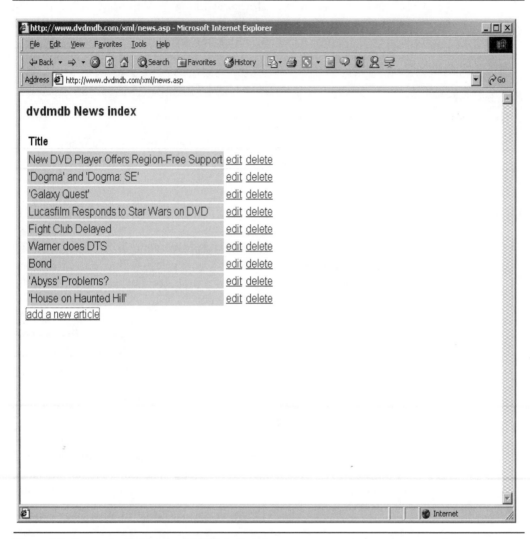

Figure 8-7: News.asp, the News publishing index page

```
set oConn = server.CreateObject("adodb.connection")
set oRec = server.CreateObject("adodb.recordset")
oConn.Open sConnStr
'find ids with this model number
set oRec = oConn.Execute (sSQL)
set OpenRecs = oRec
end function
```

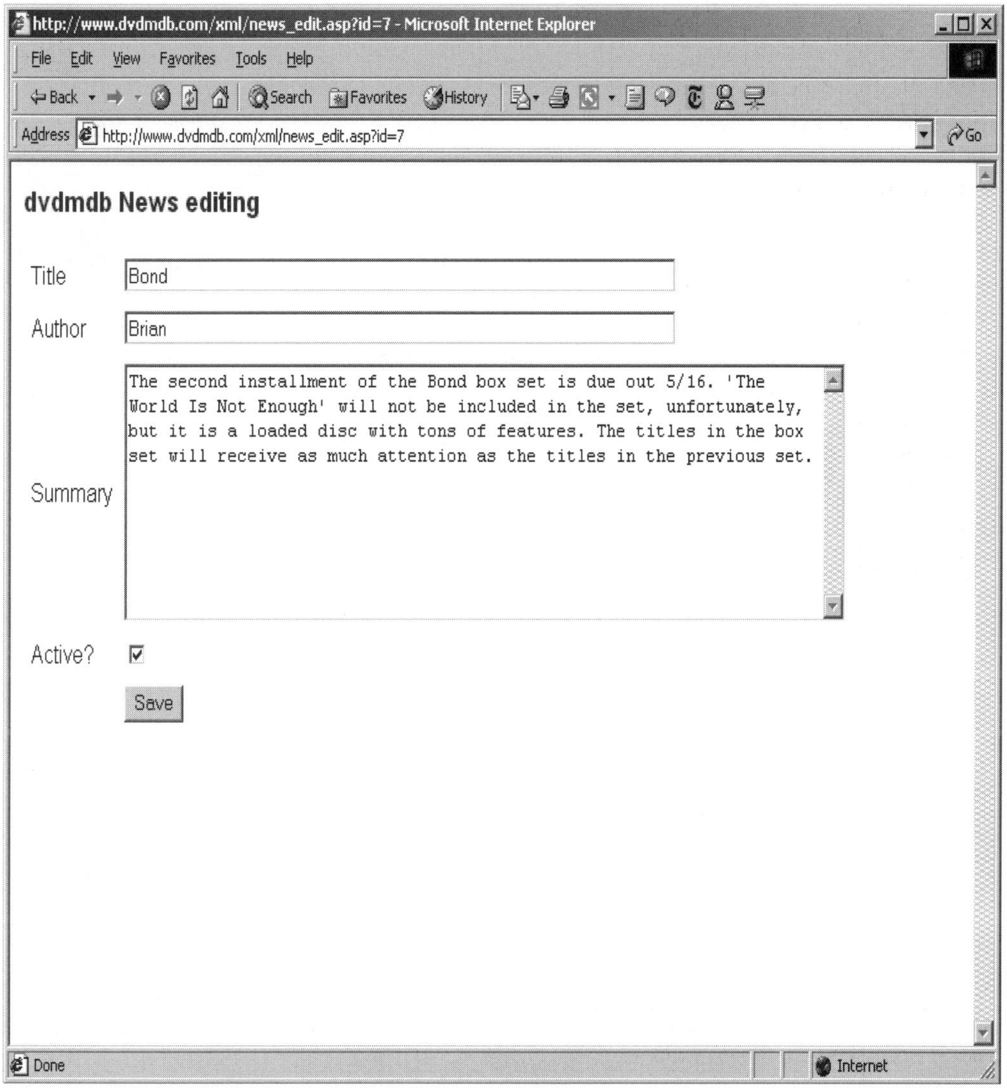

Figure 8-8: News_edit.asp, the News publishing editing page

```
function Exec(sSql,sConnStr)
set oConn = server.CreateObject("adodb.connection")
set oRec = server.CreateObject("adodb.recordset")
oConn.Open sConnstr
```

```
set oRec = oConn.Execute (sSql)
end function

function Sqlize(sSql)
Sqlize = replace(ssql,"'","''")
end function
%>
```

News.asp

Since News.asp is the index page, it is HTML with a SQL query thrown in:

```
<%@ Language=VBScript %>
<!-- #include file="common_dbtools.asp" -->
<HTML>
<HEAD>
<META NAME="GENERATOR" Content="Microsoft Visual Studio 6.0">
</HEAD>
<BODY style="font-family:arial">
<font size="4" color="midnightblue"><B>dvdmdb News
    index</B></font>
<SCRIPT language="javascript">
function delItem(id,title)
{
if (confirm('Are you sure you want to delete this item?'))
{
window.location.href = 'news_process.asp?id='+id+'&action=del';
}
}
</SCRIPT>
<BR />
<BR />
<table border=0 cellspacing=2 cellpadding=2>
<TR>
<TD><B>Title</B></TD><TD> </TD><TD> </TD>
</TR>
<%
sSql = "select * from news order by date desc"
set oRec = openrecs(sSql,sRemConn)
while not oRec.EOF
%>
<TR>
<TD bgcolor=dcdcdc><%= oRec("Title") %></TD>
<TD><a
    href="news_edit.asp?id=<%=oRec("news_id")%>">edit</a></T
    D>
```

```
<TD><a
   href="javascript:delItem(<%=oRec("news_id")%>)">delete</a>
   </TD>
</TR>

<%
oRec.Movenext
wend
%>
</table>
<TR>
<TD colspan="3"><a href="news_edit.asp">add a new
   article</a></TD>
</TR>
<P> </P>

</BODY>
</HTML>
```

You should notice that there is some JavaScript to handle the navigation, and a pretty basic SQL script to retrieve the titles and article ids of our news items.

News_edit.asp

As the page to handle both edits and updates, news_edit.asp has a pretty big responsibility. We kept news_edit.asp simple and it is a basic ASP page providing results from a query and the capability to POST to a form:

```
<!-- #include file="common_dbtools.asp" -->
<HTML>
<HEAD>
<META NAME="GENERATOR" Content="Microsoft Visual Studio 6.0">
</HEAD>
<BODY style="font-family:arial">
<font size="4" color="midnightblue"><B>dvdmdb News
   editing</B></font>
<form name="news_input" method="post"
   action="news_process.asp">
<%
'initialize variables
news_id = Request.QueryString("id")
News_Title = ""
News_Author = ""'can use a cookie with login name here
News_Summary = ""
```

```
News_Active = False

'if this is an edit, then pass along the ID and set
'the variables from the database
if news_id <> "" then
sSql = "select * from news where news_id=" &
    Request.QueryString("id")
set oRec = openrecs(sSql,sRemConn)
News_Title = oRec("Title")
News_Author = oRec("Author")
News_Summary = oRec("Summary")
if cbool(oRec("Active")) = True then
news_active = "checked"
end if
%>
<input type="hidden" name="id" value="<% =news_id %>">
<%
end if
%>
<table border=0 cellspacing=2 cellpadding=4>
<TR>
<TD>Title</TD><TD><INPUT name=news_title value="<%=
    news_title %>" size=70></TD>
</TR>
<TR>
<TD>Author</TD><TD><INPUT name=news_author value="<%=
    news_author %>" size=70></TD>
</TR>
<TR>
<TD>Summary</TD><TD><TEXTAREA name=news_summary
    rows=10 cols=70><%= news_summary %></TEXTAREA></TD>
</TR>
<TR>
<TD>Active?</TD><TD><INPUT type=checkbox name=news_active
    <% = news_active %>></TD>
</TR>
<TR>
<TD> </TD><TD><INPUT type=Submit value="Save"></TD>
</TR>
</table>
</BODY>
</HTML>
```

Notice that we are looking for an id in the querystring, and if one is provided, the editing capability is active. Otherwise, a blank form pops up and we are expected to input a new item.

News_process.asp

This is the meat and potatoes file for the system. This page handles updates, inserts, and deletes, based on what's passed in the querystring:

```
<%@ Language=VBScript %>
<!-- #include file="common_dbtools.asp" -->
<%
'determine what kind of action we are performing
if Request.QueryString("action") = "del" then
action="del"
else
if Request.Form("id") <> "" then
action="edit"
else
action="add"
end if
'set variables for database
News_Title = sqlize(Request.Form("news_title"))
News_Author = sqlize(Request.Form("news_author"))
News_Summary = sqlize(Request.Form("news_summary"))
if Request.Form("news_active") = "on" then
news_active = True
else
news_active = False
end if
end if


select case action
case "del":
sSql = "delete from news where news_id = " &
    Request.QueryString("id")
case "edit":
sSql = "update news set author= '" & news_author  & _
"', title = '" & News_Title & _
"', summary = '" & News_Summary & _
"', active = " & News_active & " where news_id = " & Request.Form("id")
case "add":
sSql = "insert into news (author,title,summary,active) values ('" & _
news_author & "','" & news_title & "','" & news_summary & "'," & _
```

```
news_active & ")"

end select
'put it in the database and return to the index page
Response.Write ssql
'Response.End
Exec sSql, sRemConn

Response.Redirect "news.asp"
%>
```

By looking at these ASP files you should realize that developing a Web site that utilizes XML does not require XML to exist in every single ASP page. The entire publishing system doesn't use one speck of XML code; that's all handled in the COM during the download process.

But wait, you say, what's the point of using XML if you don't create it at the time of uploading? Keep in mind that XML can exist as a data format, as a data delivery mechanism, and as a different markup language. In our case, we don't need to upload the data as XML.

In the future, when we go to SQL Server 2000, our model will benefit us because SQL Server 2000 will handle all of the XML conversion of our data for us.

Delivering

Don't tell my DVDmdb.com partners, but I'm going to go ahead and share a little bit of the COM code with you. This is code from the class module and it builds the news.xml page:

```
Public Function makeNews()

    Dim rs As New ADODB.Recordset
    Dim conn As New ADODB.Connection
    conn.Open "Provider=Microsoft.Jet.OLEDB.4.0;User ID=Admin;Data
      Source=D:\xml\dvdmdb.mdb;Mode=Share Deny None;Extended
      Properties="""";Jet OLEDB:System database="""";Jet
      OLEDB:Registry Path="""";Jet OLEDB:Database Password="""";Jet
      OLEDB:Engine Type=5;Jet OLEDB:Database Locking Mode=1;Jet
      OLEDB:Global Partial Bulk Ops=2;Jet OLEDB:Global Bulk
```

```
      Transactions=1;Jet OLEDB:New Database Password="""";Jet
      OLEDB:Create System Database=False;Jet OLEDB:Encrypt
      Database=False;Jet OLEDB:Don't Copy Locale on
      Compact=False;Jet OLEDB:Compact Without Replica
      Repair=False;Jet OLEDB:SFP=False;User
      Id=Admin;PASSWORD=;"
   sXML = ""
   rs.Open "select * from news", conn

   sXML = sXML & "<news>"
      sXML = sXML & "<articles>"
   While Not rs.EOF
      Date = rs("date")
      auth = rs("author")
      Title = rs("title")
      Summary = rs("summary")
      sXML = sXML & "<article date=""" & Date & """ auth = """ & auth
   & """>"
      sXML = sXML & "<title>" & Title & "</title>"
      sXML = sXML & "<summary>" & Summary
      sXML = sXML & "</summary>"

      sXML = sXML & "</article>"
      rs.MoveNext

   Wend
   sXML = sXML & "</articles>"
   sXML = sXML & "</news>"
   makeNews = sXML
End Function
```

I hope that helps you get on your way.

As a final note, all of the functional code in this book is included on the CD-ROM. Enjoy.

Summary

In this chapter, I went over the whole process, from conception to production, to develop an XML-based Web site, called DVDmdb.com. I hope you gained the knowledge you need to go out and build your own XML-based Web site.

The next two sections of the book are appendices. Appendix A covers the XML 1.0 specification, and Appendix B covers the RDF specification.

A

XML 1.0 Specification

This version:
http://www.w3.org/TR/PR-xml-971208

Previous versions:
http://www.w3.org/TR/WD-xml-961114
http://www.w3.org/TR/WD-xml-lang-970331
http://www.w3.org/TR/WD-xml-lang-970630
http://www.w3.org/TR/WD-xml-970807
http://www.w3.org/TR/WD-xml-971117

Editors:
Tim Bray (Textuality and Netscape) <tbray@textuality.com>
Jean Paoli (Microsoft) <jeanpa@microsoft.com>
C. M. Sperberg-McQueen (University of Illinois at Chicago) <cmsm-cq@uic.edu>

Status of this Document

This document is currently undergoing review by the members of the World Wide Web Consortium. It is a stable document derived from a series of working drafts produced over the last year as deliverables of the XML activity. It specifies a language created by subsetting an existing, widely used international text processing standard (Standard Generalized Markup Language, ISO 8879:1986 as amended and corrected) for use on the World Wide Web. Details of the decisions regarding which features of ISO 8879 to retain in the subset are available separately. XML is already supported by some commercial products, and there are a growing number of free implementations. Public discussions of XML are accessible online.

This specification uses the term URI, which is defined by [Berners-Lee], a work in progress expected to update [RFC1738] and [RFC1808]. Should the work not be accepted as an RFC, the references to uniform resource identifiers (URIs) in this specification will become references to uniform resource locators (URLs).

The review period for this Proposed Recommendation will end on January 5, 1998. Within 14 days from that time, the document's disposition will be announced: it may become a W3C Recommendation (possibly with minor changes), or it may revert to Working Draft status, or it may be dropped as a W3C work item. This document does not at this time imply any endorsement by the Consortium's staff or member organizations.

Abstract

The Extensible Markup Language (XML) is a simple dialect of SGML which is completely described in this document. The goal is to enable generic SGML to be served, received, and processed on the Web in the way that is now possible with HTML. XML has been designed for ease of implementation and for interoperability with both SGML and HTML.

Extensible Markup Language (XML)

Version 1.0

Table of Contents

1. Introduction
1.1 Origin and Goals
1.2 Terminology
2. Documents
2.1 Well-Formed XML Documents
2.2 Characters
2.3 Common Syntactic Constructs
2.4 Character Data and Markup
2.5 Comments
2.6 Processing Instructions
2.7 CDATA Sections
2.8 Prolog and Document Declaration
2.9 Standalone Document Declaration
2.10 White Space Handling
2.11 End-of-Line Handling
2.12 Language Identification
3. Logical Structures
3.1 Start-Tags, End-Tags, and Empty-Element Tags
3.2 Element Type Declarations
3.2.1 Element Content
3.2.2 Mixed Content
3.3 Attribute-List Declarations
3.3.1 Attribute Types
3.3.2 Attribute Defaults
3.3.3 Attribute-Value Normalization
3.4 Conditional Sections
4. Physical Structures
4.1 Character and Entity References
4.2 Entity Declarations
4.2.1 Internal Entities

4.2.2 External Entities
4.3 Parsed Entities
4.3.1 The Text Declaration
4.3.2 Well-Formed Parsed Entities
4.3.3 Character Encoding in Entities
4.4 XML Processor Treatment of Entities and References
4.4.1 Not Recognized
4.4.2 Included
4.4.3 Included If Validating
4.4.4 Forbidden
4.4.5 Notify
4.4.6 Bypassed
4.4.7 Included as PE
4.5 Construction of Internal Entity Replacement Text
4.6 Predefined Entities
4.7 Notation Declarations
4.8 Document Entity
5. Conformance
6. Notation

Appendices

A. References
A.1 Normative References
A.2 Other References
B. Character Classes
C. XML and SGML (Non-Normative)
D. Expansion of Entity and Character References (Non-Normative)
E. Deterministic Content Models (Non-Normative)
F. Autodetection of Character Encodings (Non-Normative)
G. W3C XML Working Group (Non-Normative)

1. Introduction

Extensible Markup Language, abbreviated XML, describes a class of data objects called XML documents and partially describes the behavior of computer programs which process them. XML is an application profile or restricted form of SGML, the Standard Generalized Markup Language [ISO8879]. By construction, XML documents are conforming SGML documents.

XML documents are made up of storage units called entities, which contain either parsed or unparsed data. Parsed data is made up of characters, some of which form the character data in the document, and some of which form markup. Markup encodes a description of the document's storage layout and logical structure. XML provides a mechanism to impose constraints on the storage layout and logical structure.

A software module called an **XML processor** is used to read XML documents and provide access to their content and structure. It is assumed that an XML processor is doing its work on behalf of another module, called the **application.** This specification describes the required behavior of an XML processor in terms of how it must read XML data and the information it must provide to the application.

1.1 Origin and Goals

XML was developed by an XML Working Group (originally known as the SGML Editorial Review Board) formed under the auspices of the World Wide Web Consortium (W3C) in 1996. It was chaired by Jon Bosak of Sun Microsystems with the active participation of an XML Special Interest Group (previously known as the SGML Working Group) also organized by the W3C. The membership of the XML Working Group is given in an appendix. Dan Connolly served as the WG's contact with the W3C.

The design goals for XML are:

1. XML shall be straightforwardly usable over the Internet.
2. XML shall support a wide variety of applications.
3. XML shall be compatible with SGML.
4. It shall be easy to write programs which process XML documents.
5. The number of optional features in XML is to be kept to the absolute minimum, ideally zero.
6. XML documents should be human-legible and reasonably clear.
7. The XML design should be prepared quickly.

8. The design of XML shall be formal and concise.

9. XML documents shall be easy to create.

10. Terseness in XML markup is of minimal importance.

This specification, together with associated standards (Unicode and ISO/IEC 10646 for characters, Internet RFC 1766 for language identification tags, ISO 639 for language name codes, and ISO 3166 for country name codes), provides all the information necessary to understand XML Version 1.0 and construct computer programs to process it.

This version of the XML specification is for public review and discussion. It may be distributed freely, as long as all text and legal notices remain intact.

1.2 Terminology

The terminology used to describe XML documents is defined in the body of this specification. The terms defined in the following list are used in building those definitions and in describing the actions of an XML processor:

may	Conforming documents and XML processors are permitted to but need not behave as described.
must	Conforming documents and XML processors are required to behave as described; otherwise they are in error.
error	A violation of the rules of this specification; results are undefined. Conforming software may detect and report an error and may recover from it.

fatal error	An error which a conforming XML processor must detect and report to the application. After encountering a fatal error, the processor may continue processing the data to search for further errors and may report such errors to the application. In order to support correction of errors, the processor may make unprocessed data from the document (with intermingled character data and markup) available to the application. Once a fatal error is detected, however, the processor must not continue normal processing (i.e., it must not continue to pass character data and information about the document's logical structure to the application in the normal way).
at user option	Conforming software may or must (depending on the modal verb in the sentence) behave as described; if it does, it must provide users a means to enable or disable the behavior described.
validity constraint	A rule which applies to all valid XML documents. Violations of validity constraints are errors; they must, at user option, be reported by validating XML processors.
well-formedness constraint	A rule which applies to all well-formed XML documents. Violations of well-formedness constraints are fatal errors.

match	(Of strings or names:) Two strings or names being compared must be identical. Characters with multiple possible representations in ISO/IEC 10646 (e.g. characters with both precomposed and base+diacritic forms) match only if they have the same representation in both strings. At user option, processors may normalize such characters to some canonical form. No case folding is performed. (Of strings and rules in the grammar:) A string matches a grammatical production if it belongs to the language generated by that production. (Of content and content models:) An element matches its declaration when it conforms in the fashion described in the Element Valid constraint.
for compatibility	A feature of XML included solely to ensure that XML remains compatible with SGML.
for interoperability	A non-binding recommendation included to increase the chances that XML documents can be processed by the existing installed base of SGML processors which predate the WebSGML Adaptations Annex to ISO 8879.

2. Documents

A data object is an **XML document** if it is well-formed, as defined in this specification. A well-formed XML document may in addition be valid if it meets certain further constraints.

Each XML document has both a logical and a physical structure. Physically, the document is composed of units called entities. An entity may refer to other entities to cause their inclusion in the document. A document begins in a "root" or document entity. Logically, the document is composed of declarations, elements, comments, character references, and processing instructions, all of which are indicated in the document by explicit markup. The logical and physical structures must nest properly, as described below.

2.1 Well-Formed XML Documents

A textual object is a well-formed XML document if:

1. Taken as a whole, it matches the production labeled `document`.
2. It meets all the well-formedness constraints given in this specification.
3. Each of its parsed entities is well-formed.

Document

---

[1] `document ::= prolog element Misc*`

Matching the `document` production implies that:

1. It contains one or more elements.
2. There is exactly one element, called the **root**, or document element, no part of which appears in the content of any other element. For all other elements, if the start-tag is in the content of another element, the end-tag is in the content of the same element. More simply stated, the elements, delimited by start- and end-tags, nest properly within each other.

As a consequence of this, for each non-root element `C` in the document, there is one other element `P` in the document such that `C` is in the content of `P`, but is not in the content of any other element that is in the content of `P`. `P` is referred to as the **parent** of `C`, and `C` as a **child** of `P`.

2.2 Characters

A parsed entity contains **text,** a sequence of characters, which may represent markup or character data. A **character** is an atomic unit of text as specified by ISO/IEC 10646 [ISO10646]. Legal characters are tab, carriage return, line feed, and the legal graphic characters of Unicode and ISO/IEC 10646.

The mechanism for encoding character values into bit patterns may vary from entity to entity. All XML processors must accept the UTF-8 and

---

Character Range

---

[2] Char ::= #x9 | #xA | #xD | [#x20-#D7FF] | [#xE000-
#xFFFD] | [#x10000-#x10FFFF]

/* any Unicode character, excluding the surrogate
blocks, FFFE, and FFFF. */

UTF-16 encodings of 10646; the mechanisms for signaling which of the two are in use, or for bringing other encodings into play, are discussed later, in the discussion of character encodings.

Regardless of the specific encoding used, any character in the ISO/IEC 10646 character set may be referred to by the decimal or hexadecimal equivalent of its UCS-4 code value.

2.3 Common Syntactic Constructs

This section defines some symbols used widely in the grammar.

S (white space) consists of one or more space (#x20) characters, carriage returns, line feeds, or tabs.

White Space

---

[3] S ::= (#x20 | #x9 | #xD | #xA)+

Characters are classified for convenience as letters, digits, or other characters. Letters consist of an alphabetic or syllabic base character possibly followed by one or more combining characters, or of an ideographic character. Full definitions of the specific characters in each class are given in the appendix on character classes.

A **Name** is a token beginning with a letter or one of a few punctuation characters, and continuing with letters, digits, hyphens, underscores, colons, or full stops, together known as name characters. Names beginning with the string "xml", or any string which would match (('X'|'x') ('M'|'m') ('L'|'l')), are reserved for standardization in this or future versions of this specification.

Note: The colon character within XML names is reserved for experimentation with name spaces. Its meaning is expected to be standardized at some future point, at which point those documents using the colon for experimental purposes may need to be updated. (There is no guarantee that any name-space mechanism adopted for XML will in fact use the colon as a name-space delimiter.) In practice, this means that authors should not use the colon in XML names except as part of name-space experiments, but that XML processors should accept the colon as a name character.

An Nmtoken (name token) is any mixture of name characters.

Names and Tokens

---

[4] NameChar ::= Letter | Digit | '.' | '-' | '_' | ':' | CombiningChar | Extender
[5] Name ::= (Letter | '_' | ':') (NameChar)*
[6] Names ::= Name (S Name)*

[7] Nmtoken ::= (NameChar)+
[8] Nmtokens ::= Nmtoken (S Nmtoken)*

Literal data is any quoted string not containing the quotation mark used as a delimiter for that string. Literals are used for specifying the content of internal entities (EntityValue), the values of attributes (AttValue), and external identifiers (SystemLiteral). For some purposes, the entire literal can be skipped without scanning for markup within it (SkipLit):

Literals

---

[9] EntityValue ::= '"' ([^%&"] | PEReference | Refer-
ence)* '"' | "'" ([^%&'] | PEReference | Reference)*
"'"

[10] AttValue ::= '"' ([^<&"] | Reference)* '"'

| "'" ([^<&'] | Reference)* "'"

[11] SystemLiteral ::= SkipLit

[12] PubidLiteral ::= '"' PubidChar* '"' | "'" (Pubid-
Char - "'")* "'"

[13] PubidChar ::= #x20 | #xD | #xA | [a-zA-Z0-9] | [-'()+,./:=?]

[14] SkipLit ::= ('"' [^"]* '"') | ("'" [^']* "'")

2.4 Character Data and Markup

Text consists of intermingled character data and markup. **Markup** takes the form of start-tags, end-tags, empty elements, entity references, character references, comments, CDATA section delimiters, document type declarations, and processing instructions.

All text that is not markup constitutes the **character data** of the document.

The ampersand character (&) and the left angle bracket (<) may appear in their literal form *only* when used as markup delimiters, or within a comment, a processing instruction, or a CDATA section. They are also legal within the literal entity value of an in internal entity declaration; see the section on well-formed entities. If they are needed elsewhere, they must be escaped using either numeric character references or the strings "&" and "<" respectively. The right angle bracket (>) may be represented using the string ">", and must, for compatibility, be escaped using ">" or a character reference when it appears in the string "]]>" in content, when that string is not marking the end of a CDATA section.

In the content of elements, character data is any string of characters which does not contain the start-delimiter of any markup. In a CDATA section, character data is any string of characters not including the CDATA-section-close delimiter, "]]>".

To allow attribute values to contain both single and double quotes, the apostrophe or single-quote character (') may be represented as "'", and the double-quote character (") as """.

Character Data

[15] CharData ::= [^<&] * - ([^<&] * ']]>' [^<&] *)

2.5 Comments

Comments may appear anywhere in a document outside other markup; in addition, they may appear within the document type declaration at places allowed by the grammar. They are not part of the document's character data; an XML processor may, but need not, make it possible for an application to retrieve the text of comments. For compatibility, the string "--" (double-hyphen) must not occur within comments.

Comments

[16] Comment ::= '<!--' ((Char - '-') | ('-' (Char - '-')))* '-->'

An example of a comment:

<!-- declarations for <head> & <body> -->

2.6 Processing Instructions

Processing instructions (PIs) allow documents to contain instructions for applications.

Processing Instructions

---

[17] PI ::= '<?' PITarget (S (Char* - (Char* '?>'
Char*)))? '?>'
[18] PITarget ::= Name - (('X' | 'x') ('M' | 'm') ('L'
| 'l'))

PIs are not part of the document's character data, but must be passed through to the application. The PI begins with a target (PITarget) used to identify the application to which the instruction is directed. The target names "XML", "xml", and so on are reserved for standardization in this or future versions of this specification. The XML Notation mechanism may be used for formal declaration of PI targets.

2.7 CDATA Sections

CDATA sections may occur anywhere character data may occur; they are used to escape blocks of text containing characters which would otherwise be recognized as markup. CDATA sections begin with the string "<![CDATA[" and end with the string "]]>":

CDATA Sections

---

[19] CDSect ::= CDStart CData CDEnd
[20] CDStart ::= '<![CDATA['
[21] CData ::= (Char* - (Char* ']]>' Char*))
[22] CDEnd ::= ']]>'

Within a CDATA section, only the CDEnd string is recognized as markup, so that left angle brackets and ampersands may occur in their literal form;

they need not (and cannot) be escaped using "`&lt;`" and "`&amp;`". CDA-TA sections cannot nest.

An example of a CDATA section, in which "`<greeting>`" and "`</greeting>`" are recognized as character data, not markup:

```
<![ CDATA[ <greeting>Hello, world!</greeting>]] >
```

2.8 Prolog and Document Type Declaration

XML documents may, and should, begin with an **XML declaration** which specifies the version of XML being used.

The version number "`1.0`" should be used to indicate conformance to this version of this specification; it is an error for a document to use the value "`1.0`" if it does not conform to this version of this specification. It is the intent of the XML working group to give later versions of this specification numbers other than "`1.0`", but this intent does not indicate a commitment to produce any future versions of XML, nor if any are produced, to use any particular numbering scheme. Since future versions are not ruled out, this construct is provided as a means to allow the possibility of automatic version recognition, should it become necessary. Processors may signal an error if they receive documents labeled with versions they do not support.

The function of the markup in an XML document is to describe its storage and logical structure and to associate attribute-value pairs with its logical structure. XML provides a mechanism, the document type declaration, to define constraints on the logical structure and to support the use of pre-defined storage units. An XML document is **valid** if it has an associated document type declaration and if the document complies with the constraints expressed in it.

The document type declaration must appear before the first element in the document.

Prolog

---

[23] prolog ::= XMLDecl? Misc* (doctypedecl Misc*)?
[24] XMLDecl ::= '<? xml' VersionInfo EncodingDecl?
SDDecl? S? '?>'

[25] VersionInfo ::= S 'version' Eq ('"VersionNum"' |
"'VersionNum'")

[26] Eq ::= S? '=' S?

[27] VersionNum ::= ([a-zA-Z0-9_.:] | '-')+

[28] Misc ::= Comment | PI | S

For example, the following is a complete XML document, well-formed but not valid:

<?xml version="1.0"?>
<greeting>Hello, world!</greeting>

---

and so is this:

<greeting>Hello, world!</greeting>

The XML **document type declaration** contains or points to markup declarations that provide a grammar for a class of documents. This grammar is known as a document type definition, or **DTD**. The document type declaration can point to an external subset (a special kind of external entity) containing markup declarations, or can contain the markup declarations directly in an internal subset, or can do both. The DTD for a document consists of both subsets taken together.

A **markup declaration** is an element type declaration, an attribute-list declaration, an entity declaration, or a notation declaration. These declarations may be contained in whole or in part within parameter entities, as described in the well-formedness and validity constraints below. For fuller information, see the section on physical structure.

Document Type Definition

---

[29] `doctypedecl ::= '<!DOCTYPE' S Name (S Exter-nalID)? S? ('[' (markupdecl | PEReference | S)* ']' S?)? '>'` [vc: Root Element Type]
[30] `markupdecl ::= elementdecl | AttlistDecl | Enti-tyDecl | NotationDecl | PI | Comment` [vc: Proper Declaration/PE Nesting] [wfc: PEs in Internal Sub-set]

Validity Constraint - Root Element Type	The `Name` in the document type declaration must match the element type of the root element.
Validity Constraint - Proper Declara-tion/PE Nesting	Parameter-entity replacement text must be prop-erly nested with markup declarations. That is to say, if either the first character or the last character of a markup declaration (`markupdecl` above) is contained in the replacement text for a parameter-entity reference, both must be contained in the same replacement text.
Well-Formedness Constraint - PEs in Internal Subset	In the internal DTD subset, parameter-entity refer-ences can occur only where markup declarations can occur, not within markup declarations. (This does not apply to references that occur in external parameter entities or to the external subset.)

Like the internal subset, the external subset and any external parameter en-tities referred to in the DTD must consist of a series of complete markup declarations of the types allowed by the non-terminal symbol `markup-`

decl, interspersed with white space or parameter-entity references. However, portions of the contents of the external subset or of external parameter entities may conditionally be ignored by using the conditional section construct; this is not allowed in the internal subset.

External Subset

```
[31] extSubset ::= ( markupdecl | conditionalSect |
PEReference | S )*
```

The external subset and external parameter entities also differ from the internal subset in that in them, parameter-entity references are recognized *within* markup declarations, not only *between* markup declarations.

An example of an XML document with a document type declaration:

```
<?xml version="1.0"?>
<!DOCTYPE greeting SYSTEM "hello.dtd">
<greeting>Hello, world!</greeting>
```

The system identifier "hello.dtd" gives the URI of a DTD for the document.

The declarations can also be given locally, as in this example:

```
<?xml version="1.0" encoding="UTF-8" ?>
<!DOCTYPE greeting [
<!ELEMENT greeting (#PCDATA)>
]>
<greeting>Hello, world!</greeting>
```

If both the external and internal subsets are used, the internal subset is considered to occur before the external subset. This has the effect that entity and attribute-list declarations in the internal subset take precedence over those in the external subset.

2.9 Standalone Document Declaration

Markup declarations can affect the content of the document, as passed from an XML processor to an application; examples are attribute defaults and entity declarations. The standalone document declaration, which may appear as a component of the XML declaration, signals that a document is not affected by the presence of such markup declarations (perhaps because there are none).

Standalone Document Declaration

```
[32] SDDecl ::= S 'standalone' Eq "'" ('yes' | 'no')
"'" | S 'standalone' Eq '"' ('yes' | 'no') '"' [ vc:
Standalone Document Declaration ]
```

In a standalone document declaration, the value "yes" indicates that there are no markup declarations external to the document entity (either in the DTD external subset, or in an external parameter entity referenced from the internal subset) which affect the information passed from the XML processor to the application. The value "no" indicates that there are or may be such external markup declarations. Note that the standalone document declaration only denotes the presence of external *declarations*; the presence, in a document, of references to external *entities*, when those entities are internally declared, does not change its standalone status.

If there are no external markup declarations, the standalone document declaration has no meaning. If there are are external markup declarations but there is no standalone document declaration, the value "no" is assumed.

Any XML document for which standalone="no" holds can be converted algorithmically to a standalone document, which may be desirable for some network delivery applications.

| **Validity Constraint - Standalone Document Declaration** | The standalone document declaration must have the value "`no`" if any external markup declarations contain declarations of

◆ attributes with default values, if elements to which these attributes apply appear in the document without specifications of values for these attributes, or

◆ entities (other than `amp`, `lt`, `gt`, `apos`, `quot`), if references to those entities appear in the document, or

◆ attributes with values subject to normalization, where the attribute appears in the document with a value which will change as a result of normalization, or

◆ element types with element content, if white space occurs directly within any instance of those types. |

An example XML declaration with a standalone document declaration:

```
<?xml version="1.0" standalone='yes'?>
```

2.10 White Space Handling

In editing XML documents, it is often convenient to use "white space" (spaces, tabs, and blank lines, denoted by the nonterminal S in this specification) to set apart the markup for greater readability. Such white space is typically not intended for inclusion in the delivered version of the document. On the other hand, "significant" white space that must be retained in the delivered version is common, for example in poetry and source code.

An XML processor must always pass all characters in a document that are not markup through to the application. A validating XML processor must distinguish white space in element content from other non-markup characters and signal to the application that white space in element content is not significant.

A special attribute named "`xml:space`" may be inserted in documents to signal an intention that the element to which this attribute applies requires all white space to be treated as significant by applications.

In valid documents, this attribute, like any other, must be declared if it is used. When declared, it must be given as an enumerated type whose only possible values are "`default`" and "`preserve`".

The value "`default`" signals that applications' default white-space processing modes are acceptable for this element; the value "`preserve`" indicates the intent that applications preserve all the white space. This declared intent is considered to apply to all elements within the content of the element where it is specified, unless overriden with another instance of the "`xml:space`" attribute.

The root element of any document is considered to have signaled no intentions as regards application space handling, unless it provides a value for this attribute or the attribute is declared with a default value.

For example:

```
<!ATTLIST poem xml:space (default|preserve) 'pre-
serve'>
```

2.11 End-of-Line Handling

XML parsed entities are often stored in computer files which, for editing convenience, are organized into lines. These lines are typically separated by some combination of the characters CR (#xD) and LF (#xA).

To simplify the tasks of applications, wherever an external parsed entity or the literal entity value of an internal parsed entity contains either the literal two-character sequence "#xD#xA" or a standalone literal #xD, an XML processor must pass to the application the single character #xA. (This behavior can conveniently be produced by normalizing all line breaks to #xA on input, before parsing.)

2.12 Language Identification

In document processing, it is often useful to identify the natural or formal language in which the content is written.

A special attribute named "xml:lang" may be inserted in documents to specify the language used in the contents and attribute values of any element in an XML document. The values of the attribute are language identifiers as defined by [RFC1766], "Tags for the Identification of Languages":

Language Identification

```
[33] LanguageID ::= Langcode ('-' Subcode)*

[34] Langcode ::= ISO639Code | IanaCode | UserCode

[35] ISO639Code ::= ([a-z] | [A-Z]) ([a-z] | [A-Z])

[36] IanaCode ::= ('i' | 'I') '-' ([a-z] | [A-Z])+
[37] UserCode ::= ('x' | 'X') '-' ([a-z] | [A-Z])+
[38] Subcode ::= ([a-z] | [A-Z])+
```

The Langcode may be any of the following:

- ♦ a two-letter language code as defined by [ISO639], "Codes for the representation of names of languages"
- ♦ a language identifier registered with the Internet Assigned Numbers Authority (IANA); these begin with the prefix "i-" (or "I-")

♦ a language identifier assigned by the user, or agreed on between parties in private use; these must begin with the prefix "x-" or "X-" in order to ensure that they do not conflict with names later standardized or registered with IANA

There may be any number of Subcode segments; if the first subcode segment exists and the Subcode consists of two letters, then it must be a country code from [ISO3166], "Codes for the representation of names of countries." If the first subcode consists of more than two letters, it must be a subcode for the language in question registered with IANA, unless the Langcode begins with the prefix "x-" or "X-".

It is customary to give the language code in lower case, and the country code (if any) in upper case. Note that these values, unlike other names in XML documents, are case insensitive.

For example:

```
<p xml:lang="en">The quick brown fox jumps over the
lazy dog.</p>
<p xml:lang="en-GB">What colour is it?</p>
<p xml:lang="en-US">What color is it?</p>
<sp who="Faust" desc='leise' xml:lang="de">
<l>Habe nun, ach! Philosophie,</l>
<l>Juristerei, und Medizin</l>
<l>und leider auch Theologie</l>
<l>durchaus studiert mit heißem Bemüh'n.</l>
</sp>
```

The intent declared with xml:lang is considered to apply to all elements within the content of the element where it is specified, unless overridden with another instance of xml:lang.

In valid documents, this attribute must be declared as described elsewhere in this specification; a typical declaration will take the form

---

xml:lang NMTOKEN #IMPLIED

---

but specific default values may also be given, if appropriate. In a collection of French poems for English students, with glosses and notes in English, the xml:lang attribute might be declared this way:

```
<!ATTLIST poem xml:lang NMTOKEN 'fr'>
<!ATTLIST gloss xml:lang NMTOKEN 'en'>
<!ATTLIST note xml:lang NMTOKEN 'en'>
```

---

3. Logical Structures

Each XML document contains one or more **elements**, the boundaries of which are either delimited by start-tags and end-tags, or, for empty elements, by an empty-element tag. Each element has a type, identified by name, sometimes called its "generic identifier" (GI), and may have a set of attribute specifications. Each attribute specification has a name and a value.

Element

```
[39] element ::= EmptyElemTag | STag content ETag[ wfc:
Element Type Match ]
```

This specification does not constrain the semantics, use, or (beyond syntax) names of the element types and attributes, except that names beginning with a match to (('X'|'x')('M'|'m')('L'|'l')) are reserved for standardization in this or future versions of this specification.

Well-Formedness Constraint - Element Type Match	The `Name` in an element's end-tag must match the element type in the start-tag.

3.1 Start-Tags, End-Tags, and Empty-Element Tags

The beginning of every non-empty XML element is marked by a **start-tag.**

Start-tag

```
[40] STag ::= '<' Name (S Attribute)* S? '>'[ wfc:
Unique Att Spec ]
[41] Attribute ::= Name Eq AttValue[ vc: Attribute
Value Type ] [ wfc: No External Entity References ] [
wfc: No < in Attribute Values ]
```

The `Name` in the start- and end-tags gives the element's **type.** The `Name-AttValue` pairs are referred to as the **attribute specifications** of the element, with the `Name` in each pair referred to as the **attribute name** and the content of the `AttValue` (the characters between the ' or " delimiters) as the **attribute value.**

Well-Formedness Constraint - Unique Att Spec	No attribute name may appear more than once in the same start-tag or empty-element tag.
Validity Constraint - Attribute Value Type	The attribute must have been declared; the value must be of the type declared for it. (For attribute types, see the discussion of attribute-list declarations.)
Well-Formedness Constraint - No External Entity References	Attribute values cannot contain direct or indirect entity references to external entities.

Well-Formedness Constraint - No < in Attribute Values	The replacement text of any entity referred to directly or indirectly in an attribute value (other than <) must not contain a <.

An example of a start-tag:

<termdef id="dt-dog" term="dog">

The end of every element that begins with a start-tag must be marked by an **end-tag** containing a name that echoes the element's type as given in the start-tag:

End-tag

[42] ETag ::= '</' Name S? '>'

An example of an end-tag:

</termdef>

The text between the start-tag and end-tag is called the element's **content:**

Content of Elements

[43] content ::= (element | CharData | Reference | CDSect | PI | Comment)*

If an element is **empty**, it must be represented either by a start-tag immediately followed by an end-tag or by an empty-element tag. An **empty-element tag** takes a special form:

Tags for Empty Elements

```
[44] EmptyElemTag ::= '<' Name (S Attribute)* S? '/>'[
wfc: Unique Att Spec ]
```

Empty-element tags may be used for any element which has no content, whether or not it is declared using the keyword EMPTY.

Examples of empty elements:

```
<IMG align="left"
src="http://www.w3.org/Icons/WWW/w3_home" />
<br></br>
<br/>
```

3.2 Element Type Declarations

The element structure of an XML document may, for validation purposes, be constrained using element type and attribute-list declarations.

An element type declaration constrains the element's content.

Element type declarations often constrain which element types can appear as children of the element. At user option, an XML processor may issue a warning when a declaration mentions an element type for which no declaration is provided, but this is not an error.

An **element type declaration** takes the form:

Element Type Declaration

[45] `elementdecl` ::= `'<!ELEMENT'` S Name S `contentspec`
S? `'>'` [vc: Unique Element Type Declaration]
[46] `contentspec` ::= `'EMPTY'` | `'ANY'` | Mixed | children
[vc: Element Valid]

where the `Name` gives the element type being declared.

Validity Constraint - Unique Element Type Declaration	No element type may be declared more than once.
Validity Constraint - Element Valid	An element is valid if there is a declaration matching `elementdecl` where the `Name` matches the element type, and one of the following holds:
	1. The declaration matches `EMPTY` and the element has no content. 2. The declaration matches `children` and the sequence of child elements belongs to the language generated by the regular expression in the content model. 3. The declaration matches `mixed` and the content consists of character data and child elements whose types match names in the content model. 4. The declaration matches `ANY`, and the types of any child elements have been declared.

Examples of element type declarations:

```
<!ELEMENT br EMPTY>
<!ELEMENT p (#PCDATA|emph)* >
<!ELEMENT %name.para; %content.para; >
<!ELEMENT container ANY>
```

3.2.1 Element Content

An element type has **element content** when elements of that type must contain only child elements (no character data). In this case, the constraint includes a content model, a simple grammar governing the allowed types of the child elements and the order in which they are allowed to appear. The grammar is built on content particles (cps), which consist of names, choice lists of content particles, or sequence lists of content particles:

Element-content Models

```
[47] children ::= (choice | seq) ('?' | '*' | '+')?
[48] cp ::= (Name | choice | seq) ('?' | '*' | '+')?
[49] choice ::= '(' S? cp ( S? '|' S? cp )* S? ')'[ vc:
Proper Group/PE Nesting ]
[50] seq ::= '(' S? cp ( S? ',' S? cp )* S? ')'[ vc:
Proper Group/PE Nesting ]
```

where each Name is the type of an element which may appear as a child. Any content particle in a choice list may appear in the element content at the location where the choice list appears in the grammar; content particles occurring in a sequence list must each appear in the element content in the order given in the list. The optional character following a name or list governs whether the element or the content particles in the list may occur one or more (+), zero or more (*), or zero or one times (?). The syntax and meaning are identical to those used in the productions in this specification.

The content of an element matches a content model if and only if it is possible to trace out a path through the content model, obeying the sequence, choice, and repetition operators and matching each element in the content against an element type in the content model. For compatibility, it is an error if an element in the document can match more than one occurrence of an element type in the content model. For more information, see the appendix on deterministic content models.

Validity Constraint - Proper Group/PE Nesting	Parameter-entity replacement text must be properly nested with parenthetized groups. That is to say, if either of the opening or closing parentheses in a `choice`, `seq`, or `Mixed` construct is contained in the replacement text for a parameter entity, both must be contained in the same replacement text. For interoperability, if a parameter-entity reference appears in a `choice`, `seq`, or `Mixed` construct, its replacement text should not be empty, and neither the first nor last non-blank character of the replacement text should be a connector (| or ,).

Examples of element-content models:

```
<!ELEMENT spec (front, body, back?)>
<!ELEMENT div1 (head, (p | list | note)*, div2*)>
<!ELEMENT dictionary-body (%div.mix; | %dict.mix;)*>
```

3.2.2 Mixed Content

An element type has **mixed content**, when elements of that type may contain character data, optionally interspersed with child elements. In this case, the types of the child elements may be constrained, but not their order or their number of occurrences:

Mixed-content Declaration

---

[51] Mixed ::= '(' S? '#PCDATA' (S? '|' S? Name)* S?
')*' | '(' S? '#PCDATA' S? ')' [vc: Proper Group/PE
Nesting] [vc: No Duplicate Types]

---

where the Names give the types of elements that may appear as children.

Validity Constraint - No Duplicate Types	The same name must not appear more than once in a single mixed-content declaration.

Examples of mixed content declarations:

```
<!ELEMENT p (#PCDATA|a|ul|b|i|em)*>
<!ELEMENT p (#PCDATA | %font; | %phrase; | %special;
| %form;)* >
<!ELEMENT b (#PCDATA)>
```

3.3 Attribute-List Declarations

Attributes are used to associate name-value pairs with elements. Attribute specifications may appear only within start-tags and empty-element tags; thus, the productions used to recognize them appear in the discussion of start-tags. Attribute-list declarations may be used:

- ♦ To define the set of attributes pertaining to a given element type.
- ♦ To establish type constraints for these attributes.
- ♦ To provide default values for attributes.

Attribute-list declarations specify the name, data type, and default value (if any) of each attribute associated with a given element type:

Attribute-list Declaration

---

[52] `AttlistDecl ::= '<!ATTLIST' S Name AttDef* S? '>'`
[53] `AttDef ::= S Name S AttType S Default`

The `Name` in the `AttlistDecl` rule is the type of an element. At user option, an XML processor may issue a warning if attributes are declared for an element type not itself declared, but this is not an error. The `Name` in the `AttDef` rule is the name of the attribute.

When more than one `AttlistDecl` is provided for a given element type, the contents of all those provided are merged. When more than one definition is provided for the same attribute of a given element type, the first declaration is binding and later declarations are ignored. For interoperability, writers of DTDs may choose to provide at most one attribute-list declaration for a given element type, at most one attribute definition for a given attribute name, and at least one attribute definition in each attribute-list declaration. For interoperability, an XML processor may at user option issue a warning when more than one attribute-list declaration is provided for a given element type, or more than one attribute definition is provided for a given attribute, but this is not an error.

3.3.1 Attribute Types

XML attribute types are of three kinds: a string type, a set of tokenized types, and enumerated types. The string type may take any literal string as a value; the tokenized types have varying lexical and semantic constraints, as noted:

Attribute Types

---

[54] AttType ::= StringType | TokenizedType | Enumer-
atedType
[55] StringType ::= 'CDATA'
[56] TokenizedType ::= 'ID'[vc: ID][vc: One ID per
Element Type][vc: ID Attribute Default] | 'IDREF'
[vc: IDREF] | 'IDREFS'[vc: IDREF] | 'ENTITY'[vc:
Entity Name] | 'ENTITIES'[vc: Entity Name] |
'NMTOKEN'[vc: Name Token] | 'NMTOKENS'[vc: Name
Token]

Validity Constraint - ID	Values of this type must match the Name produc-tion. A name must not appear more than once in an XML document as a value of this type; i.e., ID val-ues must uniquely identify the elements which bear them.
Validity Constraint - One ID per Element Type	No element type may have more than one ID attribute specified.
Validity Constraint - ID Attribute Default	An ID attribute must have a declared default of #IMPLIED or #REQUIRED.
Validity Constraint - IDREF	Values of type IDREF must match the Name pro-duction, and values of type IDREFS must match the Names) production; each Name must match the value of an ID attribute on some element in the XML document; i.e. IDREF values must match the value of some ID attribute.

Validity Constraint - Entity Name	Values of type ENTITY must match the production for Name; values of type ENTITIES must match Names; each Name must match the name of an unparsed entity declared in the DTD.
Validity Constraint - Name Token	Values of type NMTOKEN must consist of a string matching the Nmtoken nonterminal; values of type NMTOKENS must match Nmtokens.

The XML processor must normalize attribute values before passing them to the application, as described in the section on attribute-value normalization.

Enumerated attributes can take one of a list of values provided in the declaration. There are two kinds of enumerated types:

Enumerated Attribute Types

```
[57] EnumeratedType ::= NotationType | Enumeration
[58] NotationType ::= 'NOTATION' S '(' S? Name (S? '|'
Name)* S? ')' [ vc: Notation Attributes ]
[59] Enumeration ::= '(' S? Nmtoken (S? '|' S? Nmto-
ken)* S? ')' [ vc: Enumeration ]
```

Validity Constraint - Notation Attributes	Values of this type must match one of the notation names included in the declaration; all notation names in the declaration must be declared.
Validity Constraint - Enumeration	Values of this type must match one of the Nmtoken tokens in the declaration.

For interoperability, the same Nmtoken should not occur more than once in the enumerated attribute types of a single element type.

3.3.2 Attribute Defaults

An attribute declaration provides information on whether the attribute's presence is required, and if not, how an XML processor should react if a declared attribute is absent in a document.

Attribute Defaults

---

[60] Default ::= '#REQUIRED' | '#IMPLIED' | (('#FIXED' S)? AttValue)[vc: Attribute Default Legal] [wfc: No < in Attribute Values]

Validity Constraint - Attribute Default Legal	The declared default value must meet the lexical constraints of the declared attribute type.

#REQUIRED means that the document is not valid should the processor encounter a start-tag for the element type in question which specifies no value for this attribute. #IMPLIED means that if the attribute is omitted from an element of this type, the XML processor must inform the application that no value was specified; no constraint is placed on the behavior of the application.

If the attribute is neither #REQUIRED nor #IMPLIED, then the AttValue value contains the declared **default** value. If #FIXED is present, the document is not valid if the attribute is present with a different value from the default. If a default value is declared, when an XML processor encounters an omitted attribute, it is to behave as though the attribute were present with the declared default value.

Examples of attribute-list declarations:

```
<!ATTLIST termdef
id ID #REQUIRED
name CDATA #IMPLIED>
<!ATTLIST list
type (bullets|ordered|glossary) "ordered">
<!ATTLIST form
method CDATA #FIXED "POST">
```

3.3.3 Attribute-Value Normalization

Before the value of an attribute is passed to the application, the XML processor must normalize it as follows:

- First, strings marking line ends or boundaries (or, on some systems, record boundaries) in the attribute value and in any entities referred to in it must be replaced by single space (#x20) characters. (See also the section on end-of-line handling.)
- Second, character references and references to internal parsed entities must be expanded. References to external entities are an error.
- Finally, if the attribute is not of type CDATA, all strings of white space must be normalized to single space characters (#x20), and leading and trailing white space must be removed.

All attributes for which no declaration has been read should be treated by a non-validating parser as if declared CDATA.

3.4 Conditional Sections

Conditional sections are portions of the document type declaration external subset which are included in, or excluded from, the logical structure of the DTD based on the keyword which governs them.

Conditional Section

```
[61] conditionalSect ::= includeSect | ignoreSect
[62] includeSect ::= '<![ ' S? 'INCLUDE' S? '[ ' extSub-
set ']]>'
[63] ignoreSect ::= '<![ ' S? 'IGNORE' S? '[ ' ignore-
SectContents* ']]>'
[64] ignoreSectContents ::= Ignore ('<![ ' ignoreSect-
Contents ']]>' Ignore)*
[65] Ignore ::= Char* - (Char* ('<![ ' | ']]>') Char*)
```

Like the internal and external DTD subsets, a conditional section may contain one or more complete declarations, comments, processing instructions, or nested conditional sections, intermingled with white space.

If the keyword of the conditional section is "INCLUDE", then the processor must treat the contents of the conditional section as part of the document. If the keyword is "IGNORE", then the contents of the conditional section are not treated as part of the document. Note that for reliable parsing, the contents of even ignored conditional sections must be read in order to detect nested conditional sections and ensure that the end of the outermost (ignored) conditional section is properly detected. If a conditional section with a keyword of "INCLUDE" occurs within a larger conditional section with a keyword of "IGNORE", both the outer and the inner conditional sections are ignored.

If the keyword of the conditional section is a parameter-entity reference, the parameter entity must be replaced by its content before the processor decides whether to include or ignore the conditional section.

An example:

```
<!ENTITY % draft 'INCLUDE' >
<!ENTITY % final 'IGNORE' >


<![ %draft;[
<!ELEMENT book (comments*, title, body, supple-
ments?)>
]]>
<![ %final;[
<!ELEMENT book (title, body, supplements?)>
]]>
```

4. Physical Structures

An XML document may consist of one or many virtual storage units. These are called **entities**; they all have **content** and are all (except for the document entity, see below, and the external DTD subset) identified by **name**. Each XML document has one entity called the document entity, which serves as the starting point for the XML processor and may contain the whole document.

Entities may be either parsed or unparsed. A **parsed entity's** contents are referred to as its replacement text; this text is considered an integral part of the document.

An **unparsed entity** is a resource whose contents may or may not be text, and if text, may not be XML. Each unparsed entity has an associated notation, identified by name. Beyond a requirement that an XML processor make the notation's name and associated identifiers available to the application, XML places no constraints on the contents of unparsed entities.

Parsed entities are invoked by name using entity references; unparsed entities by name, given in the value of ENTITY or ENTITIES attributes.

General entities are parsed entities for use within the document content. In this specification, general entities are sometimes referred to with the unqualified term *entity* when this leads to no ambiguity. Parameter entities are parsed entities for use within the DTD. These two types of entities use different forms of reference and are recognized in different contexts.

4.1 Character and Entity References

A **character reference** refers to a specific character in the ISO/IEC 10646 character set, e.g. one not directly accessible from available input devices.

Character Reference

---

[66] CharRef ::= '&#' [0-9] + ';' | '&#x' [0-9a-fA-F] +
';'[wfc: Legal Character]

Well-Formedness Constraint - Legal Character	Characters referred to using character references must be legal according to the nonterminal Char.

If the character begins with "&#x", the digits and letters up to the terminating ";" provide a hexadecimal representation of the character's value in ISO/IEC 10646. If it begins just with "&#", the digits up to the terminating ";" provide a decimal representation of the character's value.

An **entity reference** refers to the content of a named entity. References to general entities use ampersand (&) and semicolon (;) as delimiters. **Parameter-entity references** use percent-sign (%) and semicolon (;) as delimiters.

Entity Reference

```
[67] Reference ::= EntityRef | CharRef
[68] EntityRef ::= '&' Name ';'[ wfc: Entity Declared
] [ vc: Entity Declared ] [ wfc: Parsed Entity ] [
wfc: No Recursion ]
[69] PEReference ::= '%' Name ';'[ wfc: Entity
Declared ] [ vc: Entity Declared ] [ wfc: Parsed
Entity ] [ wfc: No Recursion ] [ wfc: In DTD ]
```

Well-Formedness Constraint - Entity Declared	In a document without any DTD, a document with only an internal DTD subset which contains no parameter entity references, or a document with "standalone='yes'", the Name given in the entity reference must match the name given in the declaration of the entity, except that well-formed documents need not declare any of the following entities: amp, lt, gt, apos, quot. The declaration of a parameter entity must precede any reference to it. Similarly, the declaration of a general entity must precede any reference to it which appears in a default value in an attribute-list declaration. Note that if entities are declared in the external subset or in external parameter entities, a non-validating processor is not obligated to read and process their declarations; for such documents, the rule that an entity must be declared is not a well-formedness constraint.

Validity Constraint - Entity Declared	In a document with an external subset or external parameter entities with "`standalone='no'`", the `Name` given in the entity reference must match the name given in the declaration of the entity. For interoperability, valid documents should declare the entities `amp`, `lt`, `gt`, `apos`, `quot`, in the form specified in the section on predefined entities. The declaration of a parameter entity must precede any reference to it. Similarly, the declaration of a general entity must precede any reference to it which appears in a default value in an attribute-list declaration.
Well-Formedness Constraint - Parsed Entity	An entity reference must not contain the name of an unparsed entity. Unparsed entities may be referred to only in attribute values declared to be of type `ENTITY` or `ENTITIES`.
Well-Formedness Constraint - No Recursion	A parsed entity must not contain a recursive reference to itself, either directly or indirectly.
Well-Formedness Constraint - In DTD	Parameter-entity references may only appear in the DTD.

Examples of character and entity references:

```
Type <key>less-than</key> (&#x3C;) to save options.
This document was prepared on &docdate; and
is classified &security-level;.
```

Example of a parameter-entity reference:

4.2 Entity Declarations

Entities are declared thus:

```
<!ENTITY % ISOLat2
SYSTEM "http://www.xml.com/iso/isolat2-xml.entities"
>
%ISOLat2;
```

Entity Declaration

```
[70] EntityDecl ::= GEDecl /* General entities */ |
PEDecl /* Parameter entities */
[71] GEDecl ::= '<!ENTITY' S Name S EntityDef S? '>'
[72] PEDecl ::= | '<!ENTITY' S '%' S Name S PEDef S?
'>' /* Parameter entities */
[73] EntityDef ::= EntityValue | ExternalDef
[74] PEDef ::= EntityValue | ExternalID
```

The `Name` identifies the entity in an entity reference or, in the case of an unparsed entity, in the value of an `ENTITY` or `ENTITIES` attribute. If the same entity is declared more than once, the first declaration encountered is binding; at user option, an XML processor may issue a warning if entities are declared multiple times.

4.2.1 Internal Entities

If the entity definition is an `EntityValue`, the defined entity is called an **internal entity**. There is no separate physical storage object, and the content of the entity is given in the declaration. Note that some processing of entity and character references in the literal entity value may be required to produce the correct replacement text: see Construction of Internal Entity Replacement Text.

An internal entity is a parsed entity.

Example of an internal entity declaration:

4.2.2 External Entities

If the entity is not internal, it is an **external entity**, declared as follows:

```
<!ENTITY Pub-Status "This is a pre-release of the
specification.">
```

External Entity Declaration

```
[75] ExternalDef ::= ExternalID NDataDecl?
[76] ExternalID ::= 'SYSTEM' S SystemLiteral | 'PUBLIC'
S PubidLiteral S SystemLiteral
[77] NDataDecl ::= S 'NDATA' S Name[ vc: Notation
Declared ]
```

If the `NDataDecl` is present, this is an unparsed entity; otherwise it is a parsed entity.

Validity Constraint - Notation Declared	The `Name` must match the declared name of a notation.

The `SystemLiteral` that follows the keyword `SYSTEM` is called the entity's **system identifier**. It is a URI, which may be used to retrieve the entity. Note that the hash mark ("#") and fragment identifier frequently used with URIs are not, formally, part of the URI itself; an XML processor may signal an error if a fragment identifier is given as part of a system identifier. Unless otherwise provided by information outside the scope of this specification (e.g. a special XML element type defined by a particular DTD, or a processing instruction defined by a particular application specification), relative URIs are relative to the location of the resource within which the entity declaration occurs. Relative URIs in entity declarations within the internal DTD subset are thus relative to the location of the document; those in entity declarations in the external subset are relative to the location of the files containing the external subset.

In addition to a system identifier, an external identifier may include a **public identifier**. An XML processor attempting to retrieve the entity's content may use the public identifier to try to generate an alternative URI. If the processor is unable to do so, it must use the URI specified in the system literal. Before a match is attempted, all strings of white space in the public identifier must be normalized to single space characters (#x20), and leading and trailing white space must be removed.

Examples of external entity declarations:

```
<!ENTITY open-hatch
SYSTEM "http://www.textuality.com/boilerplate/Open-
Hatch.xml">
<!ENTITY open-hatch
PUBLIC "-//Textuality//TEXT Standard open-hatch
boilerplate//EN"
"http://www.textuality.com/boilerplate/Open-
Hatch.xml">
<!ENTITY hatch-pic
SYSTEM "../grafix/OpenHatch.gif"
NDATA gif >
```

4.3 Parsed Entities

4.3.1 The Text Declaration

External parsed entities may each begin with a **text declaration.**

Text Declaration

[78] TextDecl ::= '<?xml' VersionInfo? EncodingDecl S? '?>'

Note that the text declaration must be provided literally, not by reference to a parsed entity.

No text declaration may appear at any position other than the front of an external parsed entity.

4.3.2 Well-Formed Parsed Entities

The document entity is well-formed if it matches the production labeled `document`. An external general parsed entity is well-formed if it matches the production labeled `ExtParsedEnt`. An external parameter entity is well-formed if it matches the production labeled `ExtPE`.

Well-Formed External Parsed Entity

```
[79] ExtParsedEnt ::= TextDecl? content
[80] ExtPE ::= TextDecl? extSubset
```

An internal general parsed entity is well-formed if its replacement text matches the production labeled `content`. Note that this cannot be checked reliably until the end of the DTD. All internal parameter entities are well-formed by definition.

A consequence of well-formedness in entities is that the logical and physical structures in an XML document are properly nested; no start-tag, end-tag, empty-element tag, element, comment, processing instruction, character reference, or entity reference can begin in one entity and end in another.

4.3.3 Character Encoding in Entities

Each external parsed entity in an XML document may use a different encoding for its characters. All XML processors must be able to read entities in either UTF-8 or UTF-16.

Entities encoded in UTF-16 must begin with the Byte Order Mark described by ISO/IEC 10646 Annex E and Unicode Appendix B (the ZERO WIDTH NO-BREAK SPACE character, #xFEFF). This is an encoding signature, not part of either the markup or the character data of the XML document. XML processors must be able to use this character to differentiate between UTF-8 and UTF-16 encoded documents.

Although an XML processor is required to read only entities in the UTF-8 and UTF-16 encodings, it is recognized that other encodings are used around the world, and it may be desired for XML processors to read entities that use them. Parsed entities which are stored in an encoding other than UTF-8 or UTF-16 must begin with a text declaration containing an encoding declaration:

Encoding Declaration

```
[81] EncodingDecl ::= S 'encoding' Eq '"' EncName '"' |
"'" EncName "'"
[82] EncName ::= [ A-Za-z]  ([ A-Za-z0-9._] | '-')* /*
Encoding name contains only Latin characters */
```

In the document entity, the encoding declaration is part of the XML declaration. The `EncName` is the name of the encoding used.

In an encoding declaration, the values `UTF-8`, `UTF-16`, `ISO-10646-UCS-2`, and `ISO-10646-UCS-4` should be used for the various encodings and transformations of Unicode / ISO/IEC 10646, the values `ISO-8859-1`, `ISO-8859-2`, ... `ISO-8859-9` should be used for the parts of ISO 8859, and the values `ISO-2022-JP`, `Shift_JIS`, and `EUC-JP` should be used for the various encoded forms of JIS X-0208-1997. XML processors may recognize other encodings; it is recommended that character encodings registered (as *charsets*) with the Internet Assigned Numbers Authority (IANA), other than those just listed, should be referred to using their registered names. Note that these registered names are defined to be case-insensitive, so processors wishing to match against them should do so in a case-insensitive way.

It is an error for an entity including an encoding declaration to be presented to the XML processor in an encoding other than that named in the declaration, or for an encoding declaration to occur other than at the beginning of an external entity.

An entity which begins with neither a Byte Order Mark nor an encoding declaration must be in the UTF-8 encoding.

If an XML processor encounters an entity with an encoding that it is unable to process, it must notify the application of this fact and cease processing, just as with a fatal error.

Examples of encoding declarations:

```
<?xml encoding='UTF-8'?>
<?xml encoding='EUC-JP'?>
```

4.4 XML Processor Treatment of Entities and References

The table below summarizes the contexts in which character references, entity references, and invocations of unparsed entities might appear and the required behavior of an XML processor in each case. The labels in the leftmost column describe the recognition context:

Reference in Content	as a reference anywhere after the start-tag and before the end-tag of an element; corresponds to the nonterminal `content`.
Reference in Attribute Value	as a reference within either the value of an attribute in a start-tag, or a default value in an attribute declaration; corresponds to the nonterminal `AttValue`.
Occurs as Attribute Value	as a `Name`, not a reference, appearing either as the value of an attribute which has been declared as type `ENTITY`, or as one of the space-separated tokens in the value of an attribute which has been declared as type `ENTITIES`.
Reference in Entity Value	as a reference within a parameter or internal entity's literal entity value in the entity's declaration; corresponds to the nonterminal `Entity-Value`.
Reference in DTD	as a reference within either the internal or external subsets of the DTD, but outside of an `Entity-Value` or `AttValue`.

	Entity Type				Character
	Parameter	Internal General	External Parsed General	Unparsed	
Reference in Content	Not recognized	Included	Included if validating	Forbidden	Included
Reference in Attribute Value	Not recognized	Included	Forbidden	Forbidden	Included
Occurs as Attribute Value	Not recognized	Forbidden	Forbidden	Notify	Not recognized
Reference in EntityValue	Included	Bypassed	Bypassed	Forbidden	Included
Reference in DTD	Included as PE	Forbidden	Forbidden	Forbidden	Forbidden

4.4.1 Not Recognized

Outside the DTD, the % character has no particular significance; thus, what would be parameter entity references in the DTD are not recognized as markup in content. Similarly, the names of unparsed entities are not recognized except when they appear in the value of an appropriately declared attribute.

4.4.2 Included

An entity is **included** when its replacement text is retrieved and and processed, in place of the reference itself, as though it were part of the document at the location the reference was recognized. The replacement text may contain both character data and (except for parameter entities) markup, which must be recognized in the usual way, except that the replacement text of entities used to escape markup delimiters (the entities amp, lt, gt, apos, quot) is always treated as data. (The string "AT&T;" expands to "AT&T;" and the remaining ampersand is not recognized as an entity-reference delimiter.) A character reference is **included** when the indicated character is processed in place of the reference itself.

4.4.3 Included If Validating

When an XML processor recognizes a reference to a parsed entity, in order to validate the document, the processor must include its replacement text. If the entity is external, and the processor is not attempting to validate the XML document, the processor may, but need not, include the entity's replacement text.

This rule is based on the recognition that the automatic inclusion provided by the SGML and XML entity mechanism, primarily designed to support modularity in authoring, is not necessarily appropriate for other applications, in particular document browsing. Browsers, for example, when encountering an external parsed entity reference, might choose to provide a visual indication of the entity's presence and retrieve it for display only on demand.

4.4.4 Forbidden

The following are forbidden, and constitute fatal errors:

- the appearance of a reference to an unparsed entity.
- the appearance of any character or general-entity reference in the DTD except within an `EntityValue` or `AttValue`.
- a reference to an external entity in an attribute value.

4.4.5 Notify

When the name of an unparsed entity appears as a token in the value of an attribute of declared type `ENTITY` or `ENTITIES`, the processor must inform the application of the associated notation name, and the notation's associated system and public (if any) identifiers.

4.4.6 Bypassed

When a general entity reference appears in the `EntityValue` in an entity declaration, it is ignored and left as is.

4.4.7 Included as PE

Just as with external parsed entities, parameter entities need only be included if validating. When a parameter-entity reference is recognized in the DTD and included, its replacement text is enlarged by the attachment of one leading and one following space (#x20) character; the intent is to constrain the replacement text of parameter entities to contain an integral number of grammatical tokens in the DTD.

4.5 Construction of Internal Entity Replacement Text

In discussing the tratment of internal entities, it is useful to distinguish two forms of the entity's value. The **literal entity value** is the quoted string actually present in the entity declaration, corresponding to the non-terminal `EntityValue`. The **replacement text** is the content of the entity, after replacement of character references and parameter-entity references.

The literal entity value as given in an internal entity declaration (`Entity-Value`) may contain character, parameter-entity, and general-entity references. Such references must be contained entirely within the literal entity value. The actual replacement text that is included as described above must contain the *replacement text* of any parameter entities referred to, and must contain the character referred to, in place of any character references in the literal entity value; however, general-entity references must be left as-is, unexpanded. For example, given the following declarations:

```
<!ENTITY % pub "&#xc9;ditions Gallimard" >
<!ENTITY rights "All rights reserved" >
<!ENTITY book "La Peste: Albert Camus,
&#xA9; 1947 %pub;. &rights;" >
```

then the replacement text for the entity "`book`" is:

```
La Peste: Albert Camus,
' 1947  ditions Gallimard. &rights;
```

The general-entity reference "`&rights;`" would be expanded should the reference "`&book;`" appear in the document's content or an attribute value.

These simple rules may have complex interactions; for a detailed discussion of a difficult example, see the appendix on expansion of entity references.

4.6 Predefined Entities

Entity and character references can both be used to **escape** the left angle bracket, ampersand, and other delimiters. A set of general entities (amp, lt, gt, apos, quot) is specified for this purpose. Numeric character references may also be used; they are expanded immediately when recognized and must be treated as character data, so the numeric character references "<" and "&" may be used to escape < and & when they occur in character data.

All XML processors must recognize these entities whether they are declared or not. For interoperability, valid XML documents should declare these entities, like any others, before using them. If the entities in question are declared, they must be declared as internal entities whose replacement text is the single character being escaped, as shown below.

```
<!ENTITY lt   "&#38;#60;">
<!ENTITY gt   "&#62;">
<!ENTITY amp  "&#38;#38;">
<!ENTITY apos "&#39;">
<!ENTITY quot "&#34;">
```

Note that the "<" and "&" characters in the declarations of "lt" and "amp" are doubly escaped to meet the requirement that entity replacement be well-formed.

4.7 Notation Declarations

Notations identify by name the format of unparsed entities, or the application to which processing instructions are addressed.

Notation declarations provide a name for the notation, for use in entity and attribute-list declarations and in attribute specifications, and an external identifier for the notation which may allow an XML processor or its client application to locate a helper application capable of processing data in the given notation.

Notation Declarations

[83] `NotationDecl ::= '<!NOTATION' S Name S (ExternalID | PublicID) S? '>'`

[84] `PublicID ::= 'PUBLIC' S PubidLiteral`

XML processors must provide applications with the name and external identifier of any notation declared and referred to in an attribute value, attribute definition, or entity declaration. They may additionally resolve the external identifier into the system identifier, file name, or other information needed to allow the application to call a processor for data in the notation described. (It is not an error, however, for XML documents to declare and refer to notations for which notation-specific applications are not available on the system where the XML processor or application is running.)

4.8 Document Entity

The **document entity** serves as the root of the entity tree and a starting-point for an XML processor. This specification does not specify how the document entity is to be located by an XML processor; unlike other entities, the document entity has no name and might well appear on a processor input stream without any identification at all.

5. Conformance

Conforming XML processors fall into two classes: validating and non-validating.

Validating and non-validating systems alike must report violations of the well-formedness constraints given in this specification.

Validating processors must report violations of the constraints expressed by the declarations in the DTD. They must also report all failures to fulfill the validity constraints given in this specification.

6. Notation

The formal grammar of XML is given in this specification using a simple Extended Backus-Naur Form (EBNF) notation. Each rule in the grammar defines one symbol, in the form

symbol ::= expression

Symbols are written with an initial capital letter if they are defined by a regular expression, or with an initial lower case letter otherwise. Literal strings are quoted.

Within the expression on the right-hand side of a rule, the following expressions are used to match strings of one or more characters:

#xN	where N is a hexadecimal integer, the expression matches the character in ISO/IEC 10646 whose canonical (UCS-4) code value, when interpreted as an unsigned binary number, has the value indicated. The number of leading zeros in the #xN form is insignificant; the number of leading zeros in the corresponding code value is governed by the character encoding in use and is not significant for XML.

`[a-zA-Z]`, `[#xN-#xN]`	matches any character with a value in the range(s) indicated (inclusive).
`[^a-z]`, `[^#xN-#xN]`	matches any character with a value outside the range indicated.
`[^abc]`, `[^#xN#xN#xN]`	matches any character with a value not among the characters given.
`"string"`	matches a literal string matching that given inside the double quotes.
`'string'`	matches a literal string matching that given inside the single quotes.

These symbols may be combined to match more complex patterns as follows, where A and B represent simple expressions:

`(expression)`	`expression` is treated as a unit and may be combined as described in this list.
`A?`	matches A or nothing; optional A.
`A B`	matches A followed by B.
`A	B`	matches A or B but not both.
`A - B`	matches any string that matches A but does not match B.
`A+`	matches one or more occurrences of A.
`A*`	matches zero or more occurrences of A.

Other notations used in the productions are:

`/* ... */`	comment.

| [wfc: ...] | well-formedness constraint; this identifies by name a constraint on well-formed documents associated with a production. |
| [vc: ...] | validity constraint; this identifies by name a constraint on valid documents associated with a production. |

Appendices

A. References

A.1 Normative References

IETF RFC 1766
IETF (Internet Engineering Task Force). *RFC 1766: Tags for the Identification of Languages*, ed. H. Alvestrand. 1995.

ISO 639
(International Organization for Standardization). *ISO 8879:1988 (E). Code for the representation of names of languages.* [Geneva]: International Organization for Standardization, 1988.

ISO 3166
(International Organization for Standardization). *ISO 3166-1:1997 (E). Codes for the representation of names of countries and their subdivisions — Part 1: Country codes* [Geneva]: International Organization for Standardization, 1997.

ISO/IEC 10646
ISO (International Organization for Standardization). *ISO/IEC 10646-1993 (E). Information technology — Universal Multiple-Octet Coded Character Set (UCS) — Part 1: Architecture and Basic Multilingual*

Plane. [Geneva]: International Organization for Standardization, 1993 (plus amendments AM 1 through AM 7).

Unicode
The Unicode Consortium. *The Unicode Standard, Version 2.0*. Reading, Mass.: Addison-Wesley Developers Press, 1996.

A.2 Other References

Aho/Ullman
Aho, Alfred V., Ravi Sethi, and Jeffrey D. Ullman. *Compilers: Principles, Techniques, and Tools*. Reading: Addison-Wesley, 1986, rpt. corr. 1988.

Berners-Lee et al.
Berners-Lee, T., R. Fielding, and L. Masinter. *Uniform Resource Identifiers (URI): Generic Syntax and Semantics*. 1997. (Work in progress; see updates to RFC1738.)

Brüggemann-Klein
Brüggemann-Klein, Anne. *Regular Expressions into Finite Automata*. Extended abstract in I. Simon, Hrsg., LATIN 1992, S. 97-98. Springer-Verlag, Berlin 1992. Full Version in Theoretical Computer Science 120: 197-213, 1993.

Brüggemann-Klein and Wood
Brüggemann-Klein, Anne, and Derick Wood. *Deterministic Regular Languages*. Universität Freiburg, Institut für Informatik, Bericht 38, Oktober 1991.

IETF RFC1738
IETF (Internet Engineering Task Force). *RFC 1738: Uniform Resource Locators (URL)*, ed. T. Berners-Lee, L. Masinter, M. McCahill. 1994.

IETF RFC1808
IETF (Internet Engineering Task Force). *RFC 1808: Relative Uniform Resource Locators*, ed. R. Fielding. 1995.

IETF RFC2141

IETF (Internet Engineering Task Force). *RFC 2141: URN Syntax*, ed. R. Moats. 1997.

ISO/IEC 8879

ISO (International Organization for Standardization). *ISO/IEC 8879-1986 (E). Information processing — Text and Office Systems — Standard Generalized Markup Language (SGML)*. First edition — 1986-10-15. [Geneva]: International Organization for Standardization, 1986.

ISO/IEC 10744

ISO (International Organization for Standardization). *ISO/IEC 10744-1992 (E). Information technology — Hypermedia/Time-based Structuring Language (HyTime)*. [Geneva]: International Organization for Standardization, 1992. *Extended Facilities Annexe*. [Geneva]: International Organization for Standardization, 1996.

B. Character Classes

Following the characteristics defined in the Unicode standard, characters are classed as base characters (among others, these contain the alphabetic characters of the Latin alphabet, without diacritics), ideographic characters, and combining characters (among others, this class contains most diacritics); these classes combine to form the class of letters. Digits and extenders are also distinguished.

The character classes defined here can be derived from the Unicode character database as follows:

♦ Name start characters must have one of the categories Ll, Lu, Lo, Lt, Nl.
♦ Name characters other than Name-start characters must have one of the categories Mc, Me, Mn, Lm, or Nd.
♦ Characters in the compatibility area (i.e. with character code greater than #xF900 and less than #xFFFE) are not allowed in XML names.
♦ Characters which have a font or compatibility decomposition (i.e. those with a "compatibility formatting tag" in field 5 of the

database -- marked by field 5 beginning with a "<") are not allowed.

- ♦ The following characters are treated as name-start characters ratehr than name characters, because the property file classifies them as Alphabetic: [#x02BB-#x02C1], #x0559, #x06E5, #x06E6.
- ♦ Characters #x20DD-#x20E0 are excluded (in accordance with Unicode, section 5.14).
- ♦ Character #x00B7 is classified as an extender, because the property list so identifies it.
- ♦ Character #x0387 is added as a name character, because #x00B7 is its canonical equivalent.
- ♦ Characters ':' and '_' are allowed as name-start characters.
- ♦ Characters '-' and '.' are allowed as name characters.

C. XML and SGML (Non-Normative)

XML is designed to be a subset of SGML, in that every valid XML document should also be a conformant SGML document. For a detailed comparison of the additional restrictions that XML places on documents beyond those of SGML, see the accompanying note, which also includes an SGML declaration which describes those constraints of XML applicable to an SGML parser.

D. Expansion of Entity and Character References (Non-Normative)

This appendix contains some examples illustrating the sequence of entity- and character-reference recognition and expansion.

If the DTD contains the declaration

```
<!ENTITY example "<p>An ampersand (&#38;#38;) may be escaped
numerically (&#38;#38;#38;) or with a general entity
(&amp;amp;).</p>" >
```

then the XML processor will recognize the character references when it parses the entity declaration, and resolve them before storing the following string as the value of the entity "example":

```
<p>An ampersand (&#38;) may be escaped
numerically (&#38;#38;) or with a general entity
(&amp;amp;).</p>
```

A reference in the document to "&example;" will cause the text to be reparsed, at which time the start- and end-tags of the "p" element will be recognized and the three references will be recognized and expanded, resulting in a "p" element with the following content (all data, no delimiters or markup):

```
An ampersand (&) may be escaped
numerically (&#38;) or with a general entity
(&amp;).
```

A more complex example will illustrate the rules and their effects fully. In the following example, the line numbers are solely for reference.

```
1 <?xml version='1.0'?>
2 <!DOCTYPE test [
3 <!ELEMENT test (#PCDATA) >
4 <!ENTITY % xx '&#37;zz;'>
5 <!ENTITY % zz '&#60;!ENTITY tricky "error-prone" >' >
6 %xx;
7 ]>
8 <test>This sample shows a &tricky; method.</test>
```

This produces the following:

- ◆ in line 4, the reference to character 37 is expanded immediately, and the parameter entity "xx" is stored in the symbol table with the value "%zz;". Since the replacement text is not rescanned, the reference to parameter entity "zz" is not recognized. (And it would be an error if it were, since "zz" is not yet declared.)

♦ in line 5, the character reference "<" is expanded immediately and the parameter entity "zz" is stored with the replacement text "<!ENTITY tricky "error-prone" >", which is a well-formed entity declaration.

♦ in line 6, the reference to "xx" is recognized, and the replacement text of "xx" (namely "%zz;") is parsed. The reference to "zz" is recognized in its turn, and its replacement text ("<!ENTITY tricky "error-prone" >") is parsed. The general entity "tricky" has now been declared, with the replacement text "error-prone".

♦ in line 8, the reference to the general entity "tricky" is recognized, and it is expanded, so the full content of the "test" element is the self-describing (and ungrammatical) string *This sample shows a error-prone method.*

E. Deterministic Content Models (Non-Normative)

For compatibility, it is required that content models in element type declarations be deterministic.

SGML requires deterministic content models (it calls them "unambiguous"); XML processors built using SGML systems may flag non-deterministic content models as errors.

For example, the content model ((b, c) | (b, d)) is non-deterministic, because given an initial b the parser cannot know which b in the model is being matched without looking ahead to see which element follows the b. In this case, the two references to b can be collapsed into a single reference, making the model read (b, (c | d)). An initial b now clearly matches only a single name in the content model. The parser doesn't need to look ahead to see what follows; either c or d would be accepted.

More formally: a finite state automaton may be constructed from the content model using the standard algorithms, e.g. algorithm 3.5 in section 3.9 of Aho, Sethi, and Ullman [Aho]. In many such algorithms, a follow set is constructed for each position in the regular expression (i.e., each leaf node in the syntax tree for the regular expression); if any position has a follow set in which more than one following position is labeled with the same element type name, then the content model is in error and may be reported as an error.

Algorithms exist which allow many but not all non-deterministic content models to be reduced automatically to equivalent deterministic models; see Brüggemann-Klein 1991 [ABK].

F. Autodetection of Character Encodings (Non-Normative)

The XML encoding declaration functions as an internal label on each entity, indicating which character encoding is in use. Before an XML processor can read the internal label, however, it apparently has to know what character encoding is in use — which is what the internal label is trying to indicate. In the general case, this is a hopeless situation. It is not entirely hopeless in XML, however, because XML limits the general case in two ways: each implementation is assumed to support only a finite set of character encodings, and the XML encoding declaration is restricted in position and content in order to make it feasible to autodetect the character encoding in use in each entity in normal cases. Also, in many cases other sources of information are available in addition to the XML data stream itself. Two cases may be distinguished, depending on whether the XML entity is presented to the processor without, or with, any accompanying (external) information. We consider the first case first.

Because each XML entity not in UTF-8 or UTF-16 format *must* begin with an XML encoding declaration, in which the first characters must be '`<?xml`', any conforming processor can detect, after two to four octets of input, which of the following cases apply. In reading this list, it may help to know that in UCS-4, '`<`' is "`#x0000003C`" and '`?`' is "`#x0000003F`", and the Byte Order Mark required of UTF-16 data streams is "`#xFEFF`".

- ◆ `00 00 00 3C`: UCS-4, big-endian machine (1234 order)
- ◆ `3C 00 00 00`: UCS-4, little-endian machine (4321 order)
- ◆ `00 00 3C 00`: UCS-4, unusual octet order (2143)
- ◆ `00 3C 00 00`: UCS-4, unusual octet order (3412)

- ◆ FE FF: UTF-16, big-endian
- ◆ FF FE: UTF-16, little-endian
- ◆ 00 3C 00 3F: UTF-16, big-endian, no Byte Order Mark (and thus, strictly speaking, in error)
- ◆ 3C 00 3F 00: UTF-16, little-endian, no Byte Order Mark (and thus, strictly speaking, in error)
- ◆ 3C 3F 78 6D: UTF-8, ISO 646, ASCII, some part of ISO 8859, Shift-JIS, EUC, or any other 7-bit, 8-bit, or mixed-width encoding which ensures that the characters of ASCII have their normal positions, width, and values; the actual encoding declaration must be read to detect which of these applies, but since all of these encodings use the same bit patterns for the ASCII characters, the encoding declaration itself may be read reliably
- ◆ 4C 6F A7 94: EBCDIC (in some flavor; the full encoding declaration must be read to tell which code page is in use)
- ◆ other: UTF-8 without an encoding declaration, or else the data stream is corrupt, fragmentary, or enclosed in a wrapper of some kind

This level of autodetection is enough to read the XML encoding declaration and parse the character-encoding identifier, which is still necessary to distinguish the individual members of each family of encodings (e.g. to tell UTF-8 from 8859, and the parts of 8859 from each other, or to distinguish the specific EBCDIC code page in use, and so on).

Because the contents of the encoding declaration are restricted to ASCII characters, a processor can reliably read the entire encoding declaration as soon as it has detected which family of encodings is in use. Since in practice, all widely used character encodings fall into one of the categories above, the XML encoding declaration allows reasonably reliable in-band labeling of character encodings, even when external sources of information at the operating-system or transport-protocol level are unreliable.

Once the processor has detected the character encoding in use, it can act appropriately, whether by invoking a separate input routine for each case, or by calling the proper conversion function on each character of input.

Like any self-labeling system, the XML encoding declaration will not work if any software changes the entity's character set or encoding without updating the encoding declaration. Implementors of character-encoding routines should be careful to ensure the accuracy of the internal and external information used to label the entity.

The second possible case occurs when the XML entity is accompanied by encoding information, as in some file systems and some network protocols. When multiple sources of information are available, their relative priority and the preferred method of handling conflict should be specified as part of the higher-level protocol used to deliver XML. Rules for the relative priority of the internal label and the MIME-type label in an external header, for example, should be part of the RFC document defining the text/xml and application/xml MIME types. In the interests of interoperability, however, the following rules are recommended.

- If an XML entity is in a file, the Byte-Order Mark and encoding-declaration PI are used (if present) to determine the character encoding. All other heuristics and sources of information are solely for error recovery.
- If an XML entity is delivered with a MIME type of text/xml, then the `charset` parameter on the MIME type determines the character encoding method; all other heuristics and sources of information are solely for error recovery.
- If an XML entity is delivered with a MIME type of application/xml, then the Byte-Order Mark and encoding-declaration PI are used (if present) to determine the character encoding. All other heuristics and sources of information are solely for error recovery.

These rules apply only in the absence of protocol-level documentation; in particular, when the MIME types text/xml and application/xml are defined, the recommendations of the relevant RFC will supersede these rules.

G. W3C XML Working Group (Non-Normative)

This specification was prepared and approved for publication by the W3C XML Working Group (WG). WG approval of this specification does not necessarily imply that all WG members voted for its approval. The current and former members of the XML WG are:

Jon Bosak, Sun (Chair); James Clark (Technical Lead); Tim Bray, Textuality and Netscape (XML Co-editor); Jean Paoli, Microsoft (XML Co-editor); C. M. Sperberg-McQueen, U. of Ill. (XML Co-editor); Dan Connolly, W3C; Steve DeRose, INSO; Dave Hollander, HP; Eliot Kimber, Highland; Eve Maler, ArborText; Tom Magliery, NCSA; Murray Maloney, Muzmo and Grif; Makoto Murata, Fuji Xerox Information Systems; Joel Nava, Adobe; Peter Sharpe, SoftQuad; John Tigue, DataChannel

B

Resource Description Framework

This Version:
http://www.w3.org/TR/1999/REC-rdf-syntax-19990222

Newest Version:
http://www.w3.org/TR/REC-rdf-syntax

Editors:
Ora Lassila `<ora.lassila@research.nokia.com>`, Nokia Research Center
Ralph R. Swick `<swick@w3.org>`, World Wide Web Consortium

Document Status

Status of This Document

This document has been reviewed by W3C Members and other interested parties and has been endorsed by the Director as a W3C Recommendation. It is a stable document and may be used as reference material or cited as a normative reference from other documents. W3C's role in making the Recommendation is to draw attention to the specification and to promote its widespread deployment. This enhances the functionality and interoperability of the Web.

The list of know errors in this specification is available at http://www.w3.org/TR/1999/REC-rdf-syntax-19990222/errata.

Comments on this specification may be sent to <www-rdf-comments@w3.org>. The archive of public comments is available at http://www.w3.org/Archives/Public/www-rdf-comments.

Table of Contents

1. Introduction
2. Basic RDF
3. Containers
4. Statements About Statements
5. Formal Model for RDF
6. Formal Grammar for RDF
7. Examples
8. Acknowledgements
9. Appendix A: Glossary
10. Appendix B: Transporting RDF
11. Appendix C: Notes about Usage
12. Appendix D: References
13. Appendix E: Changes From Previous Version

1. Introduction

The World Wide Web was originally built for human consumption, and although everything on it is *machine-readable*, this data is not *machine-understandable*. It is very hard to automate anything on the Web, and because of the volume of information the Web contains, it is not possible to manage it manually. The solution proposed here is to use *metadata* to describe the data contained on the Web. Metadata is "data about data" (for example, a library catalog is metadata, since it describes publications) or specifically in the context of this specification "data describing Web resources". The distinction between "data" and "metadata" is not an absolute one; it is a distinction created primarily by a particular application, and many times the same resource will be interpreted in both ways simultaneously.

Resource Description Framework (RDF) is a foundation for processing metadata; it provides interoperability between applications that exchange machine-understandable information on the Web. RDF emphasizes facilities to enable automated processing of Web resources. RDF can be used in a variety of application areas; for example: in *resource discovery* to provide better search engine capabilities, in *cataloging* for describing the content and content relationships available at a particular Web site, page, or digital library, by *intelligent software agents* to facilitate knowledge sharing and exchange, in *content rating*, in describing *collections of pages* that represent a single logical "document", for describing *intellectual property rights* of Web pages, and for expressing the *privacy preferences* of a user as well as the *privacy policies* of a Web site. RDF with *digital signatures* will be key to building the "Web of Trust" for electronic commerce, collaboration, and other applications.

This document introduces a model for representing RDF metadata as well as a syntax for encoding and transporting this metadata in a manner that maximizes the interoperability of independently developed Web servers and clients. The syntax presented here uses the Extensible Markup Language [XML]: one of the goals of RDF is to make it possible to specify semantics for data based on XML in a standardized, interoperable manner. RDF and XML are complementary: RDF is a model of metadata and only addresses by reference many of the encoding issues that transportation and file storage require (such as internationalization, character sets, etc.). For these issues, RDF relies on the support of XML. It is also important to understand that this XML syntax is only one possible syntax for RDF and that alternate ways to represent the same RDF data model may emerge.

The broad goal of RDF is to define a mechanism for describing resources that makes no assumptions about a particular application domain, nor defines (a priori) the semantics of any application domain. The definition of the mechanism should be domain neutral, yet the mechanism should be suitable for describing information about any domain.

This specification will be followed by other documents that will complete the framework. Most importantly, to facilitate the definition of metadata, RDF will have a class system much like many object-oriented programming and modeling systems. A collection of classes (typically authored for a specific purpose or domain) is called a *schema*. Classes are organized in a hierarchy, and offer extensibility through subclass refinement. This way, in order to create a schema slightly different from an existing one it is not necessary to "reinvent the wheel" but one can just provide incremental modifications to the base schema. Through the sharability of schemas RDF will support the reusability of metadata definitions. Due to RDF's incremental extensibility, agents processing metadata will be able to trace the origins of schemata they are unfamiliar with back to known schemata and perform meaningful actions on metadata they weren't originally designed to process. The sharability and extensibility of RDF also allows metadata authors to use multiple inheritance to "mix" definitions, to provide multiple views to their data, leveraging work done by others. In addition, it is possible to create RDF instance data based on multiple schemata from multiple sources (i.e., "interleaving" different types of metadata). Schemas may themselves be written in RDF; a companion document to this specification, [RDFSchema], describes one set of properties and classes for describing RDF schemas.

As a result of many communities coming together and agreeing on basic principles of metadata representation and transport, RDF has drawn influence from several different sources. The main influences have come from the *Web standardization community* itself in the form of HTML metadata and PICS, the *library community*, the *structured document community* in the form of SGML and more importantly XML, and also the *knowledge representation (KR) community*. There are also other areas of technology that contributed to the RDF design; these include object-oriented programming and modeling languages, as well as databases. While RDF draws from the KR community, readers familiar with that field are cautioned that RDF does not specify a mechanism for *reasoning*. RDF can be characterized as a simple frame system. A reasoning mechanism could be built on top of this frame system.

2. Basic RDF

2.1. Basic RDF Model

The foundation of RDF is a model for representing named properties and property values. The RDF model draws on well-established principles from various data representation communities. RDF properties may be thought of as attributes of resources and in this sense correspond to traditional attribute-value pairs. RDF properties also represent relationships between resources and an RDF model can therefore resemble an entity-relationship diagram. (More precisely, RDF Schemas — which are themselves instances of RDF data models — are ER diagrams.) In object-oriented design terminology, resources correspond to objects and properties correspond to instance variables.

The RDF data model is a syntax-neutral way of representing RDF expressions. The data model representation is used to evaluate equivalence in meaning. Two RDF expressions are equivalent if and only if their data model representations are the same. This definition of equivalence permits some syntactic variation in expression without altering the meaning. (See Section 6. for additional discussion of string comparison issues.)

The basic data model consists of three object types:

Resources	All things being described by RDF expressions are called *resources*. A resource may be an entire Web page; such as the HTML document "http://www.w3.org/Overview.html" for example. A resource may be a part of a Web page; e.g. a specific HTML or XML element within the document source. A resource may also be a whole collection of pages; e.g. an entire Web site. A resource may also be an object that is not directly accessible via the Web; e.g. a printed book. Resources are always named by URIs plus optional anchor ids (see [URI]). Anything can have a URI; the extensibility of URIs allows the introduction of identifiers for any entity imaginable.
Properties	A *property* is a specific aspect, characteristic, attribute, or relation used to describe a resource. Each property has a specific meaning, defines its permitted values, the types of resources it can describe, and its relationship with other properties. This document does not address how the characteristics of properties are expressed; for such information, refer to the RDF Schema specification).
Statements	A specific resource together with a named property plus the value of that property for that resource is an RDF *statement*. These three individual parts of a statement are called, respectively, the *subject*, the *predicate*, and the *object*. The object of a statement (i.e., the property value) can be another resource or it can be a literal; i.e., a resource (specified by a URI) or a simple string or other primitive datatype defined by XML. In RDF terms, a *literal* may have content that is XML markup but is not further evaluated by the RDF processor. There are some syntactic restrictions on how markup in literals may be expressed; see Section 2.2.1.

2.1.1. Examples

Resources are identified by a *resource identifier*. A resource identifier is a URI plus an optional anchor id (see Section 2.2.1.). For the purposes of this section, properties will be referred to by a simple name.

Consider as a simple example the sentence:

Ora Lassila is the creator of the resource http://www.w3.org/Home/Lassila.

This sentence has the following parts:

Subject (Resource)	http://www.w3.org/Home/Lassila
Predicate (Property)	Creator
Object (literal)	"Ora Lassila"

In this document we will diagram an RDF statement pictorially using directed labeled graphs (also called "nodes and arcs diagrams"). In these diagrams, the nodes (drawn as ovals) represent resources and arcs represent named properties. Nodes that represent string literals will be drawn as rectangles. The sentence above would thus be diagrammed as:

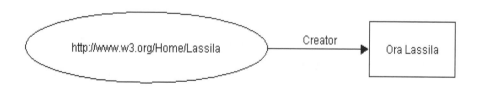

Note: The direction of the arrow is important. The arc always starts at the subject and points to the object of the statement. The simple diagram above may also be read "*http://www.w3.org/Home/Lassila has creator Ora Lassila*", or in general "*<subject> HAS <predicate> <object>*".

Now, consider the case that we want to say something more about the characteristics of the creator of this resource. In prose, such a sentence would be:

The individual whose name is Ora Lassila, email <lassila@w3.org>, is the creator of http://www.w3.org/Home/Lassila.

The intention of this sentence is to make the value of the Creator property a structured entity. In RDF such an entity is represented as another resource. The sentence above does not give a name to that resource; it is anonymous, so in the diagram below we represent it with an empty oval:

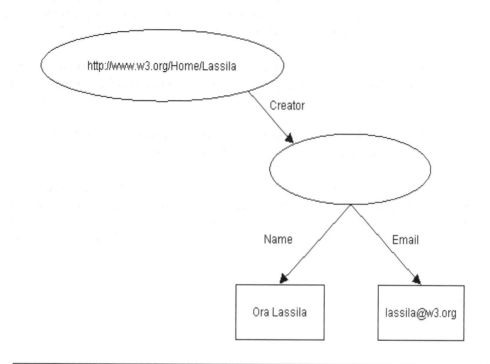

Note: corresponding to the reading in the previous note, this diagram could be read "*http://www.w3.org/Home/Lassila has creator* something *and* something *has name Ora Lassila and email lassila@w3.org*".

The structured entity of the previous example can also be assigned a unique identifier. The choice of identifier is made by the application database designer. To continue the example, imagine that an employee id is used as the unique identifier for a "person" resource. The URIs that serve as the unique keys for each employee (as defined by the organization) might then be something like `http://www.w3.org/staffId/85740`. Now we can write the two sentences:

The individual referred to by employee id 85740 is named Ora Lassila and has the email address lassila@w3.org. The resource http://www.w3.org/Home/Lassila was created by this individual.

The RDF model for these sentences is:

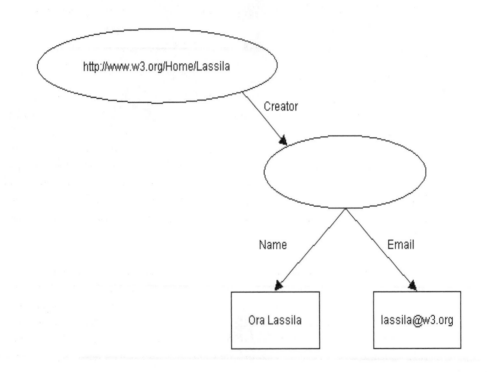

Note that this diagram is identical to the previous one with the addition of the URI for the previously anonymous resource. From the point of view of a second application querying this model, there is no distinction between the statements made in a single sentence and the statements made in separate sentences. Some applications will need to be able to make such a distinction however, and RDF supports this; see Section 4, Statements about Statements, for further details.

2.2. Basic RDF Syntax

The RDF data model provides an abstract, conceptual framework for defining and using metadata. A concrete syntax is also needed for the purposes of creating and exchanging this metadata. This specification of RDF uses the Extensible Markup Language [XML] encoding as its interchange syntax. RDF also requires the XML namespace facility to precisely associate each property with the schema that defines the property; see Section 2.2.3., Schemas and Namespaces.

The syntax descriptions in this document use the Extended Backus-Naur Form notation as defined in Section 6, Notation, of [XML] to describe the essential RDF syntax elements. The EBNF here is condensed for human readability; in particular, the italicized "*rdf*" is used to represent a variable namespace prefix rather than the more precise BNF notation "'<' NSprefix ':...'". The requirement that the property and type names in end-tags exactly match the names in the corresponding start-tags is implied by the XML rules. All syntactic flexibilities of XML are also implicitly included; e.g. whitespace rules, quoting using either single quote (') or double quote ("), character escaping, case sensitivity, and language tagging.

This specification defines two XML syntaxes for encoding an RDF data model instance. The *serialization syntax* expresses the full capabilities of the data model in a very regular fashion. The *abbreviated syntax* includes additional constructs that provide a more compact form to represent a subset of the data model. RDF interpreters are expected to implement both the full serialization syntax and the abbreviated syntax. Consequently, metadata authors are free to mix the two.

2.2.1. Basic Serialization Syntax

A single RDF statement seldom appears in isolation; most commonly several properties of a resource will be given together. The RDF XML syntax has been designed to accomodate this easily by grouping multiple statements for the same resource into a `Description` element. The `Description` element names, in an `about` attribute, the resource to which each of the statements apply. If the resource does not yet exist (i.e., does not yet have a resource identifier) then a `Description` element can supply the identifer for the resource using an `ID` attribute.

Basic RDF serialization syntax takes the form:

```
[ 1]  RDF ::= [ '<rdf:RDF>'] description* [ '</rdf:RDF>']
[ 2]  description ::= '<rdf:Description' idAboutAttr? '>'
propertyElt* '</rdf:Description>'
[ 3]  idAboutAttr ::= idAttr | aboutAttr
[ 4]  aboutAttr ::= 'about="' URI-reference '"'
[ 5]  idAttr ::= 'ID="' IDsymbol '"'
[ 6]  propertyElt ::= '<' propName '>' value '</' prop-
Name '>' | '<' propName resourceAttr '/>'
[ 7]  propName ::= Qname
[ 8]  value ::= description | string
[ 9]  resourceAttr ::= 'resource="' URI-reference '"'
[ 10]  Qname ::= [ NSprefix ':' ] name
[ 11]  URI-reference ::= string, interpreted per [ URI]
[ 12]  IDsymbol ::= (any legal XML name symbol)
[ 13]  name ::= (any legal XML name symbol)
[ 14]  NSprefix ::= (any legal XML namespace prefix)
[ 15]  string ::= (any XML text, with "<", ">", and "&"
escaped)
```

The `RDF` element is a simple wrapper that marks the boundaries in an XML document between which the content is explicitly intended to be mappable into an RDF data model instance. The `RDF` element is optional if the content can be known to be RDF from the application context.

`Description` contains the remaining elements that cause the creation of statements in the model instance. The `Description` element may be thought of (for purposes of the basic RDF syntax) as simply a place to hold the identification of the resource being described. Typically there will be more than one statement made about a resource; `Description` provides a way to give the resource name just once for several statements.

When the `about` attribute is specified with `Description`, the statements in the `Description` refer to the resource whose identifier is determined from the `about`. The value of the `about` attribute is interpreted as a URI-reference per Section 4 of [URI]. The corresponding resource identifier is obtained by resolving the URI-reference to absolute form as specified by [URI]. If a fragment identifier is included in the URI-reference then the resource identifier refers only to the subcomponent of the containing resource that is identifed by the corresponding fragment id internal to that containing resource (see anchor in [Dexter94]), otherwise the identifier refers to the entire resource specified by the URI. A `Description` element without an `about` attribute represents a new resource. Such a resource might be a surrogate, or proxy, for some other physical resource that does not have a recognizable URI. The value of the `ID` attribute of the `Description` element, if present, is the anchor id of this "in-line" resource.

If another `Description` or property value needs to refer to the in-line resource it will use the value of the `ID` of that resource in its own `about` attribute. The `ID` attribute signals the creation of a new resource and the `about` attribute refers to an existing resource; therefore either `ID` or `about` may be specified on `Description` but not both together in the same element. The values for each `ID` attribute must not appear in more than one `ID` attribute within a single document.

A single `Description` may contain more than one *propertyElt* element with the same property name. Each such propertyElt adds one arc to the graph. The interpretation of this graph is defined by the schema designer.

Within a *propertyElt*, the `resource` attribute specifies that some other resource is the value of this property; that is, the object of the statement is another resource identified by URI rather than a literal. The resource identifier of the object is obtained by resolving the `resource` attribute URI-reference in the same manner as given above for the `about` attribute. *Strings* must be well-formed XML; the usual XML content quoting and escaping mechanisms may be used if the string contains character sequences (e.g. "<" and "&") that violate the well-formedness rules or that otherwise might look like markup. See Section 6. for additional syntax to specify a property value with well-formed XML content containing markup such that the markup is not interpreted by RDF.

Property names must be associated with a schema. This can be done by qualifying the element names with a namespace prefix to unambiguously connect the property definition with the corresponding RDF schema or by declaring a default namespace as specified in [NAMESPACES].

The example sentence from Section 2.1.1

Ora Lassila is the creator of the resource http://www.w3.org/Home/Lassila.

is represented in RDF/XML as:

```
<rdf:RDF>
 <rdf:Description about="http://www.w3.org/Home/Lassila">
  <s:Creator>Ora Lassila</s:Creator>
 </rdf:Description>
</rdf:RDF>
```

Here the namespace prefix 's' refers to a specific namespace prefix chosen by the author of this RDF expression and defined in an XML namespace declaration such as:

```
xmlns:s="http://description.org/schema/"
```

This namespace declaration would typically be included as an XML attribute on the `rdf:RDF` element but may also be included with a particular `Description` element or even an individual propertyElt expression. The namespace name URI in the namespace declaration is a globally unique identifier for the particular schema this metadata author is using to define the use of the Creator property. Other schemas may also define a property named Creator and the two properties will be distinguished via their schema identifiers. Note also that a schema usually defines several properties; a single namespace declaration will suffice to make a large vocabulary of properties available for use.

The complete XML document containing the description above would be:

```
<?xml version="1.0"?>
<rdf:RDF
 xmlns:rdf="http://www.w3.org/1999/02/22-rdf-syntax-ns#"
 xmlns:s="http://description.org/schema/">
 <rdf:Description about="http://www.w3.org/Home/Lassila">
  <s:Creator>Ora Lassila</s:Creator>
 </rdf:Description>
</rdf:RDF>
```

Using the default namespace syntax defined in [NAMESPACES] for the RDF namespace itself, this document could also be written as:

```
<?xml version="1.0"?>
<RDF
 xmlns="http://www.w3.org/1999/02/22-rdf-syntax-ns#"
 xmlns:s="http://description.org/schema/">
 <Description about="http://www.w3.org/Home/Lassila">
  <s:Creator>Ora Lassila</s:Creator>
 </Description>
</RDF>
```

Furthermore, namespace declarations can be associated with an individual Description element or even an individual propertyElt element as in:

```
<?xml version="1.0"?>
<RDF xmlns="http://www.w3.org/1999/02/22-rdf-syntax-ns#">
 <Description about="http://www.w3.org/Home/Lassila">
  <s:Creator xmlns:s="http://description.org/schema/">Ora Lassila</s:Creator>
 </Description>
</RDF>
```

As XML namespace declarations may be nested, the previous example may be further condensed to:

```
<?xml version="1.0"?>
<RDF xmlns="http://www.w3.org/1999/02/22-rdf-syntax-ns#">
 <Description about="http://www.w3.org/Home/Lassila">
  <Creator xmlns="http://description.org/schema/">Ora Lassila</Creator>
 </Description>
</RDF>
```

Highly condensed expressions such as this are discouraged, however, when the RDF/XML encoding is written by hand or expected to be edited in a plain text editor. Though unambiguous, the possibility of error is greater than if explicit prefixes are used consistently. Note that an RDF/XML fragment that is intended to be inserted in other documents should declare all the namespaces it uses so that it is completely self-contained. For readability, the introductory examples in the remainder of this section omit the namespace declarations in order to not obscure the specific points being illustrated.

2.2.2. Basic Abbreviated Syntax

While the serialization syntax shows the structure of an RDF model most clearly, often it is desirable to use a more compact XML form. The RDF *abbreviated syntax* accomplishes this. As a further benefit, the abbreviated syntax allows documents obeying certain well-structured XML DTDs to be directly interpreted as RDF models.

Three forms of abbreviation are defined for the basic serialization syntax. The first is usable for properties that are not repeated within a `Description` and where the values of those properties are literals. In this case, the properties may be written as XML attributes of the `Description` element. The previous example then becomes:

```
<rdf:RDF>
 <rdf:Description about="http://www.w3.org/Home/Lassila"
 s:Creator="Ora Lassila" />
</rdf:RDF>
```

Note that since the `Description` element has no other content once the Creator property is written in XML attribute form, the XML empty element syntax is employed to elide the `Description` end-tag.

Here is another example of the use of this same abbreviation form:

```
<rdf:RDF>
 <rdf:Description about="http://www.w3.org">
  <s:Publisher>World Wide Web Consortium</s:Publisher>
  <s:Title>W3C Home Page</s:Title>
  <s:Date>1998-10-03T02:27</s:Date>
 </rdf:Description>
</rdf:RDF>
```

is equivalent for RDF purposes to

```
<rdf:RDF>
 <rdf:Description about="http://www.w3.org"
     s:Publisher="World Wide Web Consortium"
     s:Title="W3C Home Page"
     s:Date="1998-10-03T02:27"/>
</rdf:RDF>
```

Note that while these two RDF expressions are equivalent, they may be treated differently by other processing engines. In particular, if these two expressions were embedded into an HTML document then the default behavior of a non-RDF-aware browser would be to display the values of the properties in the first case while in the second case there should be no text displayed (or at most a whitespace character).

The second RDF abbreviation form works on nested `Description` elements. This abbreviation form can be employed for specific statements when the object of the statement is another resource and the values of any properties given in-line for this second resource are strings. In this case, a similar transformation of XML element names into XML attributes is used: the properties of the resource in the nested `Description` may be written as XML attributes of the propertyElt element in which that `Description` was contained.

The second example sentence from Section 2.1.1

The individual referred to by employee id 85740 is named Ora Lassila and has the email address lassila@w3.org. The resource ht-tp://www.w3.org/Home/Lassila was created by this individual.

is written in RDF/XML using explicit serialization form as

```
<rdf:RDF>
 <rdf:Description about="http://www.w3.org/Home/Lassila">
  <s:Creator rdf:resource="http://www.w3.org/staffId/85740"/>
 </rdf:Description>

 <rdf:Description about="http://www.w3.org/staffId/85740">
  <v:Name>Ora Lassila</v:Name>
  <v:Email>lassila@w3.org</v:Email>
 </rdf:Description>
</rdf:RDF>
```

This form makes it clear to a reader that two separate resources are being described but it is less clear that the second resource is used within the first description. This same expression could be written in the following way to make this relationship more obvious to the human reader. Note that to the machine, there is no difference:

```
<rdf:RDF>
 <rdf:Description about="http://www.w3.org/Home/Lassila">
  <s:Creator>
   <rdf:Description about="http://www.w3.org/staffId/85740">
<v:Name>Ora Lassila</v:Name>
<v:Email>lassila@w3.org</v:Email>
   </rdf:Description>
  </s:Creator>
 </rdf:Description>
</rdf:RDF>
```

Using the second basic abbreviation syntax, the inner `Description` element and its contained property expressions can be written as attributes of the Creator element:

```
<rdf:RDF>
 <rdf:Description about="http://www.w3.org/Home/Lassila">
  <s:Creator rdf:resource="http://www.w3.org/staffId/85740"
    v:Name="Ora Lassila"
    v:Email="lassila@w3.org" />
 </rdf:Description>
</rdf:RDF>
```

When using this abbreviation form the `about` attribute of the nested `Description` element becomes a `resource` attribute on the propertyElt element, as the resource named by the URI is in both cases the value of the Creator property. It is entirely a matter of writer's preference which of the three forms above are used in the RDF source. They all produce the same internal RDF models.

Note: The observant reader who has studied the remainder of this document will see that there are some additional relationships represented by a `Description` *element to preserve the specific syntactic grouping of statements. Consequently the three forms above are slightly different in ways not important to the discussion in this section. These differences become important only when making higher-order statements as described in Section 4.*

The third basic abbreviation applies to the common case of a `Description` element containing a `type` property (see Section 4.1 for the meaning of `type`). In this case, the resource type defined in the schema corresponding to the value of the `type` property can be used directly as an element name. For example, using the previous RDF fragment if we wanted to add the fact that the resource http://www.w3.org/staffId/85740 represents an instance of a Person, we would write this in full serialization syntax as:

```
<rdf:RDF
  xmlns:rdf="http://www.w3.org/1999/02/22-rdf-syntax-ns#"
  xmlns:s="http://description.org/schema/">
  <rdf:Description about="http://www.w3.org/Home/Lassila">
   <s:Creator>
    <rdf:Description about="http://www.w3.org/staffId/85740">
<rdf:type resource="http://description.org/schema/Person"/>
<v:Name>Ora Lassila</v:Name>
```

```
<v:Email>lassila@w3.org</v:Email>
    </rdf:Description>
   </s:Creator>
  </rdf:Description>
 </rdf:RDF>
```

and using this third abbreviated form as:

```
<rdf:RDF>
 <rdf:Description about="http://www.w3.org/Home/Lassila">
  <s:Creator>
   <s:Person about="http://www.w3.org/staffId/85740">
<v:Name>Ora Lassila</v:Name>
<v:Email>lassila@w3.org</v:Email>
   </s:Person>
  </s:Creator>
 </rdf:Description>
</rdf:RDF>
```

The EBNF for the basic abbreviated syntax replaces productions [2] and [6] of the grammar for the basic serialization syntax in the following manner:

```
[ 2a]  description ::= '<rdf:Description' idAboutAttr?
propAttr* '/>' | '<rdf:Description' idAboutAttr? pro-
pAttr* '>' propertyElt* '</rdf:Description>' | typedN-
ode
[ 6a]  propertyElt ::= '<' propName '>' value '</' prop-
Name '>' | '<' propName resourceAttr? propAttr* '/>'
[ 16]  propAttr ::= propName '="' string '"' (with embed-
ded quotes escaped)
[ 17]  typedNode ::= '<' typeName idAboutAttr? propAttr*
'/>' | '<' typeName idAboutAttr? propAttr* '>' proper-
ty* '</' typeName '>'
```

2.2.3. Schemas and Namespaces

When we write a sentence in natural language we use words that are meant to convey a certain meaning. That meaning is crucial to understanding the statements and, in the case of applications of RDF, is crucial to establishing that the correct processing occurs as intended. It is crucial that *both* the writer and the reader of a statement understand the same meaning for the terms used, such as Creator, approvedBy, Copyright, etc. or confusion will result. In a medium of global scale such as the World Wide Web it is not sufficient to rely on shared cultural understanding of concepts such as "creatorship"; it pays to be as precise as possible.

Meaning in RDF is expressed through reference to a *schema*. You can think of a schema as a kind of dictionary. A schema defines the terms that will be used in RDF statements and gives specific meanings to them. A variety of schema forms can be used with RDF, including a specific form defined in a separate document [RDFSchema] that has some specific characteristics to help with automating tasks using RDF.

A schema is the place where definitions and restrictions of usage for properties are documented. In order to avoid confusion between independent — and possibly conflicting — definitions of the same term, RDF uses the XML namespace facility. Namespaces are simply a way to tie a specific use of a word in context to the dictionary (schema) where the intended definition is to be found. In RDF, each predicate used in a statement must be identified with exactly one namespace, or schema. However, a `Description` element may contain statements with predicates from many schemas. Examples of RDF Descriptions that use more than one schema appear in Section 7.

2.3. Qualified Property Values

Often the value of a property is something that has additional contextual information that is considered "part of" that value. In other words, there is a need to qualify property values. Examples of such qualification include naming a unit of measure, a particular restricted vocabulary, or some other annotation. For some uses it is appropriate to use the property value without the qualifiers. For example, in the statement "the price of that pencil is 75 U.S. cents" it is often sufficient to say simply "the price of that pencil is 75".

In the RDF model a qualified property value is simply another instance of a structured value. The object of the original statement is this structured value and the qualifiers are further properties of this common resource. The principal value being qualified is given as the value of the *value* property of this common resource. See Section 7.3. Non-Binary Relations for an example of the use of the *value* property.

3. Containers

Frequently it is necessary to refer to a collection of resources; for example, to say that a work was created by more than one person, or to list the students in a course, or the software modules in a package. RDF containers are used to hold such lists of resources or literals.

3.1. Container Model

RDF defines three types of container objects:

Bag	An unordered list of resources or literals. *Bags* are used to declare that a property has multiple values and that there is no significance to the order in which the values are given. *Bag* might be used to give a list of part numbers where the order of processing the parts does not matter. Duplicate values are permitted.
Sequence	An ordered list of resources or literals. *Sequence* is used to declare that a property has multiple values and that the order of the values is significant. *Sequence* might be used, for example, to preserve an alphabetical ordering of values. Duplicate values are permitted.
Alternative	A list of resources or literals that represent alternatives for the (single) value of a property. *Alternative* might be used to provide alternative language translations for the title of a work, or to provide a list of Internet mirror sites at which a resource might be found. An application using a property whose value is an *Alternative* collection is aware that it can choose any one of the items in the list as appropriate.

Note: The definitions of Bag and Sequence explicitly permit duplicate values. RDF does not define a core concept of Set, which would be a Bag with no duplicates, because the RDF core does not mandate an enforcement mechanism in the event of violations of such constraints. Future work layered on the RDF core may define such facilities.

To represent a collection of resources, RDF uses an additional resource that identifies the specific collection (an *instance* of a collection, in object modeling terminology). This resource must be declared to be an instance of one of the container object types defined above. The *type* property, defined below, is used to make this declaration. The membership relation between this container resource and the resources that belong in the collection is defined by a set of properties defined expressly for this purpose. These membership properties are named simply "_1", "_2", "_3", etc. Container resources may have other properties in addition to the membership properties and the *type* property. Any such additional statements describe the container; see Section 3.3, Distributive Referents, for discussion of statements about each of the members themselves.

A common use of containers is as the value of a property. When used in this way, the statement still has a single statement object regardless of the number of members in the container; the container resource itself is the object of the statement.

For example, to represent the sentence

The students in course 6.001 are Amy, Tim, John, Mary, and Sue.

the RDF model is

Bag containers are not equivalent to repeated properties of the same type; see Section 3.5. for a discussion of the difference. Authors will need to decide on a case-by-case basis which one (repeated property statement or Bag) is more appropriate to use.

The sentence

The source code for X11 may be found at ftp.x.org, ftp.cs.purdue.edu, or ftp.eu.net.

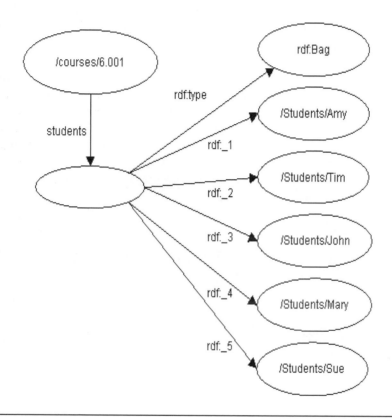

is modeled in RDF as

Alternative containers are frequently used in conjunction with language tagging. A work whose title has been translated into several languages might have its Title property pointing to an Alternative container holding each of the language variants.

3.2. Container Syntax

RDF container syntax takes the form:

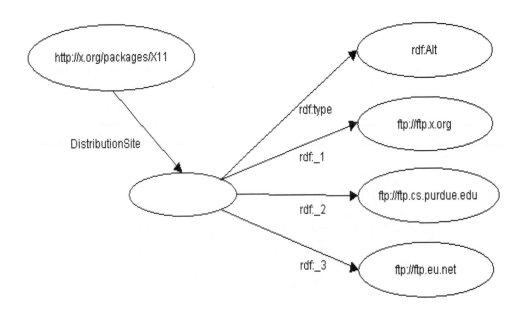

```
[18]  container ::= sequence | bag | alternative
[19]  sequence  ::=  '<rdf:Seq' idAttr?  '>'  member*
'</rdf:Seq>'
[20]  bag   ::=   '<rdf:Bag'  idAttr?   '>'   member*
'</rdf:Bag>'
[21]  alternative ::= '<rdf:Alt' idAttr? '>' member+
'</rdf:Alt>'
[22]  member ::= referencedItem | inlineItem
[23]  referencedItem ::= '<rdf:li' resourceAttr '/>'
[24]  inlineItem ::= '<rdf:li>' value '</rdf:li>'
```

Containers may be used everywhere a Description is permitted:

```
[ 1a]  RDF ::= '<rdf:RDF>' obj* '</rdf:RDF>'
[ 8a]  value ::= obj | string
[ 25]  obj ::= description | container
```

Note that RDF/XML uses `li` as a convenience element to avoid having to explicitly number each member. The `li` element assigns the properties _1, _2, and so on as necessary. The element name `li` was chosen to be mnemonic with the term "list item" from HTML.

An `Alt` container is required to have at least one member. This member will be identified by the property _1 and is the default or preferred value.

Note: The RDF Schema specification [RDFSCHEMA] also defines a mechanism to declare additional subclasses of these container types, in which case production [18] is extended to include the names of those declared subclasses. There is also a syntax for writing literal values in attribute form; see the full grammar in Section 6.

3.2.1. Examples

The model for the sentence

The students in course 6.001 are Amy, Tim, John, Mary, and Sue.

is written in RDF/XML as

```
<rdf:RDF>
  <rdf:Description about="http://mycollege.edu/courses/6.001">
    <s:students>
      <rdf:Bag>
<rdf:li resource="http://mycollege.edu/students/Amy"/>
<rdf:li resource="http://mycollege.edu/students/Tim"/>
<rdf:li resource="http://mycollege.edu/students/John"/>
<rdf:li resource="http://mycollege.edu/students/Mary"/>
<rdf:li resource="http://mycollege.edu/students/Sue"/>
      </rdf:Bag>
    </s:students>
  </rdf:Description>
</rdf:RDF>
```

In this case, since the value of the students property is expressed as a Bag there is no significance to the order given here for the URIs of each student.

The model for the sentence

The source code for X11 may be found at ftp.x.org, ftp.cs.purdue.edu, or ftp.eu.net.

is written in RDF/XML as

```
<rdf:RDF>
  <rdf:Description about="http://x.org/packages/X11">
    <s:DistributionSite>
      <rdf:Alt>
<rdf:li resource="ftp://ftp.x.org"/>
<rdf:li resource="ftp://ftp.cs.purdue.edu"/>
<rdf:li resource="ftp://ftp.eu.net"/>
      </rdf:Alt>
    </s:DistributionSite>
  </rdf:Description>
</rdf:RDF>
```

Here, any one of the items listed in the container value for DistributionSite is an acceptable value without regard to the other items.

3.3. Distributive Referents: Statements about Members of a Container

Container structures give rise to an issue about statements: when a statement is made referring to a collection, what "thing" is the statement describing? Or in other words, to what object is the statement is referring? Is the statement describing the container itself or is the statement describing the members of the container? The object being described (in the XML syntax indicated by the `about` attribute) is in RDF called the *referent*.

The following example:

```
<rdf:Bag ID="pages">
  <rdf:li resource="http://foo.org/foo.html" />
  <rdf:li resource="http://bar.org/bar.html" />
</rdf:Bag>

<rdf:Description about="#pages">
  <s:Creator>Ora Lassila</s:Creator>
</rdf:Description>
```

expresses that "Ora Lassila" is the creator of the Bag "pages". It does not, however, say anything about the individual pages, the members of the Bag. The referent of the `Description` is the container (the Bag), not its members. One would sometimes like to write a statement about each of the contained objects individually, instead of the container itself. In order to express that "Ora Lassila" is the creator of each of the pages, a different kind of referent is called for, one that *distributes* over the members of the container. This referent in RDF is expressed using the `aboutEach` attribute:

```
[ 3a]  idAboutAttr ::= idAttr | aboutAttr | aboutEachAttr
[ 26]  aboutEachAttr ::= 'aboutEach="' URI-reference '"'
```

As an example, if we wrote

```
<rdf:Description aboutEach="#pages">
  <s:Creator>Ora Lassila</s:Creator>
</rdf:Description>
```

we would get the desired meaning. We will call the new referent type a *distributive referent*. Distributive referents allow us to "share structure" in an RDF `Description`. For example, when writing several `Descriptions` that all have a number of common statement parts (predicates and objects), the common parts can be shared among all the `Descriptions`, possibly resulting in space savings and more maintainable metadata. The value of an `aboutEach` attribute must be a container. Using a distributive referent on a container is the same as making all the statements about each of the members separately.

No explicit graph representation of distributive referents is defined. Instead, in terms of the statements made, distributive referents are expanded into the individual statements about the individual container members (internally, implementations are free to retain information about the distributive referents - in order to save space, for example - as long as any querying functions work as if all of the statements were made individually). Thus, with respect to the resources "foo" and "bar", the above example is equivalent to

```
<rdf:Description about="http://foo.org/foo.html">
  <s:Creator>Ora Lassila</s:Creator>
</rdf:Description>
```

```
<rdf:Description about="http://bar.org/bar.html">
 <s:Creator>Ora Lassila</s:Creator>
</rdf:Description>
```

3.4. Containers Defined By A URI Pattern

One very frequent use of metadata is to make statements about "all pages at my Web site", or "all pages in this branch of my Web site". In many cases it is impractical or even undesirable to try to list each such resource explicitly and identify it as a member of a container. RDF therefore has a second distributive referent type. This second distributive referent type is a shorthand syntax that represents an instance of a Bag whose members are by definition all resources whose resource identifiers begin with a specified string:

```
[ 26a]  aboutEachAttr  ::= 'aboutEach="' URI-reference
'"' | 'aboutEachPrefix="' string '"'
```

The `aboutEachPrefix` attribute declares that there is a Bag whose members are all the resources whose fully resolved resource identifiers begin with the character string given as the value of the attribute. The statements in a `Description` that has the `aboutEachPrefix` attribute apply individually to each of the members of this Bag.

For example, if the two resources http://foo.org/doc/page1 and http://foo.org/doc/page2 exist then we can say that each of them has a copyright property by writing

```
<rdf:Description aboutEachPrefix="http://foo.org/doc">
 <s:Copyright>© 1998, The Foo Organization</s:Copyright>
</rdf:Description>
```

If these are the only two resources whose URIs start with that string then the above is equivalent to both of the following alternatives:

```
<rdf:Description about="http://foo.org/doc/page1">
 <s:Copyright>© 1998, The Foo Organization</s:Copyright>
</rdf:Description>
<rdf:Description about="http://foo.org/doc/page2">
 <s:Copyright>© 1998, The Foo Organization</s:Copyright>
</rdf:Description>
```

and

```
<rdf:Description aboutEach="#docpages">
  <s:Copyright>© 1998, The Foo Organization</s:Copyright>
</rdf:Description>
<rdf:Bag ID="docpages">
  <rdf:li resource="http://foo.org/doc/page1"/>
  <rdf:li resource="http://foo.org/doc/page2"/>
</rdf:Bag>
```

3.5. Containers Versus Repeated Properties

A resource may have multiple statements with the same predicate (i.e., using the same property). This is not the same as having a single statement whose object is a container containing multiple members. The choice of which to use in any particular circumstance is in part made by the person who designs the schema and in part made by the person who writes the specific RDF statements.

Consider as an example the relationship between a writer and her publications. We might have the sentence

Sue has written "Anthology of Time", "Zoological Reasoning", "Gravitational Reflections".

That is, there are three resources each of which was written independently by the same writer.

In this example there is no stated relationship between the publications other than that they were written by the same person.

On the other hand, the sentence

The committee of Fred, Wilma, and Dino approved the resolution.

says that the three committee members as a whole voted in a certain manner; it does not necessarily state that each committee member voted in favor of the article. It would be incorrect to model this sentence as three separate approvedBy statements, one for each committee member, as this

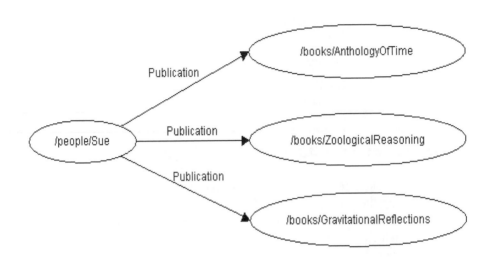

would state the vote of each individual member. Rather, it is better to model this as a single approvedBy statement whose object is a Bag containing the committee members' identities:

The choice of which representation to use, Bag or repeated property, is made by the person creating the metadata after considering the schema. If, for example, in the publications example above we wished to say that those were the complete set of publications then the schema might include a property called *publications* for that purpose. The value of the *publications* property would be a Bag listing all of Sue's works.

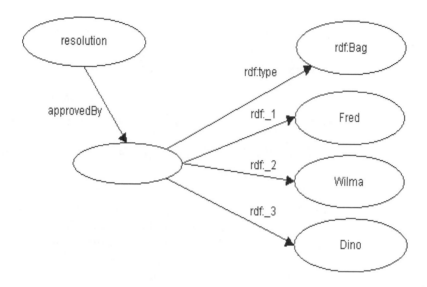

4. Statements about Statements

In addition to making statements about Web resources, RDF can be used for making statements about other RDF statements; we will refer to these as *higher-order statements*. In order to make a statement about another statement, we actually have to build a model of the original statement; this model is a new resource to which we can attach additional properties.

4.1. Modeling Statements

Statements are made about resources. A model of a statement is the resource we need in order to be able to make new statements (higher-order statements) about the modeled statement.

For example, let us consider the sentence

Ora Lassila is the creator of the resource http://www.w3.org/Home/Lassila.

RDF would regard this sentence as a fact. If, instead, we write the sentence

Ralph Swick says that Ora Lassila is the creator of the resource http://www.w3.org/Home/Lassila.

we have said nothing about the resource http://www.w3.org/Home/Lassila; instead, we have expressed a fact about a statement Ralph has made. In order to express this fact to RDF, we have to model the original statement as a resource with four properties. This process is formally called reification in the Knowledge Representation community. A model of a statement is called a *reified statement*.

To model statements RDF defines the following properties:

subject	The *subject* property identifies the resource being described by the modeled statement; that is, the value of the *subject* property is the resource about which the original statement was made (in our example, http://www.w3.org/Home/Lassila).
predicate	The *predicate* property identifies the original property in the modeled statement. The value of the *predicate* property is a resource representing the specific property in the original statement (in our example, creator).

object	The *object* property identifies the property value in the modeled statement. The value of the *object* property is the object in the original statement (in our example, "Ora Lassila").
type	The value of the *type* property describes the type of the new resource. All reified statements are instances of RDF:Statement; that is, they have a *type* property whose object is RDF:Statement. The *type* property is also used more generally to declare the type of any resource, as was shown in Section 3, "Containers".

A new resource with the above four properties represents the original statement and can both be used as the object of other statements and have additional statements made about it. The resource with these four properties is not a replacement for the original statement, it is a model of the statement. A statement and its corresponding reified statement exist independently in an RDF graph and either may be present without the other. The RDF graph is said to contain the fact given in the statement if and only if the statement is present in the graph, irrespective of whether the corresponding reified statement is present.

To model the example above, we could attach another property to the reified statement (say, "attributedTo") with an appropriate value (in this case, "Ralph Swick"). Using base-level RDF/XML syntax, this could be written as

```
<rdf:RDF
  xmlns:rdf="http://www.w3.org/1999/02/22-rdf-syntax-ns#"
  xmlns:a="http://description.org/schema/">
  <rdf:Description>
   <rdf:subject resource="http://www.w3.org/Home/Lassila" />
   <rdf:predicate resource="http://description.org/schema/Creator" />
   <rdf:object>Ora Lassila</rdf:object>
```

```
    <rdf:type resource="http://www.w3.org/1999/02/22-rdf-syntax-ns#Statement" />
    <a:attributedTo>Ralph Swick</a:attributedTo>
    </rdf:Description>
</rdf:RDF>
```

Figure 8 represents this in graph form. Syntactically this is rather verbose; in Section 4.2. we present a shorthand for making statements about statements.

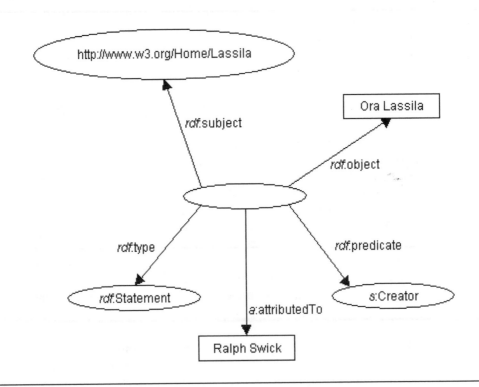

Reification is also needed to represent explicitly in the model the statement grouping implied by Description elements. The RDF graph model does not need a special construct for Descriptions; since Descriptions really are collections of statements, a Bag container is used to indicate that a set of statements came from the same (syntactic) Description. Each statement within a `Description` is reified and each of the reified statements is a member of the Bag representing that `Description`. As an example, the RDF fragment

```
<rdf:RDF>
 <rdf:Description about="http://www.w3.org/Home/Lassila" bagID="D_001">
  <s:Creator>Ora Lassila</s:Creator>
  <s:Title>Ora's Home Page</s:Title>
 </rdf:Description>
</rdf:RDF>
```

would result in the graph shown in Figure 9.

Note the new attribute `bagID`. This attribute specifies the resource id of the container resource:

```
[ 2b]  description  ::=  '<rdf:Description' idAboutAttr?
bagIDAttr? propAttr* '/>' | '<rdf:Description' idAbou-
tAttr? bagIDAttr? propAttr* '>' propertyElt* '</rdf:De-
scription>'
[ 27]  bagIDAttr ::= 'bagID="' IDsymbol '"'
```

`BagID` and `ID` should not be confused. `ID` specifies the identification of an in-line resource whose properties are further detailed in the Description. `BagID` specifies the identification of the container resource whose members are the reified statements about another resource. A `Description` may have both an `ID` attribute and a `bagID` attribute.

4.2. Syntactic Shorthand for Statements About Statements

Since attaching a `bagID` to a `Description` results in including in the model a Bag of the reified statements of the `Description`, we can use this as a syntactic shorthand when making statements about statements. For example, if we wanted to say that Ralph states that Ora is the creator of http://www.w3.org/Home/Lassila and that he also states that the title of that resource is "Ora's Home Page", we can simply add to the example above

```
<rdf:Description aboutEach="#D_001">
 <a:attributedTo>Ralph Swick</a:attributedTo>
</rdf:Description>
```

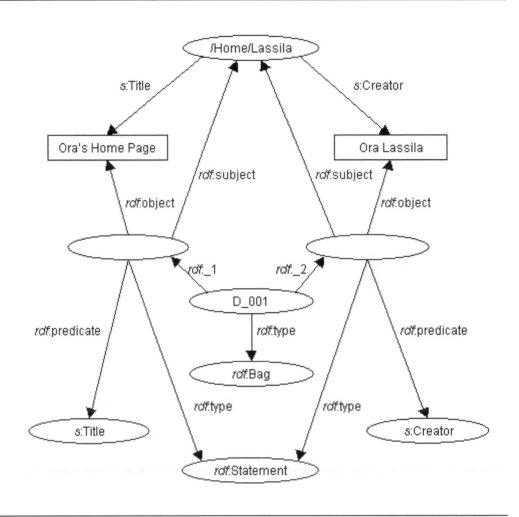

Note that this shorthand example includes additional facts in the model not represented by the example in Figure 8. This shorthand usage expresses facts about Ralph's statements and also facts about Ora's home page.

The reader is referred to Section 5 ("Formal Model") of this specification for a more formal treatment of higher-order statements and reification.

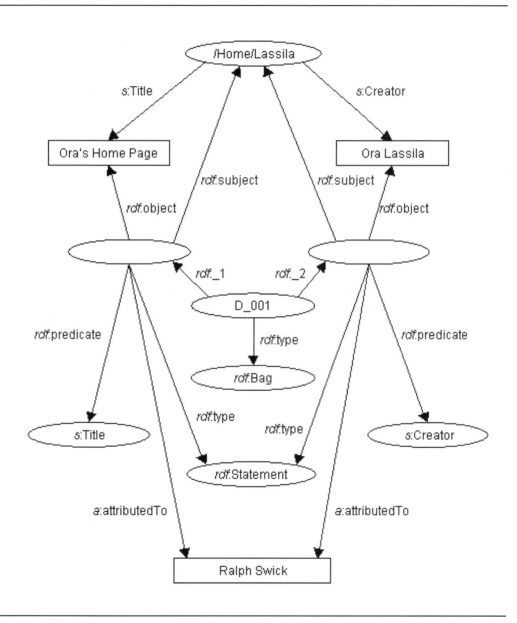

5. Formal Model for RDF

This specification shows three representations of the data model; as 3-tuples (triples), as a graph, and in XML. These representations have equivalent meaning. The mapping between the representations used in this specification is not intended to constrain in any way the internal representation used by implementations.

The RDF data model is defined formally as follows:

1. There is a set called *Resources*.
2. There is a set called *Literals*.
3. There is a subset of *Resources* called *Properties*.
4. There is a set called *Statements*, each element of which is a triple of the form
{pred, sub, obj}
Where pred is a property (member of Properties), sub is a resource (member of Resources), and obj is either a resource or a literal (member of Literals).

We can view a set of statements (members of *Statements*) as a directed labeled graph: each resource and literal is a vertex; a triple {p, s, o} is an arc from s to o, labeled by p. This is illustrated in figure 11.

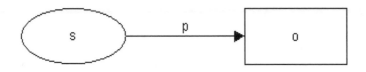

: S

This can be read either

o is the value of p for s

or (left to right)

s has a property p with a value o

or even

the p of s is o

For example, the sentence

Ora Lassila is the creator of the resource http://www.w3.org/Home/Lassila

would be represented graphically as follows:

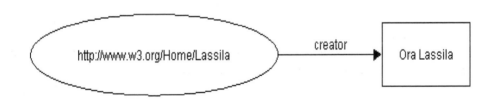

and the corresponding triple (member of *Statements*) would be

{creator, [http://www.w3.org/Home/Lassila], "Ora Lassila"}

The notation [*I*] denotes the resource identified by the URI *I* and quotation marks denote a literal.

Using the triples, we can explain how statements are reified (as introduced in Section 4). Given a statement {creator, [http://www.w3.org/Home/Lassila], "Ora Lassila"}

we can express the reification of this as a new resource X as follows:

{type, [X], [RDF:Statement]}
{predicate, [X], [creator]}
{subject, [X], [http://www.w3.org/Home/Lassila]}
{object, [X], "Ora Lassila"}

From the standpoint of an RDF processor, facts (that is, statements) are triples that are members of *Statements*. Therefore, the original statement remains a fact despite it being reified since the triple representing the original statement remains in *Statements*. We have merely added four more triples.

The property named "type" is defined to provide primitive typing. The formal definition of type is:

---

5. There is an element of *Properties* known as RDF:type.
6. Members of *Statements* of the form {RDF:type, sub, obj} must satisfy the following: sub and obj are members of *Resources*. [RDFSchema] places additional restrictions on the use of type.

Furthermore, the formal specification of reification is:

The resource r in the definition above is called the *reified statement*. When a resource represents a reified statement; that is, it has an RDF:type property with a value of RDF:Statement, then that resource must have exactly one RDF:subject property, one RDF:object property, and one RDF:predicate property.

As described in Section 3, it is frequently necessary to represent a collection of resources or literals; for example to state that a property has an ordered sequence of values. RDF defines three kinds of collections: ordered lists, called *Sequences*, unordered lists, called *Bags*, and lists that represent alternatives for the (single) value of a property, called *Alternatives*.

7. There is and element of *Resources*, not contained in *Properties*, known as RDF:Statement.

8. There are three elements in *Properties* known as RDF:predicate, RDF:subject and RDF: object.

9. Reification of a triple {pred, sub, obj} of *Statements* is an element r of *Resources* representing the reified triple and the elements s_1, s_2, s_3, and s_4 of *Statements* such that

s_1: {RDF:predicate, r, pred}
s_2: {RDF:subject, r, subj}
s_3: {RDF:object, r, obj}
s_4: {RDF:type, r, [RDF:Statement]}

Formally, these three collection types are defined by:

10. There are three elements of *Resources*, not contained in *Properties*, known as RDF:Seq, RDF:Bag, and RDF:Alt.

11. There is a subset of *Properties* corresponding to the ordinals (1, 2, 3, ...) called *Ord*. We refer to elements of *Ord* as RDF:_1, RDF:_2, RDF:_3, ...

To represent a collection *c,* create a triple {RDF:type, *c, t}* where *t* is one of the three collection types RDF:Seq, RDF:Bag, or RDF:Alt. The remaining triples {RDF:_1, *c, r_1*}, ..., {RDF:_n, *c, r_n*}, ... point to each of the members r_n of the collection. For a single collection resource there may be at most one triple whose predicate is any given element of *Ord* and the elements of *Ord* must be used in sequence starting with RDF:_1. For resources that are instances of the RDF:Alt collection type, there must be exactly one triple whose predicate is RDF:_1 and that is the default value for the Alternatives resource (that is, there must always be at least one alternative).

6. Formal Grammar for RDF

The complete BNF for RDF is reproduced here from previous sections. The precise interpretation of the grammar in terms of the formal model is also given. Syntactic features inherited from XML are not reproduced here. These include all well-formedness constraints, the use of whitespace around attributes and the '=', as well as the use of either double or single quotes around attribute values. This section is intended for implementors who are building tools that read and interpret RDF/XML syntax.

Where used below, the keywords "SHOULD", "MUST", and "MUST NOT" are to be interpreted as described in RFC 2119 [RFC2119]. However, for readability, these words do not appear in all uppercase letters in this specification.

```
[ 6.1]   RDF                        ::= [ '<rdf:RDF>'] obj*
[ '</rdf:RDF>']
[ 6.2]  obj            ::= description | container
[ 6.3]  description    ::= '<rdf:Description' idAboutAt-
tr? bagIdAttr? propAttr* '/>'| '<rdf:Description' id-
AboutAttr?   bagIdAttr?   propAttr*   '>'   propertyElt*
'</rdf:Description>' | typedNode
[ 6.4]  container      ::= sequence | bag | alternative
[ 6.5]   idAboutAttr        ::=   idAttr  |  aboutAttr  |
aboutEachAttr
[ 6.6]  idAttr         ::= ' ID="' IDsymbol '"'
[ 6.7]  aboutAttr      ::= ' about="' URI-reference '"'
[ 6.8]  aboutEachAttr  ::= ' aboutEach="' URI-reference
'"' |  ' aboutEachPrefix="' string '"'
[ 6.9]  bagIdAttr      ::= ' bagID="' IDsymbol '"'

[ 6.10] propAttr       ::= typeAttr | propName '="' string
'"' (with embedded quotes escaped)
[ 6.11] typeAttr       ::= ' type="' URI-reference '"'
[ 6.12] propertyElt    ::= '<' propName idAttr? '>' value
'</' propName '>' | '<' propName idAttr? parseLiteral
'>' literal '</' propName '>' | '<' propName idAttr?
parseResource '>' propertyElt* '</' propName '>' | '<'
propName idRefAttr? bagIdAttr? propAttr* '/>'
[ 6.13] typedNode           ::= '<' typeName idAboutAttr?
```

```
                bagIdAttr? propAttr* '/>' | '<' typeName idAboutAttr?
                bagIdAttr? propAttr* '>' propertyElt* '</' typeName '>'
[ 6.14]  propName          ::= Qname
[ 6.15]  typeName          ::= Qname
[ 6.16]  idRefAttr         ::= idAttr | resourceAttr
[ 6.17]  value             ::= obj | string
[ 6.18]  resourceAttr      ::= ' resource="' URI-reference
'"'
[ 6.19]  Qname             ::= [ NSprefix ':' ] name
[ 6.20]  URI-reference     ::= string, interpreted per [ URI]
[ 6.21]  IDsymbol          ::= (any legal XML name symbol)
[ 6.22]  name              ::= (any legal XML name symbol)
[ 6.23]  NSprefix          ::= (any legal XML namespace pre-
fix)
[ 6.24]  string            ::= (any XML text, with "<", ">",
and "&" escaped)
[ 6.25]  sequence          ::= '<rdf:Seq' idAttr? '>' member*
'</rdf:Seq>'| '<rdf:Seq' idAttr? memberAttr* '/>'
[ 6.26]  bag               ::= '<rdf:Bag' idAttr? '>' member*
'</rdf:Bag>' | '<rdf:Bag' idAttr? memberAttr* '/>'
[ 6.27]  alternative       ::= '<rdf:Alt' idAttr? '>' member+
'</rdf:Alt>' | '<rdf:Alt' idAttr? memberAttr? '/>'
[ 6.28]  member            ::= referencedItem | inlineItem
[ 6.29]  referencedItem    ::= '<rdf:li' resourceAttr '/>'
[ 6.30]  inlineItem        ::= '<rdf:li' '>' value </rdf:li>'
| '<rdf:li' parseLiteral '>' literal </rdf:li>' |
'<rdf:li' parseResource '>' propertyElt* </rdf:li>'
[ 6.31]  memberAttr        ::= ' rdf:_n="' string '"' (where
n is an integer)
[ 6.32]  parseLiteral      ::= ' parseType="Literal"'
[ 6.33]  parseResource     ::= ' parseType="Resource"'
[ 6.34]  literal           ::= (any well-formed XML)
```

The formal namespace name for the properties and classes defined in this specification is http://www.w3.org/1999/02/22-rdf-syntax-ns#. When an RDF processor encounters an XML element or attribute name that is declared to be from a namespace whose name begins with the string "http://www.w3.org/TR/REC-rdf-syntax" and the processor does not recognize the semantics of that name then the processor is required to skip (i.e., generate no tuples for) the entire XML element, including its content, whose name is unrecognized or that has an attribute whose name is unrecognized.

Each propertyElt *E* contained by a `Description` element results in the creation of a triple {p,r,v} where:

1. p is the expansion of the namespace-qualified tag name (Generic Identifier) of E. This expansion is generated by concatenating the namespace name given in the namespace declaration with the LocalPart of the qualified name.

2. r is

   ♦ the resource whose identifier is given by the value of the `about` attribute of the `Description` or
   ♦ a new resource whose identifier is the value of the `ID` attribute of the `Description`, if present; else the new resource has no identifier.

3. If *E* is an empty element (no content), v is the resource whose identifier is given by the `resource` attribute of *E*. If the content of *E* contains no XML markup or if `parseType="Literal"` is specified in the start tag of *E* then v is the content of *E* (a literal). Otherwise, the content of *E* must be another `Description` or container and v is the resource named by the (possibly implicit) `ID` or `about` of that `Description` or container.

The `parseType` attribute changes the interpretation of the element content. The `parseType` attribute should have one of the values 'Literal' or 'Resource'. The value is case-sensitive. The value 'Literal' specifies that the element content is to be treated as an RDF/XML literal; that is, the content must not be interpreted by an RDF processor. The value 'Resource' specifies that the element content must be treated as if it were the content of a `Description` element. Other values of `parseType` are reserved for future specification by RDF. With RDF 1.0 other values must be treated as identical to 'Literal'. In all cases, the content of an element having a `parseType` attribute must be well-formed XML. The content of an element having a `parseType="Resource"` attribute must further match the production for the content of a `Description` element.

The RDF Model and Syntax Working Group acknowledges that the parse-Type='Literal' mechanism is a minimum-level solution to the requirement to express an RDF statement with a value that has XML markup. Additional complexities of XML such as canonicalization of whitespace are not yet well defined. Future work of the W3C is expected to resolve such issues in a uniform manner for all applications based on XML. Future versions of RDF will inherit this work and may extend it as we gain insight from further application experience.

URI-References are resolved to resource identifiers by first resolving the URI-reference to absolute form as specified by [URI] using the base URI of the document in which the RDF statements appear. If a fragment identifier is included in the URI-reference then the resource identifier refers only to a subcomponent of the containing resource; this subcomponent is identifed by the corresponding anchor id internal to that containing resource and the extent of the subcomponent is defined by the fragment identifier in conjunction with the content type of the containing resource, otherwise the resource identifier refers to the entire item specified by the URI.

Note: Although non-ASCII characters in URIs are not allowed by [URI], [XML] specifies a convention to avoid unnecessary incompatibilities in extended URI syntax. Implementors of RDF are encouraged to avoid further incompatibility and use the XML convention for system identifiers. Namely, that a non-ASCII character in a URI be represented in UTF-8 as one or more bytes, and then these bytes be escaped with the URI escaping mechanism (i.e., by converting each byte to %HH, where HH is the hexadecimal notation of the byte value).

The `Description` element itself represents an instance of a Bag resource. The members of this Bag are the resources corresponding to the reification of each of the statements in the `Description`. If the `bagID` attribute is specified its value is the identifier of this Bag, else the Bag is anonymous.

When `about` is specified with `Description`, the statements in the `Description` refer to the resource named in the `about`. A `Description` element without an `about` attribute represents an in-line resource. This in-line resource has a resource identifier formed using the value of the base URI of the document containing the RDF statements plus an anchor id equal to the value of the `ID` attribute of the `Description` element, if present. When another `Description` or property value refers to the in-line resource it will use the value of the `ID` in an `about` attribute. When the other `Description` refers to the Bag of resources corresponding to the reified statements it will use the value of `bagID` in an `about` attribute. Either `ID` or `about` may be specified on `Description` but not both together in the same element. The values for each `ID` and `bagID` attribute must not appear in more than one such attribute within a document nor may the same value be used in an `ID` and a `bagID` within a single document.

When `aboutEach` is specified with `Description`, the statements in the `Description` refer to each of the members of the container named by `aboutEach`. The triples {p,r,v} represented by each contained propertyElt *E* as described above are duplicated for each r that is a member of the container.

When `aboutEachPrefix` is specified with `Description`, the statements in the `Description` refer to each of the members of an anonymous Bag container. The members of this Bag container are all the resources whose absolute form resource identifiers begin with the character string given as the value of `aboutEachPrefix`. The absolute form resource identifier is produced by resolving the URI according to the algorithm in Section 5.2., Resolving Relative References to Absolute Form, in [URI]. The triples {p,r,v} represented by each contained propertyElt *E* as described above are duplicated for each r that is a member of the container.

`Seq`, `Bag`, and `Alt` each represent an instance of a Sequence, Bag, or Alternative container resource type respectively. A triple {RDF:type,c,t} is created where c is the collection resource and t is one of RDF:Seq, RDF:Bag, or RDF:Alt. The members of the collection are denoted by `li`. Each `li` element *E* corresponds to one member of the collection and results in the creation of a triple {p,c,v} where:

1. p is assigned consecutively according to the (XML) order of lexical appearance of each member starting with "RDF:_1" for each container.

2. c is the collection resource. The `ID` attribute, if specified, provides the URI fragment identifier for c.

3. (same as rule 3 above) If *E* is an empty element (no content), v is the resource whose resource identifier is given by the `resource` attribute of *E*. If the content of *E* contains no XML markup or if `parseType="Literal"` is specified in the start tag of *E* then v is the content of *E* (a literal). Otherwise, the content of *E* must be another `Description` or container and v is the resource named by the(possibly implicit) `ID` or `about` of that `Description` or container.

The URI identifies (after resolution) the target resource; i.e., the resource to which the `Description` applies or the resource that is included in the container. The `bagID` attribute on a `Description` element and the `ID` attribute on a container element permit that `Description` or container to be referred to by other `Descriptions`. The `ID` on a container element is the name that is used in a `resource` attribute on a property element to make the collection the value of that property.

Within propertyElt (production [6.12]), the URI used in a `resource` attribute identifies (after resolution) the resource that is the object of the statement (i.e., the value of this property). The value of the `ID` attribute, if specified, is the identifier for the resource that represents the reification of the statement. If an RDF expression (that is, content with RDF/XML markup) is specified as a property value the object is the resource given by the `about` attribute of the contained `Description` or the (possibly implied) `ID` of the contained `Description` or container resource. `Strings` must be well-formed XML; the usual XML content quoting and escaping mechanisms may be used if the string contains character sequences (e.g. "<" and "&") that violate the well-formedness rules or that otherwise might look like markup. The attribute `parseType="Literal"` specifies that the element content is an RDF literal. Any markup that is part of this content is included as part of the literal and not interpreted by RDF.

It is recommended that property names always be qualified with a namespace prefix to unambiguously connect the property definition with the corresponding schema.

As defined by XML, the character repertoire of an RDF string is ISO/IEC 10646 [ISO10646]. An actual RDF string, whether in an XML document or in some other representation of the RDF data model, may be stored using a direct encoding of ISO/IEC 10646 or an encoding that can be mapped to ISO/IEC 10646. Language tagging is part of the string value; it is applied to sequences of characters within an RDF string and does not have an explicit manifestation in the data model.

Two RDF strings are deemed to be the same if their ISO/IEC 10646 representations match. Each RDF application must specify which one of the following definitions of 'match' it uses:

a. the two representations are identical, or
b. the two representations are canonically equivalent as defined by The Unicode Standard [Unicode].

Note: The W3C I18N WG is working on a definition for string identity matching. This definition will most probably be based on canonical equivalences according to the Unicode standard and on the principle of early uniform normalization. Users of RDF should not rely on any applications matching using the canonical equivalents, but should try to make sure that their data is in the normalized form according to the upcoming definitions.

This specification does not state a mechanism for determining equivalence between literals that contain markup, nor whether such a mechanism is guaranteed to exist.

The `xml:lang` attribute may be used as defined by [XML] to associate a language with the property value. There is no specific data model representation for `xml:lang` (i.e., it adds no triples to the data model); the language of a literal is considered by RDF to be a part of the literal. An application may ignore language tagging of a string. All RDF applications must specify whether or not language tagging in literals is significant; that is, whether or not language is considered when performing string matching or other processing.

Attributes whose names start with "`xmlns`" are namespace declarations and do not represent triples in the data model. There is no specific data model representation for such namespace declarations.

Each property and value expressed in XML attribute form by productions [6.3] and [6.10] is equivalent to the same property and value expressed as XML content of the corresponding `Description` according to production [6.12]. Specifically; each XML attribute *A* specified with a `Description` start tag other than the attributes `ID`, `about`, `aboutEach`, `aboutEachPrefix`, `bagID`, `xml:lang`, or any attribute starting with the characters `xmlns` results in the creation of a triple {p,r,v} where:

1. p is the expansion of the namespace-qualified attribute name of *A*. This expansion is generated by concatenating the namespace name given in the namespace declaration with the LocalPart of the qualified name and then resolving this URI according to the algorithm in Section 5.2., Resolving Relative References to Absolute Form, in [URI].

2. r is the resource whose resource identifer is given by the value of the `about` attribute, resolved as specified above, or whose anchor id is given by the value of the `ID` attribute of the Description or is a member of the collection specified by the `aboutEach` or `aboutEachPrefix` attribute.

3. v is the attribute value of *A* (a literal).

Grammatically, production [6.11] is just a special case of the propName production [6.10]. The value of the `type` attribute is interpreted as a URI-reference and expanded in the same way as the value of the `resource` attribute. Use of [6.11] is equivalent to using *rdf:type* as an element (property) name together with a `resource` attribute.

The typedNode form (production [6.13]) may be used to represent instances of resources of specific types and to further describe those resources. A `Description` expressed in typedNode form by production [6.13] is equivalent to the same `Description` expressed by production [6.3] with the same `ID`, `bagID`, and `about` attributes plus an additional type property in the `Description` where the value of the type property is the resource whose identifier is given by the fully expanded and resolved URI corresponding to the typeName of the typedNode. Specifically, a typedNode represents a triple {RDF:type,n,t} where n is the resource whose identifier is given by the value of the `about` attribute (after resolution) or whose anchor id is given by the value of the `ID` attribute of the typedNode element, and t is the expansion of the namespace-qualified tag name. The remainder of the typedNode attributes and content is handled as for `Description` elements above.

Properties and values expressed in XML attribute form within an empty XML element E by productions [6.10] and [6.12] are equivalent to the same properties and values expressed as XML content of a single Description element D which would become the content of E. The referent of D is the value of the property identified by the XML element name of E according to productions [6.17], [6.2], and [6.3]. Specifically; each propertyElt start tag containing attribute specifications other than ID, resource, bagID, xml:lang, or any attribute starting with the characters xmlns results in the creation of the triples $\{p, r_1, r_2\}$, $\{p_{a1}, r_2, v_{a1}\}$, ..., $\{p_{an}, r_2, v_{an}\}$ where

1. p is the expansion of the namespace-qualified tag name.
2. r_1 is the resource being referred to by the element containing this propertyElt expression.

3. r_2 is the resource named by the resource attribute if present or a new resource. If the ID attribute is given it is the identifier of this new resource.
4. p_{a1} ... p_{an} are the expansion of the namespace-qualified attribute names.
5. v_{a1} ... v_{an} are the corresponding attribute values.

The value of the bagID attribute, if specified, is the identifier for the Bag corresponding to the Description D; else the Bag is anonymous.

7. Examples

The following examples further illustrate features of RDF explained above.

7.1. Sharing Values

A single resource can be the value of more than one property; that is, it can be the object of more than one statement and therefore pointed to by more than one arc. For example, a single Web page might be shared between several documents and might then be referenced more than once in a "sitemap". Or two different (ordered) sequences of the same resources may be given.

Consider the case of specifying the collected works of an author, sorted once by publication date and sorted again alphabetically by subject:

```
<RDF xmlns="http://www.w3.org/1999/02/22-rdf-syntax-ns#">
 <Seq ID="JSPapersByDate">
  <li resource="http://www.dogworld.com/Aug96.doc"/>
  <li resource="http://www.webnuts.net/Jan97.html"/>
  <li resource="http://www.carchat.com/Sept97.html"/>
 </Seq>
 <Seq ID="JSPapersBySubj">
  <li resource="http://www.carchat.com/Sept97.html"/>
  <li resource="http://www.dogworld.com/Aug96.doc"/>
  <li resource="http://www.webnuts.net/Jan97.html"/>
 </Seq>
</RDF>
```

This XML example also uses the default namespace declaration syntax to elide the namespace prefix.

7.2. Aggregates

To further illustrate aggregates, consider an example of a document with two authors specified alphabetically, a title specified in two different languages, and having two equivalent locations on the Web:

```
<rdf:RDF
 xmlns:rdf="http://www.w3.org/1999/02/22-rdf-syntax-ns#"
 xmlns:dc="http://purl.org/metadata/dublin_core#">
 <rdf:Description about="http://www.foo.com/cool.html">
  <dc:Creator>
   <rdf:Seq ID="CreatorsAlphabeticalBySurname">
<rdf:li>Mary Andrew</rdf:li>
<rdf:li>Jacky Crystal</rdf:li>
   </rdf:Seq>
  </dc:Creator>

  <dc:Identifier>
   <rdf:Bag ID="MirroredSites">
<rdf:li rdf:resource="http://www.foo.com.au/cool.html"/>
<rdf:li rdf:resource="http://www.foo.com.it/cool.html"/>
   </rdf:Bag>
  </dc:Identifier>
```

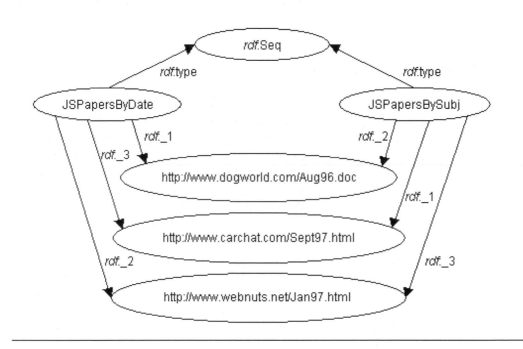

```
            <dc:Title>
              <rdf:Alt>
    <rdf:li xml:lang="en">The Coolest Web Page</rdf:li>
    <rdf:li xml:lang="it">Il Pagio di Web Fuba</rdf:li>
              </rdf:Alt>
            </dc:Title>
           </rdf:Description>
         </rdf:RDF>
```

This example illustrates the use of all three types of collection. The order of the creators is deemed significant so the *Sequence* container is used to hold them. The locations on the Web are equivalent; order is not significant, therefore a *Bag* is used. The document has only a single title and that title has two variants, so the *Alternatives* container is used.

Note: In many cases, it is impossible to have a preferred language among various language alternatives; all languages are considered to be strictly equivalent. In these cases, the description author should use a `Bag` instead of an `Alt` container.

7.3. Non-Binary Relations

The RDF data model intrinsically only supports binary relations; that is, a statement specifies a relation between two resources. In the following examples we show the recommended way to represent higher arity relations in RDF using just binary relations. The recommended technique is to use an intermediate resource with additional properties of this resource giving the remaining relations. As an example, consider the subject of one of John Smith's recent articles — library science. We could use the Dewey Decimal Code for library science to categorize that article. Dewey Decimal codes are far from the only subject categorization scheme, so to hold the classification system relation we identify an additional resource that is used as the value of the subject property and annotate this resource with an additional property that identifies the categorization scheme that was used. As specified in Section 2.3., the RDF core includes a *value* property to denote the principal value of the main relation. The resulting graph might look like:

which could be exchanged as:

```
<RDF
 xmlns="http://www.w3.org/1999/02/22-rdf-syntax-ns#"
 xmlns:rdf="http://www.w3.org/1999/02/22-rdf-syntax-ns#"
 xmlns:dc="http://purl.org/metadata/dublin_core#"
 xmlns:l="http://mycorp.com/schemas/my-schema#">
 <Description about="http://www.webnuts.net/Jan97.html">
  <dc:Subject
    rdf:value="020 - Library Science"
    l:Classification="Dewey Decimal Code"/>
 </Description>
</RDF>
```

Note: In the example above two namespace declarations exist for the same namespace. This is frequently needed when default namespaces are declared so that attributes that do not come from the namespace of the element may be specified, as is the case with the rdf:value attribute in the dc:Subject element above.

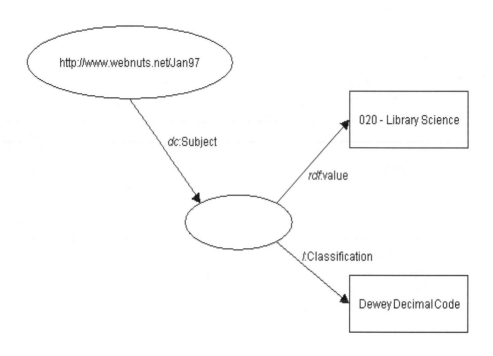

Figure 2: A ternary relation

A common use of this higher-arity capability is when dealing with units of measure. A person's weight is not just a number such as "200", it also includes the unit of measure used. In this case we might be using either pounds or kilograms. We could use a relationship with an additional arc to record the fact that John Smith is a rather strapping gentleman:

which can be exchanged as:

```
<RDF
 xmlns="http://www.w3.org/1999/02/22-rdf-syntax-ns#"
 xmlns:rdf="http://www.w3.org/1999/02/22-rdf-syntax-ns#"
 xmlns:n="http://www.nist.gov/units/">
 <Description about="John_Smith">
  <n:weight rdf:parseType="Resource">
   <rdf:value>200</rdf:value>
```

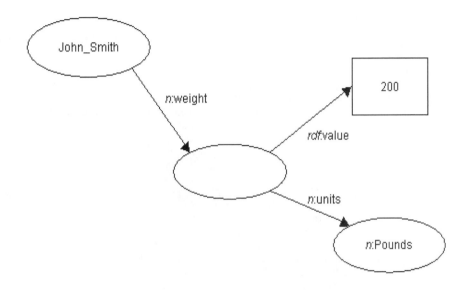

```
        <n:units rdf:resource="http://www.nist.gov/units/Pounds"/>
      </n:weight>
    </Description>
  </RDF>
```

provided the resource "Pounds" is defined in a NIST schema with the URI http://www.nist.gov/units/Pounds.

7.4. Dublin Core Metadata

The Dublin Core metadata is designed to facilitate discovery of electronic resources in a manner similar to a library card catalog. These examples represent the simple description of a set of resources in RDF using vocabularies defined by the Dublin Core Initiative. *Note: the specific Dublin Core RDF vocabulary shown here is not intended to be authoritative. The Dublin Core Initiative is the authoritative reference.*

Here is a description of a Web site home page using Dublin Core properties:

```
<rdf:RDF
 xmlns:rdf="http://www.w3.org/1999/02/22-rdf-syntax-ns#"
 xmlns:dc="http://purl.org/metadata/dublin_core#">
 <rdf:Description about="http://www.dlib.org">
  <dc:Title>D-Lib Program - Research in Digital Libraries</dc:Title>
  <dc:Description>The D-Lib program supports the community of people
  with research interests in digital libraries and electronic
  publishing.</dc:Description>
  <dc:Publisher>Corporation For National Research Initiatives</dc:Publisher>
  <dc:Date>1995-01-07</dc:Date>
  <dc:Subject>
   <rdf:Bag>
<rdf:li>Research; statistical methods</rdf:li>
<rdf:li>Education, research, related topics</rdf:li>
<rdf:li>Library use Studies</rdf:li>
   </rdf:Bag>
  </dc:Subject>
  <dc:Type>World Wide Web Home Page</dc:Type>
  <dc:Format>text/html</dc:Format>
  <dc:Language>en</dc:Language>
 </rdf:Description>
</rdf:RDF>
```

The second example is of a published magazine.

```
<rdf:RDF
 xmlns:rdf="http://www.w3.org/1999/02/22-rdf-syntax-ns#"
 xmlns:dc="http://purl.org/metadata/dublin_core#"
 xmlns:dcq="http://purl.org/metadata/dublin_core_qualifiers#">
 <rdf:Description about="http://www.dlib.org/dlib/may98/05contents.html">
  <dc:Title>DLIB Magazine - The Magazine for Digital Library Research
   - May 1998</dc:Title>
  <dc:Description>D-LIB magazine is a monthly compilation of
  contributed stories, commentary, and briefings.</dc:Description>
  <dc:Contributor rdf:parseType="Resource">
   <dcq:AgentType
rdf:resource="http://purl.org/metadata/dublin_core_qualifiers#Editor"/>
   <rdf:value>Amy Friedlander</rdf:value>
  </dc:Contributor>
  <dc:Publisher>Corporation for National Research Initiatives</dc:Publisher>
  <dc:Date>1998-01-05</dc:Date>
  <dc:Type>electronic journal</dc:Type>
```

```
        <dc:Subject>
          <rdf:Bag>
<rdf:li>library use studies</rdf:li>
<rdf:li>magazines and newspapers</rdf:li>
          </rdf:Bag>
        </dc:Subject>
        <dc:Format>text/html</dc:Format>
        <dc:Identifier>urn:issn:1082-9873</dc:Identifier>
        <dc:Relation rdf:parseType="Resource">
          <dcq:RelationType
rdf:resource="http://purl.org/metadata/dublin_core_qualifiers#IsPartOf"/>
          <rdf:value resource="http://www.dlib.org"/>
        </dc:Relation>
      </rdf:Description>
    </rdf:RDF>
```

The third example is of a specific article in the magazine referred to in the previous example.

```
<rdf:RDF
  xmlns:rdf="http://www.w3.org/1999/02/22-rdf-syntax-ns#"
  xmlns:dc="http://purl.org/metadata/dublin_core#"
  xmlns:dcq="http://purl.org/metadata/dublin_core_qualifiers#">
  <rdf:Description about=
  "http://www.dlib.org/dlib/may98/miller/05miller.html">
    <dc:Title>An Introduction to the Resource Description Framework</dc:Title>
    <dc:Creator>Eric J. Miller</dc:Creator>
    <dc:Description>The Resource Description Framework (RDF) is an
    infrastructure that enables the encoding, exchange and reuse of
    structured metadata. rdf is an application of xml that imposes needed
    structural constraints to provide unambiguous methods of expressing
    semantics. rdf additionally provides a means for publishing both
    human-readable and machine-processable vocabularies designed to
    encourage the reuse and extension of metadata semantics among
    disparate information communities. the structural constraints rdf
    imposes to support the consistent encoding and exchange of
    standardized metadata provides for the interchangeability of separate
    packages of metadata defined by different resource description
    communities. </dc:Description>
    <dc:Publisher>Corporation for National Research Initiatives</dc:Publisher>
    <dc:Subject>
      <rdf:Bag>
<rdf:li>machine-readable catalog record formats</rdf:li>
<rdf:li>applications of computer file organization and
access methods</rdf:li>
      </rdf:Bag>
    </dc:Subject>
    <dc:Rights>Copyright @ 1998 Eric Miller</dc:Rights>
    <dc:Type>Electronic Document</dc:Type>
    <dc:Format>text/html</dc:Format>
```

```
<dc:Language>en</dc:Language>
<dc:Relation rdf:parseType="Resource">
  <dcq:RelationType
rdf:resource="http://purl.org/metadata/dublin_core_qualifiers#IsPartOf"/>
    <rdf:value resource="http://www.dlib.org/dlib/may98/05contents.html"/>
  </dc:Relation>
 </rdf:Description>
</rdf:RDF>
```

Note: Schema developers may be tempted to declare the values of certain properties to use a syntax corresponding to the XML Namespace qualified name abbreviation. We advise against using these qualified names inside property values as this may cause incompatibilities with future XML datatyping mechanisms. Furthermore, those fully versed in XML 1.0 features may recognize that a similar abbreviation mechanism exists in user-defined entities. We also advise against relying on the use of entities as there is a proposal to define a future subset of XML that does not include user-defined entities.

7.5. Values Containing Markup

When a property value is a literal that contains XML markup, the following syntax is used to signal to the RDF interpreter not to interpret the markup but rather to retain it as part of the value. The precise representation of the resulting value is not specified here.

In the following example, the value of the Title property is a literal containing some MATHML markup.

```
<rdf:Description
 xmlns:rdf="http://www.w3.org/1999/02/22-rdf-syntax-ns#"
 xmlns:dc="http://purl.org/metadata/dublin_core#"
 xmlns="http://www.w3.org/TR/REC-mathml"
 rdf:about="http://mycorp.com/papers/NobelPaper1">

 <dc:Title rdf:parseType="Literal">
  Ramifications of
    <apply>
    <power/>
    <apply>
<plus/>
<ci>a</ci>
<ci>b</ci>
```

```
        </apply>
        <cn>2</cn>
      </apply>
      to World Peace
    </dc:Title>
    <dc:Creator>David Hume</dc:Creator>
  </rdf:Description>
```

7.6. PICS Labels

The Platform for Internet Content Selection (PICS) is a W3C Recommendation for exchanging descriptions of the content of Web pages and other material. PICS is a predecessor to RDF and it is an explicit requirement of RDF that it be able to express anything that can be expressed in a PICS label.

Here is an example of how a PICS label might be expressed in RDF form. *Note that work to re-specify PICS itself as an application of RDF may follow the completion of the RDF specification, thus the following example should not be considered an authoritative example of a future PICS schema.* This example comes directly from [PICS]. Note that a PICS Rating Service Description is exactly analogous to an RDF Schema; the categories described in such a Ratings Service description file are equivalent to properties in the RDF model.

```
<rdf:RDF
  xmlns:rdf="http://www.w3.org/1999/02/22-rdf-syntax-ns#"
  xmlns:pics="http://www.w3.org/TR/xxxx/WD-PICS-labels#"
  xmlns:gcf="http://www.gcf.org/v2.5">
  <rdf:Description about="http://www.w3.org/PICS/Overview.html" bagID="L01"
    gcf:suds="0.5"
    gcf:density="0"
    gcf:color.hue="1"/>

  <rdf:Description about="http://www.w3.org/PICS/Underview.html" bagID="L02"
    gcf:subject="2"
    gcf:density="1"
    gcf:color.hue="1"/>

  <rdf:Description aboutEach="#L01"
    pics:by="John Doe"
    pics:on="1994.11.05T08:15-0500"
    pics:until="1995.12.31T23:59-0000"/>

  <rdf:Description aboutEach="#L02"
```

```
      pics:by="Jane Doe"
      pics:on="1994.11.05T08:15-0500"
      pics:until="1995.12.31T23:59-0000"/>
    </rdf:RDF>
```

Note that `aboutEach` is used to indicate that the PICS label options refer to the individual (rating) statements and not to the container in which those statements happen to be supplied.

[PICS] also defines a type called a *generic label*. A PICS generic label is a label that applies to every page within a specified portion of the Web site.

Below is an example of how a PICS generic label would be written in RDF, using the `aboutEachPrefix` collection constructor. This example is drawn from the "Generic request" example in Appendix B of [PICS]:

```
<rdf:RDF
  xmlns:rdf="http://www.w3.org/1999/02/22-rdf-syntax-ns#"
  xmlns:pics="http://www.w3.org/TR/xxxx/WD-PICS-labels#"
  xmlns:ages="http://www.ages.org/our-service/v1.0/">
  <rdf:Description aboutEachPrefix="http://www.w3.org/WWW/" bagID="L03"
    ages:age="11"/>

  <rdf:Description aboutEach="#L03"
    pics:by="abaird@w3.org"/>
</rdf:RDF>
```

The property `age` with the value "11" appears on every resource whose URI starts with the string "http://www.w3.org/WWW/". The reified statement corresponding to each such statement ("The age of *[I] is 11")* has a property stating that "abaird@w3.org" was responsible for creating those statements.

7.7. Content Hiding For RDF inside HTML

RDF, being well-formed XML, is suitable for direct inclusion in an HTML document when the user agent follows the HTML recommendations for error handling in invalid documents. When a fragment of RDF is incorporated into an HTML document some browsers will render any exposed string content. Exposed string content is anything that appears between the ">" that ends one tag and the "<" that begins the next tag. Generally, multiple consecutive whitespace characters including end-of-line characters are rendered as a single space.

The RDF abbreviated syntax can frequently be used to write property values that are strings in XML attribute form and leave only whitespace as exposed content. For example, the first part of the Dublin Core example from Section 7.4. could be written as:

```
<rdf:RDF
  xmlns:rdf="http://www.w3.org/1999/02/22-rdf-syntax-ns#"
  xmlns:dc="http://purl.org/metadata/dublin_core#">
  <rdf:Description about="http://www.dlib.org"
    dc:Title="D-Lib Program - Research in Digital Libraries"
    dc:Description="The D-Lib program supports the community of people
     with research interests in digital libraries and electronic
     publishing."
    dc:Publisher="Corporation For National Research Initiatives"
    dc:Date="1995-01-07"/>
</rdf:RDF>
```

Rewriting to avoid exposed content will work for most common cases. One common but less obvious case is container descriptions. Consider the first part of the example in Section 7.2.:

```
<rdf:RDF
  xmlns:rdf="http://www.w3.org/1999/02/22-rdf-syntax-ns#"
  xmlns:dc="http://purl.org/metadata/dublin_core#">
  <rdf:Description about="http://www.foo.com/cool.html">
   <dc:Creator>
    <rdf:Seq ID="CreatorsAlphabeticalBySurname">
<rdf:li>Mary Andrew</rdf:li>
<rdf:li>Jacky Crystal</rdf:li>
    </rdf:Seq>
   </dc:Creator>
  </rdf:Description>
</rdf:RDF>
```

To rewrite this with no exposed content, we use the following form:

```
<rdf:RDF
  xmlns:rdf="http://www.w3.org/1999/02/22-rdf-syntax-ns#"
  xmlns:dc="http://purl.org/metadata/dublin_core#">
  <rdf:Description about="http://www.foo.com/cool.html">
   <dc:Creator>
    <rdf:Seq ID="CreatorsAlphabeticalBySurname"
rdf:_1="Mary Andrew"
rdf:_2="Jacky Crystal"/>
```

```
      </dc:Creator>
    </rdf:Description>
  </rdf:RDF>
```

Note here that the `li` element cannot be used as an attribute due to the XML rule forbidding multiple occurrences of the same attribute name within a tag. Therefore we use the explicit RDF *Ord properties; in effect manually expanding the `li` element.*

A complete HTML document containing RDF metadata describing itself is:

```
<html>
<head>
 <rdf:RDF
   xmlns:rdf="http://www.w3.org/1999/02/22-rdf-syntax-ns#"
   xmlns:dc="http://purl.org/metadata/dublin_core#">
   <rdf:Description about="">
    <dc:Creator>
<rdf:Seq ID="CreatorsAlphabeticalBySurname"
 rdf:_1="Mary Andrew"
 rdf:_2="Jacky Crystal"/>
    </dc:Creator>
   </rdf:Description>
 </rdf:RDF>
</head>
<body>
<P>This is a fine document.</P>
</body>
</html>
```

The HTML document above should be accepted by all browsers compliant with HTML 3.2 and later and should only render the characters "This is a fine document."

8. Acknowledgements

This specification is the work of the W3C RDF Model and Syntax Working Group. This Working Group has been most ably chaired by Eric Miller of the Online Computer Library Center and Bob Schloss of IBM. We thank Eric and Bob for their tireless efforts in keeping the group on track and we especially thank OCLC, IBM, and Nokia for supporting them and us in this endeavor.

The members of the Working Group who helped design this specfication, debate proposals, provide words, proofread numerous drafts and ultimately reach consensus are: Ron Daniel (DATAFUSION), Renato Iannella (DSTC), Tsuyoshi SAKATA (DVL), Murray Maloney (Grif), Bob Schloss (IBM), Naohiko URAMOTO (IBM), Bill Roberts (KnowledgeCite), Arthur van Hoff (Marimba), Charles Frankston (Microsoft), Andrew Layman (Microsoft), Chris McConnell (Microsoft), Jean Paoli (Microsoft), R.V. Guha (Netscape), Ora Lassila (Nokia), Ralph LeVan (OCLC), Eric Miller (OCLC), Charles Wicksteed (Reuters), Misha Wolf (Reuters), Wei Song (SISU), Lauren Wood (SoftQuad), Tim Bray (Textuality), Paul Resnick (University of Michigan), Tim Berners-Lee (W3C), Dan Connolly (W3C), Jim Miller (W3C, emeritus), Ralph Swick (W3C). Dan Brickley (UK Bristol) joined the RDF Schema activity and brought us lots of sage advice in the final stages of this work. Martin Dürst (W3C) reviewed several working drafts and made a number of suggestions for improvement on behalf of the W3C Internationalization Working Group. Janne Saarela (W3C) performed a priceless service by creating a 'clean room' implementation from our working drafts.

This document is the collective work of the Working Group. The editors are indebted to the Working Group for helping to create and polish this specification.

Appendix A. Glossary

The following terms are used in this specification with varying degrees of intuitive meaning and precise meaning. The summary definitions here are for guidance only; they are non-normative. Where appropriate, the location in the document of the precise definition is given also.

Arc	A representation of a property in a graph form; specifically the edges in a directed labeled graph.

Attribute	A characteristic of an object. In Chapter 6 this term refers to a specific XML syntactic construct; the `name="value"` portions of an XML tag.
Element	As used here, this term refers to a specific XML syntactic construct; i.e., the material between matching XML start and end tags.
Literal	The most primitive value type represented in RDF, typically a string of characters. The content of a literal is not interpreted by RDF itself and may contain additional XML markup. Literals are distinguished from Resources in that the RDF model does not permit literals to be the subject of a statement.
Node	A representation of a resource or a literal in a graph form; specifically, a vertex in a directed labeled graph.
Property	A specific attribute with defined meaning that may be used to describe other resources. A property plus the value of that property for a specific resource is a *statement* about that resource. A property may define its permitted values as well as the types of resources that may be described with this property.

<u>Resource</u>	An abstract object that represents either a physical object such as a person or a book or a conceptual object such as a color or the class of things that have colors. Web pages are usually considered to be physical objects, but the distinction between physical and conceptual or abstract objects is not important to RDF. A resource can also be a component of a larger object; for example, a resource can represent a specific person's left hand or a specific paragraph out of a document. As used in this specification, the term resource refers to the whole of an object if the URI does not contain a fragment (anchor) id or to the specific subunit named by the fragment or anchor id.
<u>Statement</u>	An expression following a specified grammar that names a specific resource, a specific property (attribute), and gives the value of that property for that resource. More specifically here, an *RDF statement* is a statement using the RDF/XML grammar specified in this document.
<u>Triple</u>	A representation of a statement used by RDF, consisting of just the property, the resource identifier, and the property value in that order.

Appendix B. Transporting RDF

Descriptions may be associated with the resource they describe in one of four ways:

1. The Description may be contained within the resource ("embedded"; e.g. in HTML).
2. The Description may be external to the resource but supplied by the transfer mechanism in the same retrieval transaction as that which returns

the resource ("along-with"; e.g. with HTTP GET or HEAD).

3. The Description may be retrieved independently from the resource, including from a different source ("service bureau"; e.g. using HTTP GET).

4. The Description may contain the resource ("wrapped"; e.g. RDF itself).

All resources will not support all association methods; in particular, many kinds of resources will not support embedding and only certain kinds of resources may be wrapped.

A human- or machine-understandable description of an RDF schema may be accessed through content negotiation by dereferencing the schema URI. If the schema is machine-understandable it may be possible for an application to learn some of the semantics of the properties named in the schema on demand. The logic and syntax of RDF schemas are described in a separate document, [RDFSchema].

The recommended technique for embedding RDF expressions in an HTML document is simply to insert the RDF in-line as shown in Example 7.7. This will make the resulting document non-conformant to HTML specifications up to and including HTML 4.0 but the W3C expects that the HTML specification will evolve to support this. Two practical issues will arise when this technique is employed with respect to browsers conforming to specifications of HTML up to and including HTML 4.0. Alternatives are available to authors in these cases; see [XMLinHTML]. It is up to the author to choose the appropriate alternative in each circumstance.

1. Some HTML 2.0 browsers will assume a </HEAD> tag immediately before the first RDF element that appears within <HEAD>.

Authors concerned about very old browsers may place all RDF expressions at the end of the document head.

2. All HTML browsers conforming to specifications up to and including HTML 4.0 will render any content appearing in RDF property values expressed as XML elements (i.e., production [6.12]).

Authors concerned about preventing their RDF content from rendering in old browsers may use the abbreviated syntax (propAttr form) to move the property value into an attribute. Not all properties can be expressed this way.

In the event that none of the alternatives above provides the capabilities desired by the author, the RDF expressions may be left external to the HTML document and linked with an HTML <LINK> element. The recommended relation type for this purpose is REL="meta"; e.g.

```
<LINK rel="meta" href="mydocMetadata.DC.RDF">
```

Appendix C: Notes about Usage

C.1. Property Names

The RDF serialization and abbreviated syntaxes use XML as their encoding. XML elements and attributes are case sensitive, so RDF property names are therefore also case sensitive. This specification does not require any specific format for property names other than that they be legal XML *names*. For its own identifiers, RDF has adopted the convention that all property names use "InterCap style"; that is, the first letter of the property name and the remainder of the word is lowercase; e.g. *subject*. When the property name is a composition of words or fragments of words, the words are concatenated with the first letter of each word (other than the first word) capitalized and no additional punctutation; e.g. *subClassOf*.

C.2. Namespace URIs

RDF uses the proposed XML namespace mechanism to implement globally unique identifiers for all properties. In addition, the namespace name serves as the identifier for the corresponding RDF schema. The namespace name is resolved to absolute form as specified by the algorithm in Section 5.2., Resolving Relative References to Absolute Form, in [URI]. An RDF processor can expect to use the schema URI to access the schema content. This specification places no further requirements on the content that might be supplied at that URI, nor how (if at all) the URI might be modified to obtain alternate forms or a fragment of the schema.

Appendix D: References

[Dexter94]
F. Halasz and M. Schwarz. The Dexter Hypertext Reference Model. Communications of the ACM, 37(2):30–39, February 1994. Edited by K. Gr¿nb ck and R. Trigg. http://www.acm.org/pubs/citations/journals/cacm/1994-37-2/p30-halasz/

[HTML]
HTML 4.0 Specification, Raggett, Le Hors, Jacobs eds, World Wide Web Consortium Recommendation; http://www.w3.org/TR/REC-html40/

[ISO10646]
ISO/IEC 10646. The applicable version of this standard is defined in the XML specification [XML].

[NAMESPACES]
Namespaces in XML; Bray, Hollander, Layman eds, World Wide Web Consortium Recommendation; http://www.w3.org/TR/1999/REC-xml-names-19990114.

[PICS]
PICS Label Distribution Label Syntax and Communication Protocols, Version 1.1, W3C Recommendation 31-October-96; http://www.w3.org/TR/REC-PICS-labels.

[RDFSchema]
Resource Description Framework (RDF) Schemas; Brickley, Guha, Layman eds., World Wide Web Consortium Working Draft; http://www.w3.org/TR/1998/WD-rdf-schema

[RFC2119]
Key words for use in RFCs to Indicate Requirement Levels; S. Bradner, March 1997; RFC2119.

[Unicode]
The Unicode Standard. The applicable version of this standard is the version defined by the XML specification [XML].

[URI]
Uniform Resource Identifiers (URI): Generic Syntax; Berners-Lee, Fielding, Masinter, Internet Draft Standard August, 1998; RFC2396.

[XML]
Extensible Markup Language (XML) 1.0; World Wide Web Consortium Recommendation; http://www.w3.org/TR/REC-xml.

[XMLinHTML]
XML in HTML Meeting Report; Connolly, Wood eds.; World Wide Web Consortium Note; http://www.w3.org/TR/NOTE-xh.

Appendix E: Changes

Some typographic changes were made after the Proposed Recommendation was published. The known errata in the previous version as of the time of publication have been corrected. A small clarifying change to the final paragraph of Section 6 was also made.

Ora Lassila <ora.lassila@research.nokia.com>

Ralph R. Swick <swick@w3.org>

Revision History:

17-February-1999: prepare for publication as W3C Recommendation.

5-January-1999: publish as W3C Proposed Recommendation.

16-December-1998: final draft intended as Proposed Recommendation.

30-October-1998: incorporate Last Call review comments, add parseType, improve the I18N wordings.

8-October-1998: final cleanup, move changes to Appendix E, publish as Last Call.

7-October-1998: reserve a bit of schema URI space for futureproofing, add rdf:value.

2-October-1998: major renaming; statements, predicates, subjects, objects.

4-September-1998: instanceOf -> type, revise higher-arity relations model, add node identifier.

19-August-1998: Add '_' to Ord property names.

12-August-1998: Update to newer XML namespace declaration syntax. Add content to Section 7.

20-July-1998: More typos fixed. Third public draft

15-July-1998: Incorporate comments and fix typos. Initial letter of property names changed to lowercase

15-June-1998: Major rewrite and reorganization

16-February-1998: Editorial cleanup, prep for second public distribution
6-February-1998: Editorial cleanup, add and revise some examples
11-January-1998: Renaming and collapsing of several elements
14-November-1997: Further refinement, especially regarding assertions
3-November-1997: Edits in preparation for second public distribution
2-October-1997: First public draft
1-October-1997: Edits in preparation for first public distribution
1-August-1997: First draft to Working Group

Last updated: $Date: 1999/02/24 14:45:07 $

Index

A

Absolute location terms, 22
ABSTRACT element, 63
Access, 87
Active Channel
    example of, 73–74
    how it works, 60–61
    implementing, 61–66
Active Server Pages (ASP), 5, 87, 112, 126
    error handling, 116–117
    looking at contents, 114–115
    retrieving data, 115–116
    using XMLDOM, 113–114
ActiveX, 4

Adept Editor, 35
ADO, 126
Adobe
    FrameMaker+SGML, 4, 36–37
    Photoshop, 52
Alternative, 263
Ampersand, use of, 190, 229
ancestor, 23
Apache, 90
ArborText, 35
Arrays, 44, 46–47
Astoria, 37–38
<A> tag, 19
Attribute defaults, 213–214
Attribute name, 203
Attribute-list declarations, 209–214
Attribute specifications, 203
Attribute types, 123, 210–212
Attribute value, 203
    normalization, 214
Aurora, 84
Authoring tools
    Adept Editor, 35
    Dreamweaver, 32–33
    FrameMaker+SGML, 36–37
    SGML, 36
    Visual XML, 34–35
    XMetaL, 34
    XML Notepad, 33–34
    XML Pro, 35
Autodesk, 54
Auto-Graphics Inc., 37

B

Bag, 263
Berners-Lee, Tim, 4

Bitmap graphics, 51
Bluestone XML Suite, 91–93
Bosak, Jon, 5, 183
Brackets, use of angle, 190, 229
Bray, Tim, 42
Bypassed, 228

C

C, 87
C++, 87, 104
Cascading Style Sheets, 14, 20
CDATA sections, 192–193
CDF Generator, 61
CGI, 87
Channel Definition Format (CDF), 5
    Active Channel, example of, 73–
    74
    Active Channel, how it works,
    60–61
    Active Channel, implementing,
    61–66
    element definitions, 66–73
    purpose of, 60
CHANNEL/Channel element, 62,
69–70
Character classes, 235–236
Character data, 190–191
Character encoding in entities, 223–
225
    autodetection, 239–242
Character references, 217–220
    expansion of, 237–238
Characters, 187–188
Chemical Markup Language (CML),
5, 12
child, 23, 187

Child elements
    Channel, 69–70
    Item, 70, 71
    Schedule, 71
    shared by Channel and Item, 68
Chrystal Software, 37
Clark, James, 118
Colon, use of, 189
Command-line, using the, 29–31
Comments, 191
common_dbtools.asp, 170–172
compute, 44, 46
    structure, 47–49
Conditional expressions, 47
Conditional sections, 214–216
Conformance, 231
Connolly, Dan, 183
Content, 204
Content management tools
    Astoria, 37–38
    ObjectStore, 38–39
    Oracle 8i, 38
    SGML Database Editorial System, 37
Content models, deterministic, 239
ConText, 133
Cooper, Clark, 110
Corel, 36

D

Data Islands, 82–83
Data Source Object (DSO), 79–90, 83
Data sources, creating, 125–129
DB2, 91
descendant, 23

Document entity, 231
Document Object Model (DOM), 83
    DOMParser, 30
    nodes in a tree, 101–104
    requirements, 96–101
Documents
    CDATA sections, 192–193
    character data and markup, 190–191
    characters, 187–188
    comments, 191
    common syntactic constructs, 188–190
    document type declaration, 193–197
    end-of-lines, 199–200
    language identification, 200–202
    processing instructions, 192
    standalone document declaration, 197–198
    valid, 17–18
    version number, 193
    well-formed, 18, 186, 187
    white space, 198–199
Document Type Declaration, 3, 116, 193–197
Document Type Definition (DTD), 14–15, 194
DOMParser, 30
Draw programs, 52
Dreamweaver, 32–33, 65
DVDmdb.com
    building the front page, 157–158
    creating the XSL, 158–169
    database, 144–148
    delivering, 177–178

documents, 148–169
news, 153–155
objective, 142–144
prices, 155–157
publishing system, 170–178
reviews, 150–153
uploading, 170–177

E
Editable objects, 53
Element content, 207–208
Elements, 202
ElementType, 123
Element type declarations, 205–209
Empty-element tags, 204–205
Enabler, 88
End-of-lines, 199–200
End-tags, 204
Entities, 186, 216–217
    character encoding in, 223–225
    declarations, 220–222
    document, 231
    expansion of, 237–238
    external, 221–222
    internal, 220–221
    parsed, 222–225
    predefined, 229–230
    processor treatment of, 225–228
    references, 217–220
Enumerated attribute types, 212
Error handling
    Active Server Pages, 116–117
    Visual Basic, 108–109
Escape, 229
Event handlers, 118
Expressions, conditional versus

mathematical, 47–48
Extended Backus-Naur Form
    (EBNF), 231
Extensible Forms Description Lan-
    guage (XFDL). See XFDL
Extensible Markup Language. See
    XML
External entities, 221–222

F
following, 23
Forbidden, 227
Form global options, 43
FrameMaker+SGML, 4, 36–37
FrontPage, 4
fsibling, 23
Function calls, 48

G
General entities, 217
Generic identifier (GI), 202
Groups, 53

H
HoTMetaL, 34
href, 20
HREF, 70, 72
html, 22
HTML, 4–5

I
IBM, 5, 6, 88
id, 22
iFS (Internet File System) support,
    131–132
Included, 227

Included as PE, 228
Included If Validating, 227
Informix, 87, 90, 91
Internal entities, 220–221, 228–229
Internet Explorer 3.0, 78
Internet Explorer 4.0, 79–80
Internet Explorer 5.0, 6, 80–84
IsClonable, 70
Item element, 70–71
Items, XFDL, 43–44

J

Java, 4, 104
    Oracle 8i platform for, 133–134
JavaScript, 4, 30
Java Server Pages, 87
JDBC, 91
JUMBO, 12

L

Language identification, 200–202
Linking, 18
    elements, 19
    out-of-line, 20–21
    simple and extended, 20
    XLinks, 19–21
    XPointers, 21–23
Literals, 189–190
LOGO/Logo element, 63–64, 72

M

Macromedia, 54
    Dreamweaver, 32–33, 65
Markup, 190
Markup declaration, 194–194

Markup language, creating your own, 12–13
Mathematical expressions, 47–48
MathML (Mathematical Markup Language), 5, 12
    implementation, 59–60
    presentational tags, 58–59
    purpose of, 57
    semantic tags, 58
    software, 59
Microsoft, 5, 60
    Access, 87
    CDF Generator, 61
    IIS Web servers, 90
    Paint, 52
    SQL Server, 90, 91, 134–138
    XML Notepad, 33–34
Mixed content, 208–209
Morel, Pierre, 34
Mozilla, 87
Murray-Rust, Peter, 5, 12

N

Name(s), 188–189
    tokens and, 189
Namespaces, 24, 82
Natural-language query mechanism, 90
Netscape, 6, 60, 90
Netscape Navigator 3.0, 78
Netscape Navigator 6.0, 84–86
News.asp, 173–174
News_edit.asp, 174–175
News_process.asp, 175–177
news.xml, 153–155
Notation declarations, 230–231, 231–

233
Notations, 230
Notify, 228
Not Recognized, 226
Novell, 36

O
ODBC, 91, 126
Object Model, 79
ObjectStore, 38–39
Options, XFDL, 44–47
Oracle, 87, 90, 91
Oracle 8i, 38
    iFS support, 131–132
    parser, 131
    platform for Java, 133–134
    XML support, 130–133
origin(), 22
ownerDocument, 124

P
Paint programs, 52
parent, 187
Parsed entities, 216, 222–225
ParseError/parseError, 108–109,
116–117
Parsers/parsing, 30, 79, 82
    Oracle, 131
Perl (Practical Extraction and
Reporting Language), 87, 104, 109–
112
Photoshop, 52
PHP, 104, 117–119
PowerDesigner, 144
preceding, 23
Presentational tags, 58–59

Prices, 155–157
Processing instructions (PIs), 192
Processor treatment of entities and
references, 225–228
Properties, 248
psibling, 23
Public identifier, 222
Push technology, 60
Python, 29, 87, 104

Q
Quotes, use of, 191

R
Raster graphics, 51
ReadyState property, 107
References
    processor treatment of, 225–228
    types of, 233–235
Relative location terms, 22–23
Replacement text, 228–229
Resource Description Framework
(RDF), 74–75, 84
    basic model, 247–252
    container model, 263–265
    containers defined by URI, 270–
271
    containers versus repeated prop-
erties, 271–273
    container syntax, 265–268
    examples, 293–305
    glossary, 306–307
    grammar, 284–293
    model, 279–284
    notes about usage, 309–310
    property values, 262

purpose of, 245–247
referents, 268–270
schemas and namespaces, 261–262
statements, 273–279
syntax, abbreviated, 257–261
syntax, serialization, 253–257
transporting, 308–309
Resources, 248
Reviews, 150–153
Roberts, Brian, 142
Robots, 9
root(), 22, 187

S

SCHEDULE/Schedule element, 63, 71–72
Schema(s)
    defined, 14, 122–123
    information access, 124–125
    XML, 15–16, 83, 122–125
Semantic tags, 58
Sequence, 263
Server, XML on, 87–88
SGML (standard generalized markup language), 3–4
    Database Editorial System, 37
    non-normative, 236–237
    WordPerfect, 36
Simple character data, 44, 46
Smart Editor, 37
SoftQuad, 34
SQL Server, 90, 91, 134–138
Standalone document declaration, 197–198
Start-tags, 203–204

Statements, 248
StoryServer, 5–6, 89–90
Strings, quoted, 48
Sybase, 87, 90, 91
System identifier, 221

T

Tags, 8–9
    empty-element, 204–205
    end, 204
    presentational 58–59
    semantic, 58
    start, 203–204
Text declaration, 222–223
TITLE element, 63
Tracking element, 73
Type, 203

U

Universal Forms Description Language (UFDL), 42
UNIX, 84
Unparsed entity, 216
Usage, 71
UserSchedule element, 71
UWI.Com, 42

V

Validating processors, 231
Valid documents, 17–18
Value, 48
Vector graphics, defined, 51–52
Vector Markup Language (VML), 51
    benefits of, 54–55
    design requirements, 55–56
    implementation, 55

vector graphics and, 52–54
Vignette, StoryServer, 5–6, 89–90
VISIO, 54
Visual Basic, 104, 105–109
Visual-XML, 34–35, 92–93

W
Wall, Larry, 109
Waterloo Maple, 5
Web browsers
    Internet Explorer 3.0, 78
    Internet Explorer 4.0, 79–80
    Internet Explorer 5.0, 80–84
    Mozilla, 87
    Netscape Navigator 3.0, 78
    Netscape Navigator 6.0, 84–86
Well-formed documents, 18, 186, 187
Well-formed parsed entities, 223
White space, 47, 48, 188, 198–199
WordPerfect SGML, 36
World Wide Web Consortium (W3C), 12, 242

X
XFDL (Extensible Forms Description Language)
    compute structure, 47–49
    conditional versus mathematical expression, 47–48
    development of, 42
    form structure, 42–47
    items, 43–44
    options, 44–47
    reproducing documents, 47
    sample forms, 49–51

XLinks, 19–21
XLL (Extensible Linking Language), 18
XMetaL, 34
XML (Extensible Markup Language)
    benefits of, 2
    conformance, 231
    data sharing and, 12
    defined, 8–9
    documents, 186–202
    first draft of, 5
    goals of, 9–11, 183–184
    history of, 3–6
    how it works, 13
    logical structures, 202–216
    non-normative, 236–237
    notation, 231–233
    origins of, 183–184
    physical structures, 216–231
    reasons for using, 11
    terminology, 184–186
XMLDOM, 105–106, 113–114
XMLDOMDocument, 124
XMLDOMNode, 124
XML Object Model (XOM), 79, 112
XML Pro, 35
XML processor, 183
XML-Server, 91–92
xmlproc, 29
Xparse, 30
XPointers, 21
    absolute location terms, 22
    relative location terms, 22–23
    support, 23
XSL, 16–17
    creating, 158–169

processing, 82
support, 82